African Philosophy

African Philosophy

New and Traditional Perspectives

Edited by
Lee M. Brown

OXFORD
UNIVERSITY PRESS
2004

OXFORD

UNIVERSITY PRESS

Oxford New York
Auckland Bangkok Buenos Aires Cape Town Chennai
Dar es Salaam Delhi Hong Kong Istanbul Karachi Kolkata
Kuala Lumpur Madrid Melbourne Mexico City Mumbai Nairobi
São Paulo Shanghai Taipei Tokyo Toronto

Copyright © 2004 by Oxford University Press, Inc.

Published by Oxford University Press, Inc.
198 Madison Avenue, New York, New York 10016
www.oup.com

Oxford is a registered trademark of Oxford University Press

Library of Congress Cataloging-in-Publication Data
African philosophy : new and traditional perspectives /
edited by Lee M. Brown.
p. cm.
Includes bibliographical references and index.
ISBN 0-19-511440-X; ISBN 0-19-511441-8 (pbk.)
1. Philosophy, African. I. Brown, Lee M.
B5305.A374 2003
199′.67—dc21   2003048695

2 4 6 8 9 7 5 3 1
Printed in the United States of America
on acid-free paper

PREFACE

During the past two decades, the idea of there being an African philosophy has undergone significant scrutiny. Criticisms have largely come from three fronts. First, it has been alleged that philosophy is written and that since traditional African cultures were rooted in oral traditions they could not produce philosophy. Second, it has been alleged that philosophy is rooted in critical inquiry, and that since what is usually characterized as traditional African philosophical thought is associated with folk wisdom or sagacious edicts, it is not philosophy. This objection has two components. It alleges that philosophy is rooted in epistemology—in concerns about what it is to know that something is true—and that traditional African cultures have shown no evidence of a systematic analysis of what could constitute knowledge. Similarly, it alleges that philosophy is also rooted in metaphysics—in concerns about what it is for something to be true or to be real or to exist, and that traditional African cultures have shown no evidence of a systematic analysis of metaphysical concerns. Third, it has been alleged that philosophical concerns are universal and as such they are not specific to a culture, population, or location.

When carefully scrutinized, none of these criticisms proves fatal to the notion that there were philosophical perspectives within traditional African cultures—at root the controversy is really about just that—or that there exists a philosophical phenomenon that can be appropriately characterized as African. As in the case of other philosophical traditions tied to locations and populations, African philosophy is the philosophy that reflects the philosophical concerns that are manifested in African conceptual languages. Greek, Asian, and American philosophies are notable philosophical traditions tied to locations and to conceptual concerns within their respective populations. It will become obvious through reading the essays in this collection that African cultures were concerned with epistemological and metaphysical issues before the infusion of Judaic, Islamic, and Christian religious perspectives and before being influenced by Greek and Western ideologies in wider ways. It seems short-sighted to view philosophical thought as beginning within Ancient Greek culture and to hold that those who do not come out of that lineage or who have different concerns have no philosophical perspectives or have perspectives that do not merit scholarly consideration. Moreover, epistemology and metaphysics are merely two of many areas that philosophy encompasses. Given the effects of colonial oppression, postcolonial African cultures are very much concerned about the impositions of Western conceptions of ethics, justice, fairness, rights, compassion, and humaneness. It is thought that in many respects, those conceptions appear to stand in contrast to precolonial conceptions found in traditional African cultures. In addition, not all philosophical concerns are universal. Some are local in that they are they language-relative. Such concerns may emerge in an effort to capture cultural idioms.

Concerning what counts as doing philosophy, the oral traditions that grounded the distribution of information within early African cultures ought not to count against there being philosophical thought or philosophical perspectives within traditional African cultures. Were we to be consistent and hold that traditional African thought cannot be philosophical, because philosophical thought is thought that is written or is non-sagacious in character, we could not count Socrates, Buddha, or Jesus as having engaged in philosophical thought. None wrote about what they taught or thought, and the general character of much of what came forth from Buddha and Jesus was sagacious. Moreover, that which is characterized as sagacious does not simply emerge without critical inquiry and significant reflection. One can find more probing discussions about the controversy in the writings of Kwame Anthony Appiah, Joseph Asike, Richard Bell, Segun Gbadegesin, Kwame Gyekye, Paulin Hountondji, D. A. Masolo, John Mbiti, Albert Mosley, V. Y. Mudimbe, Olusegun Oladipo, Tsenay Serequeberhan, Kwasi Wiredu, and others. At present, this controversy has lost much of its luster and concerns of greater substance are currently being formally addressed by African intellectuals.

This collection of essays addresses epistemological and metaphysical issues that are specific to the traditional conceptual languages of sub-Saharan Africa. By "traditional" I mean "without the infusion of foreign influence—most notably without the infusion of Judaic, Islamic, Christian, Greek, and Western conceptual schemes into sub-Saharan cultures." The primary focus of the collection is on traditional African conceptions of mind, person, personal identity, truth, knowledge, understanding, objectivity, destiny, free will, causation, and reality. The collection encompasses metaphysical and epistemological concerns from various traditional African folk philosophical perspectives. Among those perspectives are Akan, Azande, Bokis, Igbo, Luo, and Yoruba. The contributors are: Leke Adeofe, K. Anthony Appiah, Lee Brown, Segun Gbadegesin, D. A. Masolo, Albert Mosley, Ifeanyi Menkiti, and Kwasi Wiredu. Their perspectives, where appropriate, address current concerns in Western philosophy of psychology, philosophy of mind, philosophy of science, philosophy of language, metaphysics, and epistemology. The underlying intent is to bring Western philosophy into contact with traditional African folk philosophy in a fruitful way— a way that will encourage and enable those from each tradition to learn from the other and by so doing, foster a more humane understanding of how to see ourselves, each other, and the world at large.

ACKNOWLEDGMENTS

The contributing authors must be thanked for fashioning their essays to accommodate the purpose of this book. My deepest gratitude goes to Dr. David R. Kurtzman for his insightful feedback during the editing of the manuscript. I thank Prof. Frederick Schmitt for encouraging me to undertake this project, and the reference librarians Dr. Lorraine Haricombe, Dr. Alfred Kagan, and Joan M. Barnes for their assistance in my compiling the bibliography of source material of epistemological and metaphysical perspectives in African philosophical thought. I thank Julia M. L. Brown for contributing her interpretative artistry to the cover of this book. I also thank the University of Illinois, Howard University, and the Daihonzan Chozen-ji for supporting this project.

CONTENTS

CONTRIBUTORS

Leke Adeofe
Department of Philosophy
Triton College

K. Anthony Appiah
Department of Philosophy
Princeton University

Lee M. Brown
Department of Philosophy
Howard University

Segun Gbadegesin
Department of Philosophy
Howard University

D. A. Masolo
Department of Philosophy
University of Louisville

I. A. Menkiti
Department of Philosophy
Wellesley College

Albert Mosley
Department of Philosophy
Smith College

Kwasi Wiredu
Department of Philosophy
University of South Florida

African Philosophy

ONE

INTRODUCTION

*Seeing through the Conceptual Languages
of Others*

Among the goals of this collection is to provide accurate and well-developed characterizations of some of the salient epistemological and metaphysical concerns that have shaped the conceptual languages of sub-Saharan Africa. Another goal is to enable readers to enhance their functional understanding and their appreciation of the epistemological and metaphysical perspectives that have driven traditional African philosophical thought. Among the motives for striving toward such goals is obedience to an ancient Western injunction. Socrates and Plato urged that we must know ourselves, and although those two philosophers did not say so, one of the necessary routes toward self-knowledge is knowledge of others. Self-knowledge and knowledge of others are coeval in human individuals, and this kind of knowledge leads us toward the recognition of the importance of knowledge of other cultures. Moreover, seeing ourselves through the conceptual lenses of others enables us to have a more informed view of ourselves, and the derived knowledge empowers us to enable others more appropriately.

Most of what has been made known through literature about traditional African philosophical thought emerged through Eurocentric characterizations of African cultures. Those characterizations emerged primarily from the perspectives of Western anthropologists and Christian-trained African theologians and clerics, who interpreted and translated traditional African conceptual idioms into Western conceptual idioms. The process was either poorly informed or self-serving, and much of what was characterized as African thought was a Western invention. The characterizations did not emerge by viewing traditional African conceptual idioms through the conceptual lens of traditional Africans. Instead, Eurocentric languages were superimposed upon African cultures without an informed or dedicated commitment to preserving the integrity of African conceptual idioms, and without clear and accurate understanding of the underlying ontological commitments that grounded those idioms.[1]

Moreover, the institutionalization of racialism within Western cultures tainted honest efforts to be objective when studying African philosophical thought.[2] The cultures of sub-Saharan Africa were viewed by Western colonizers and missionaries as primitive, backward, and in need of radical reconstruction. In contrast to Western religions, traditional African religions were viewed as grounded upon superstition and metaphysical fantasy, and the cultures on the whole were viewed as having little value outside of the resources that could be extracted for Western use. Within Western cultures, those sentiments became an institutionalized lens through which African cultures and Africans came to be viewed. Such sentiments were fostered by the racist perspectives of well-respected philosophers such as Georg Hegel, David Hume, and Immanuel Kant. Because of their stature within the Western intellectual community, their stereotypes of the "essential dispositions" of Africans helped fuel racialism and served to marginalize any intellectual activity by those of obvious African descent. Like most stereotypes, theirs were far from accurate. That is to say, there is no causal link between the amount of melanin in an individual's body and in the ability of an individual to waltz, to appreciate fine wines, to be ethical, or to engage in abstract reasoning. In brief, racialism is a false theory. Moreover, people of African descent—not unlike any other population with a language—have long engaged in philosophical thought, and their perspectives have much to contribute to many of the concerns that have plagued Western philosophy for the past 2,500 years. Not taking seriously the philosophical concerns within other cultures can severely limit the ability of Western philosophy to evolve or otherwise grow. Their having a sagacious format or their not being rooted in Western ideology is no compelling reason for discounting their merit or their ability to enable Westerners to enrich their common conceptual base. Significant growth often occurs when we look at ourselves though the lenses of others. Sometimes that growth amounts merely to greater confirmation of existing perspectives, and that can be a good thing to have happen. Other times, seeing as do others precipitates a significant change in our own view, and if it is wisdom we seek that too can be a good thing to have happen.

Philosophy begins with experience, and at some point, our experiences and emergent concepts become influenced by our dispositions and by our beliefs about what is real, what is necessary, what is possible, and what is true. Our conceptual language provides the format that structures how and what we come to understand as real, as necessary, as possible, and as true.[3] With the advent of new perspectives, challenges to older perspectives emerge that require clarification or resolution. Reflections upon such concerns form a significant component of philosophical discourse, and in many respects reflecting upon such concerns can be characterized as reflecting upon concerns that are universal. That which is real or necessary or possible or true is universal, while that which is taken to be real, necessary, possible, or true may be otherwise. Given that philosophy, as an activity, is the pursuit of wisdom, the concern of philosophy is acquiring knowledge and its implications regarding what is real, necessary, possible, and true.

Our conceptual language provides the format that structures how and what we come to understand as real, as possible, and as true. However, there are arenas in which language itself seems to fail us. This can occur when perplexities emerge because language has fostered an implication that is not consistent with our intuitions, or because language does not accurately capture or otherwise reflect what we have in mind. Concerning the latter, there are times when a painting or non-lyrical musical composition can better capture what we have in mind than can words. Also, some concepts—"knowledge" and "game" are notable examples—do not seem to be readily analyzable or amenable to being provided necessary and sufficient conditions for appropriate usage.[4] Concerning the former, in opposition to perspectives in artificial intelligence, a thermostat is not conscious. Also, no matter the clarity of the proof, the unending decimal fraction consisting only of an infinite number of nines proceeded by a decimal point does not obviously designate the number one.[5]

Just as the early adaptations of emergent populations to vastly different environments and ecosystems fostered the emergence of biological diversity, they also fostered cultural diversity. The diversity in languages was reflective of what was needed for adapting to specific environments and to existing cultural influences that had implications for efforts to adapt. Reflecting those adaptations, the emergent cultures and their associated conceptual languages differed in ontological commitments, in how those commitments were given an order, and in what was viewed as most fundamental for grappling with issues of vital human concern: those concerns that impinged upon one's quality of life and upon one's longevity and upon one's quest to find purpose and meaning in life. Accordingly, they also differed in what could count as being known and how. Still, underlying those differences are ancient concerns about what is real, what is necessary, what is possible, and what counts as knowing and what counts as truth. It is perhaps through viewing the world through the conceptual lenses of others that we can realize a collective human experience and subsequently realize significant progress in personal and in interpersonal human development. Having such a realization requires having a richer understanding of the conceptual idioms of others.

Philosophers are those who seek wisdom, and to have wisdom one must have truth in hand and one must not only understand why the truths are as such, but also see their implications for the rest of what is known and what is valued. Little wisdom can be realized if one's perspectives are confined as were those of the challenged persons attempting to gain knowledge of the elephant by touching only one part while being unwilling to learn from others. To appreciate the philosophical perspectives of other cultures, one must come to understand those perspectives from the points of view of those who hold them. Granted, unless one is intimately familiar with a culture, it is often difficult to appreciate or even to understand the how and why of the ontological and epistemological commitments that ground the perspectives upon which a culture is built. But unless the effort is made, one's knowledge is likely to be only superficial, and so little genuine appreciation will be realized.[6] This phenomenon is not merely specific to cases where there are significant cultural differences. It is also prevalent within a culture when there are incompatible variations in ontological and epistemological commitments. A brief example will show how this occurs even within the natural sciences.

Significant technological progress has occurred when something previously dismissed or otherwise ignored was given full hearing. One such case is when physical theory was in conflict with human experience, and human experience was characterized as silly, self-indulgent, misguided, and delusional. It was not until the early 1980s that many otherwise very astute engineers and physicists were able to hear differences between audio cables and between amplifiers with identical measured specifications and performance characteristics.[7] According to physical theory, the human ear is not capable of detecting or otherwise distinguishing differences in the quality of signals whose only difference is distortion that is less than 0.05%. Accordingly, for any two functionally equivalent amplifiers whose distortion products remained below 0.05%, there is no audible distortion or difference that can be discerned.[8] Similarly, since the measurable total harmonic distortion products of audio cables is less than the residual of existing test equipment, 0.001%, the ear is not able to discern any difference between functionally equivalent audio cables.

Still, avid audiophiles claimed to be able to hear differences between audio equipment that test results—in conjunction with the associated theory—imply cannot be discerned. Moreover, many audiophiles claimed to be able to recognize specific audio equipment solely on the basis of the audible distortions it added to reproduced music. Here we have a case where well-entrenched and well-supported physical theories within the natural sciences tell us what is not possible, while personal experience suggests otherwise. Those who believed the theories could not hear differences between equipment with the same measured results, and they could not hear distortion contributed by equipment whose measured results were below the threshold of theoretical audibility. However, in the late 1970s, a new method of gathering information about the distortion products of audio devices was developed. That method showed that many amplifiers with measured total harmonic distortion below 0.01% actually had transient intermodulation distortion products greater than 5%. Transient intermodulation distortion was a new-found distortion. Its recognition showed that the dynamic performance of audio devices could not be reliably discerned by using the existing standard methods.[9] Strangely, accompanying the acceptance of the more accurate method of measuring distortion was an increase in hearing astuteness of those who had previously accepted the old theories. One of the consequences of the new-found awareness by previous believers of the old theory is that amplifier and cable design changed within the audio industry, and more musically accurate devices became available to the general public. Both Norwood Hanson and Thomas Kuhn have aptly pointed out that what we are capable of seeing depends upon the beliefs we bring to our experiences.[10] The richer our concepts, the more access we have to the objects that make up the universe. Seeing life through the conceptual lenses of others can increase the depth and enrich the breadth of our conceptual scheme. Such growth fosters the development of wisdom.

Among the more problematic concerns that emerge when deciding between theories from different cultural traditions is that there are factors involved that make knowing which is true exceedingly difficult to discern. Unless we know what is intended by the use of the words within a language, there is little chance of discerning whether any claims within the language are true. Concerning the essays in this collection, although it is not explicitly stated, a theme common to all is that a word that is shared among different cultures can have different extensions while being taken to have the same sense. This phenomenon is not consistent with the tenet that sense determines reference. If we hold the latter to be correct, then we need to reevaluate our perspectives on the extent to which a translation or reduction of one cultural idiom to another can be said to be complete or one of synonymy. This brings into question the extent to which we can be sure that our understanding of the conceptual languages of others is accurate, and that brings into question the appropriateness of making comparative judgments about the merits of the philosophical perspectives of other cultures. This is not a tacit support of skepticism. It is instead a reminder that our ability to appreciate or otherwise understand the content of the conceptual languages of others turns on the extent to which we are able to view the content from the perspectives of the native users of the language.

In "Akan and Euro-American Concepts of the Person," K. Anthony Appiah explores these issues from the perspective of trying to discern conceptions of what it is to be a person when those conceptions are from different cultural traditions. His focus is upon conceptions of the person within Western and within Akan traditions. He discusses six obstacles to realizing which of the two traditional conceptions of the person is most accurate. In so doing, he notes that there may be no non–question-begging way of comparing theories, since the theories themselves play central roles in our coming to understand how each is to be used. In other words, how each is to be used determines the extensions of its concepts, and that condition plays a critical role in determining the extent to which one theory can be said to map onto the objects subsumed by the other.

Even if question begging were itself not an issue, there still remain questions about how to discern which conceptualization is most accurate, since each will fail to capture something of significance. There can also be cases when both are equally accurate, but about different things, and the issue then comes to deciding what things most matter. As to what most matters, discerning that often comes down to what is most valued by the reducing culture. If having powers to bring about changes in others by casting spells is not significant within a culture, then reducing talk about witches to talk about psychotics works well. However, psychotics do not have the powers purportedly had by witches, so something fairly significant gets lost when witches become mere psychotics—people with a specific kind of delusional perspective on life. There are at least two notable dangers with such reductions. First, they can destroy components of a culture that are essential to the survival of the culture, and often what is gained by the reduction does not offset the loss that results from the reduction. Second, replacement idioms typically have problems of their own and they themselves are typically replaced in some future by something else. Such transitions get us further away from being able to understand what was of significance in the original conceptual language, and that gets us further away from being able to understand what was important to the people of the culture out of which the language emerged. This is perhaps most alarming, since the fundamental questions that people are asking today are those that were asked scores of translations ago. Perhaps were we better able to see how they grappled with their concerns, we could get a better handle on how to grapple with ours. Such insights are nearly impossible when the other's conceptual language is not taken as seriously as our own.

In "Truth and an African Language," Kwasi Wiredu compares conceptions of truth within Akan and Western languages. He treats truth as a primarily epistemological rather than an ontological concept. Even so, he does not disregard the ontological concerns that are part of epistemological inquiries. Although objects, situations, and their relations to, say, a person are the subjects of that which is claimed to be true, when speaking literally, neither an object nor a situation nor a subject can be said to be a truth. Wiredu views truth as something about that which is claimed to be reality. He argues that truth has to do with judgments and that those judgments accord, in some sense, with reality. The focus of his essay is on the nature of the judgment that is seen as essential for ascertaining truth.

Wiredu's essay provides an interesting and accessible tour of Frege's and of Tarski's criteria for something's being true. During his investigation, he explores Western conceptions of truth, with a focus upon the correspondence, coherence, and pragmatic theories of truth. The exploration then makes a transition to Dewey's characterization of truth as warranted assertibility, and Wiredu subsequently shows how the concept of truth within the Akan language can be an aid to clear thinking about how to come to know what can be characterized as truth. Wiredu suggests that a possible unification of the three competing Western theories of truth can be realized by an infusion of the Akan conception of truth. However, he notes that some philosophical problems are not universal, and that they are instead language relative and as such their existence depends upon the peculiarities of the culture in which the language is rooted. He cautions us to be cognizant of this so that we will be less prone to take language-dependent issues for universal issues. This exemplifies one variety of case in which a philosophy can be one of a specific culture—when the concerns are indigenous to the cultural and linguistic idioms of a people.

In traditional Yoruba thought, a necessary condition for an individual to be a person is that it has taken on a destiny. In "An Outline of a Theory of Destiny," Segun Gbadegesin puts forth the thesis that when viewed under the guise of modern philosophical rigor, the traditional Yoruba concept of destiny seems to bring with it more conceptual problems than its usage is otherwise thought to help explain. His concerns are with an apparent inconsistency in held beliefs, within traditional folk African culture, about what it means to have a destiny. Among those concerns is how one makes sense of the tenet that having a destiny fixes one's life experiences with the tenet that one can be held responsible for one's actions. He is concerned also with what it means to choose a destiny, and with whether it is appropriate to say of something that does not have a destiny that it is a person. Associated with that concern is the issue of whether the person that emerged from the process of getting a destiny is responsible for having its destiny and accountable for how it subsequently lives. Given traditional Yoruba perspectives on personhood, something becomes a person only when it has chosen a destiny for its life. Since that process occurs during life in utero, questions are raised about what it is that actually chooses a destiny. A person emerges only after the selection is made, and life in utero is not the life of something that is typically thought to be capable of making quality-of-life decisions. He contends that it is not wholly obvious that one can be held accountable for something that one did not do or for something for which one lacked the required tools, and that both seem to be operative during the purported choosing of one's destiny.

One of the underlying concerns in Gbadegesin's essay is how best to account for holding a person accountable for behaviors that he or she did not obviously choose. Grounding this concern are broader issues about the extent to which an individual can be said to have willingly participated in something before becoming a person and about whether such participation supports the having of a depth of consciousness and wisdom that is typically associated with Plato's contention that individuals have knowledge while in utero. Gbadegesin specifically addresses related concerns about reincarnation and about surviving as an ancestral spirit after death. Since essential to being a person is the having of a chosen destiny, and since it is not wholly obvious that a chosen destiny is a thing that can survive the death of a body, it is not wholly obvious that the person who was fashioned by its destiny can survive in spiritual form after death. This is problematic in large part because destiny is not viewed as something that is by nature spiritual and because on some traditional conceptualizations, since destiny and *ori* are the same—or in the least, destiny is contained in the *ori*—when the *ori* dies, so dies the destiny. "*Ori*" in Yoruba is usually translated "head," but clearly these translation issues are closely interrelated. A Westerner usually does not speak of the head's dying apart from the body's dying, except when talking in metaphor. There are other perspectives on this issue and some are discussed in depth in "Understanding and Ontology in Traditional African Thought" and in "Personal Identity in African Metaphysics."

The concerns with which Gbadegesin wrestles are weighty, and they have significant implications for Western concerns about having free will in light of determinism. Also, efforts by Western theologians to reconcile omniscience with free will are fraught with similar difficulties. It is Gbadegesin's contention that believing in destiny is not irrational and that the Yoruba concept of destiny deserves more investigation before any such charges can be made justifiably. He suggests that viewing one's life as having a destiny gives it purpose and direction and that since one's destiny can be made more to one's liking through known types of practices, the quality of one's life can be joyous and fruitful even though it is fundamentally determined before birth. Perhaps most interesting about the kind of destiny that Gbadegesin seems to embrace is that it is flexible, in the sense that it can be influenced by those who approach life in a manner that is respectful of the phenomena that are ultimately responsible for the formation of destinies. Still, as traditionally conceived, the notion that individuals have destinies is problematic, but it is no more problematic than the free-will–determinism problem, and it raises no more difficulties than are raised by fatalism within some protestant traditions. I leave it to the reader to discern whether said perspectives are any less compelling than those associated with efforts to reconcile free will with either determinism or omniscience. With respect to either of these two phenomena, that which is fixed by omniscience or by deterministic chains is not amenable to being altered. Hence, in light of either, it can be said that one's belief that one could have done otherwise can be viewed as illusionary as another's belief that one's actions are destined. The truth of the matter is still not known, and perhaps the discussions contained in Gbadegesin's essay will promote less jaundiced perspectives when evaluating the merits of conceptual languages that are different from one's own.

In "Personal Identity in African Metaphysics" Leke Adeofe explores some of the issues involved in discerning what it is to be a person within the context of a Yoruba metaphysical worldview. Those issues are viewed in light of Western conceptions of personal identity. His concerns are: What is the nature of persons? What is it for a person to be the same persisting entity across time? What relationship, if any, exists between an individual's first-person subjective experiences and our objective third-person perspective? Adeofe's primary focus is on the extent to which his characterization of the Yoruba theory of reality has provided integrated responses to personal identity questions. He characterizes Yoruba thought as having a tripartite conception of persons, while arguing that it does not fall prey to criticisms that have plagued notable Western conceptions of persons. Variants of the continuity and persistence theories that are associated with Kant, Descartes, and Hume are discussed in light of Yoruba conceptions of persons. Adeofe also explores the Lockean idea of linking social roles to personal identity and suggests that the Yoruba characterization provides a more promising conception. He argues that the Yoruba conceptual language provides a tested conception of human existence that is sufficient for clarifying personal identity concerns within Western culture.

D. A. Masolo's "The Concept of the Person in Luo Modes of Thought" begins with a characterization of salient influences of European colonialism on traditional conceptual idioms of Luo modes of thought. He discusses what he sees as external cultural impositions that function as obstacles to acquiring an accurate understanding of ontological commitments in traditional African cultures. His early focus is upon what Rosalind Shaw, V. Y. Mudimbe, and others have characterized as the European construction of previously inexistent realities in traditional African ontology. Those constructions are characterized as inventions that emerged through the imposition of Eurocentric taxonomies on African cultures. Also discussed are contributions of

European anthropologists and European-trained African theologians and clerics to the translations of traditional African cultural idioms into Eurocentric idioms. Masolo suggests that their characterizations were self-serving and inaccurate and that the subsequent infusions into colonial and postcolonial African cultures have distorted African cultural idioms and have given Westerners inaccurate characterizations of the ontological commitments within traditional African cultures.

Masolo goes into great detail to distinguish traditional African conceptual idioms from those presented as African via Eurocentric interpretations. Although there is discussion of the colonial influences upon ethical and political perspectives within traditional African thought, Masolo's discussions are primarily focused on concerns in the areas of metaphysics and epistemology. Therein, he focuses upon conceptions of personhood and personal identity. He contends that in many African systems of thought, conceptions of individual identity often exceed the confinement of the two Cartesian categories—mind and body—that are offered by Westerners to explain individual capacities to think and act in objectively discernable ways. Masolo notes that Jackson and Karp and Wiredu and Gyekye have argued that several African communities think of personhood as constituted of several more categories.[11] He suggests that this raises questions about what constitutes human agency and about how various senses of responsibility can be used to explain both everyday and extraordinary occurrences.

In keeping with such concerns, Masolo examines the concept of *jouk* that is found among the Southern (Kenya) and Central (Uganda) Luo. He focuses upon the implications of the concept for understanding what constitutes personhood, for grounding the principles of moral discourse and judgment, and for determining the principles of social geography of the Luo world. He discusses the similarities and the differences between Luo, Yoruba, and Akan ontological commitments and claims that they are notable. It is claimed that each ontology has efficacy within each of the cultural domains. In addition, Masolo suggests that within each culture there is a firm commitment to the belief that underlying the experiential world is a reality that gives order to our experiences. In concluding, Masolo suggests that perhaps by focusing upon that which is substantially common to all, we can develop a more fruitful perspective for solving some of the problems that are still dominating concerns in Western philosophy.

Ifeanyi Menkiti adds another dimension to the concerns raised by Masolo. Menkiti argues that the ontological commitments within traditional African cultures are not grounded upon supernaturalism. He suggests that characterizing the theoretical posits within traditional African cultures as supernatural posits infuses Western idioms into traditional African conceptual languages. In "Physical and Metaphysical Understanding: Nature, Agency, and Causation in African Traditional Thought," Menkiti sheds light upon a flawed but deeply entrenched Western perspective that has significantly influenced how the ontological commitments within African cultures have been viewed. Within Western cultures there exists the tenet that traditional African conceptual schemes are pre-theoretic and hence lack the foundations that are required for explaining natural phenomena. That perspective is offered to account for the flawed position that those belonging to traditional African cultures do not understand natural phenomena because African perspectives on how and why phenomena occur are rooted in mere superstition and metaphysical fantasy and as such lack the theoretical grounding that permits a genuine understanding of how and why phenomena occur.

Understanding natural phenomena requires seeing the phenomenon to be explained and the phenomenon offered to explain it as being subsumed within a theoretical framework. For causal explanation, the event to be explained and that which caused it must be linked by a true generalization—one that makes sense within our conceptual scheme. From a Western perspective, claiming that the man died because a spell was cast upon him makes no sense when the man was drowned by a crocodile. Without its making sense, no genuine understanding takes place, and it is because of the inability of Westerners to achieve an understanding from the offered explanations within traditional African cultures that African cultures are viewed as not having an understanding of natural phenomena.

The claim that a cast spell caused a person's death is viewed as evidence for believing that traditional Africans are superstitious and that their ontological commitments are not amenable to the kind of empirical grounding that is required for theory formation and for subsequently explaining natural phenomena. Menkiti challenges this perspective and argues that traditional African culture is largely misunderstood. To that end he argues that it is not rooted in supernaturalism and that its metaphysics are empirically grounded. He provides compelling reasons for Westerners to acquire a more informed perspective on traditional African thought, and he suggests that there is much that Westerners can learn from traditional African thought that will better enable solving salient philosophical concerns within

Western culture. Particularly noteworthy about Menkiti's discussion is his bringing to light how one's ontological commitments determine what can be seen and valued. It is not only our physiology—our hard wiring—that determines the limits of our experiences, it is also our worldview. Just as boiling water can rid it of contained bacteria that cause illness, boiling water can rid it of contained demons that cause illness. This is not to say that demons and bacteria are one and the same. It is also not to say that they are radically different. It is to say merely that each, in a sense, is a characterization of the same phenomenon and that it is often our uninformed responses to those characterizations that determine how we view and treat those whose expressed ontological commitments differ from our own. Perhaps by acquiring a better understanding of why demons are viewed as harmful while germs are not and of why germs are viewed as harmful while demons are not, we can acquire a better understanding of human nature and of our propensity to posit only the unobservables that make sense to us, during our efforts to account for the phenomena that perhaps reside in all of nature, but are only noticed within specific conceptual schemes.

In "Witchcraft, Science, and the Paranormal in Contemporary African Philosophy," Albert Mosley explores the traditional African philosophical foundations that have given rise to current perspectives on the supernatural within contemporary African philosophical thought. He argues against the comparative Western tenet that while Western ontology is grounded upon facts about nature, traditional African ontology is rooted in mere metaphysical fantasy. Mosley objects to critiquing African ontology outside of the contextual framework that gives it structure and meaning. Moreover, it can be argued that almost any effort to analyze concepts outside of the scheme that provides the foundations for their meanings will result in unjustifiable biases. This is the case even within modern science. For example, in, *How the Laws of Physics Lie*, Nancy Cartwright suggests that when taken literally, almost all the laws of nature are false. If she is correct, and the law statements that science offers as true are otherwise, how ought we to proceed when attempting to access the extent to which a purported relationship between types of events obtains? Having such information is often important when assessing what to believe or do within specific situations. In fairness to Western science, when a law statement is assessed outside of the boundary conditions that fashion the arena in which its claim purports truth, that law statement can be said to be too broad—to be saying more than what would have been otherwise understood were the boundary conditions made obvious.

The gas laws of Charles and Boyle reflect the behavior of ideal gases, and as such, one is not likely to realize the precise predicted value of the gas laws when using gases that are not ideal. Similarly, when building an electronic circuit with resistors, one should not be surprised when the results fail to follow Ohm's law. Most resistors are not linear and as such they have capacitance or inductance, and either can affect current or voltage in ways that are not reflected by the stated value of the resistor. Still, accurate and reliable circuitry is designed on the basis of physical theories that employ law statements that characterize relations that are not as precise as found readily in nature. The success of such projects is rooted in there being an understanding of the specifications of the objects over which a universal generalization ranges. For example, without reservation we can apply the general rule that unless one is very skilled at differentiating types of mushrooms, picking a mushroom from the wild and eating it is dangerous. While it is not true that all wild mushrooms are lethal, it is true that most mushrooms of specific types cause death when ingested.

Given the apparent looseness in how seemingly exceptionless generalizations are interpreted and subsequently used, we can perhaps say that those who embrace the laws of nature understand that there is variability within the types of relations that law statements characterize and that when that variability is considered, the resultant claim by a subsuming law statement is true. For example, we can say with certainty, that were the value of the resistor 1 ohm at all frequencies, then the current for any applied frequency would be 1 ampere for an applied 1 volt potential. However, when a resistor has an associated parallel capacitance, there will be frequencies where current flow will be greater than 1 ampere for an applied 1 volt potential. Also, as a matter of practice, where the current is greater than 1 ampere for the same applied voltage, one can deduce that a capacitance or inductance is associated with the resistor and one can deduce its value—all things considered.

It seems safe to say that accepting law statements within science as true requires some degree of generosity. Can such generosity be extended to the law statements and theories within traditional African culture that make use of magic, witchcraft, and incorporeal spirits to account for observed phenomena? Mosley argues that it should, and that implies—if he is correct—that it can. However, it is not wholly obvious that the generosity can be extended. The law statements that emerge from Western science are rooted in empirical inquiry. They are testable and confirmable. The generalizations that emerge from positing magic, witchcraft, and incorporeal spirits are not obviously testable or otherwise confirmable through empirical methods, and hence it can be argued that there is no obvious viable basis for assessing their truth. Mosley's essay tackles this problem, and his arguments are in many respects compelling. When one looks at his position in light of Western religious tenets, his position has even greater plausibility. Much of Western religion is rooted in faith—where to have faith is to believe without empirical evidence. Mosley argues for a more inclusive view of both knowledge and the scientific enterprise wherein non-experimental evidence and societal perspectives factor into how research is to proceed and into what can be discerned as true and as justification for accepting a proposition as true.

In "Understanding and Ontology in Traditional African Thought," I discuss how the ontological commitments within modern Western culture can be viewed as no less problematic than those within traditional African cultures. Each posits unobservable entities to explain the experiential world, and in neither is there ready access to those posits that are held as grounding or as otherwise determining what is experienced. I look at the conceptions of persons in each tradition and suggest there is something of significance that each tradition can learn from the other. Concerning what is meant by "person," upon careful scrutiny it becomes apparent that "person" as used in Western culture is not coextensive with "person" in traditional African culture. What would be called a person in Western culture might not be called a person in African culture, while what would be called a person in African culture would be called a person in Western culture. The asymmetry speaks to telling difficulties associated with capturing African conceptual language within Western conceptual language—with replacing African conceptual language with Western theoretical idioms. It speaks also to the need for caution and perhaps charity when making judgments about what should count as significant or as well grounded when evaluating conceptual schemes that are not one's own.[12] Concerning the view that traditional African ontology is rooted in mere superstition or metaphysical fantasy, a careful viewing will reveal that Western ontology can be characterized similarly. It is not simply obvious that one rather than the other has a firmer foundation. Moreover, there seems to be something of significance that African ontology can lend to Western conceptual language during efforts to account for how a person's mind can affect its body and for how something can be the same throughout its existence. According to traditional African thought, all persons are in some sense physical, and it is that aspect of personhood that can lend explanatory efficacy to the Western practice of attributing causal efficacy to incorporeal beings and to the associated spiritual world that plays a fundamental role in grounding Western culture. When we consider that our best science tells us that matter and energy are in principle interchangeable, that $E = MC^2$, the traditional African characterization of ancestral spirits as quasi-material seems far less fantastic than might initially be thought by someone who is being introduced to the philosophical perspectives in traditional sub-Saharan cultures.

It will be evident to the careful and sympathetic reader that the purposes of the authors represented in this book are less polemical than they are irenic. It is among our aims to provide the opportunity for a new dialogue between practitioners of varying methods of accomplishing philosophical tasks. And it is with the hope that increased understanding of each other will be the result of that dialogue, that each of us has rendered these contributions to the study of humanity and its nature.

Notes

1. Ontological concerns are concerns about what makes up the furniture of the universe—the stuff, if you will, that we count as real as opposed to imaginary or fictitious. By definition, unicorns are not real—they cannot exist as actual objects in the world in which we live. Even if a single-horned horse were excavated, it could not be a unicorn. If we are speaking and writing literally, the occurrence of a unicorn is neither likely nor biologically possible in the world we inhabit. An ontological commitment is a disposition to accept and a willingness to use specific conceptual idioms or characterizations of reality as true of the world in which we live.

2. Racialism is the theory that human races exist and that the biology that gives rise to the phenotypes that permit racial classification also gives rise to essential qualities such as intellectual, spiritual, ethical, and aesthetic dispositions. Racism is racialism accompanied by the belief that one's membership in a particular race makes one biologically superior to those in another race. Typically, accompanying that belief is the belief that one's racial superiority gives one the right to oppress those believed to be racially inferior. Neither theory is true.

3. This is not intended as an exhaustive list of philosophical concerns.

4. For concerns about what counts as knowledge, see discussions of "the Gettier Problem." Edmund Gettier's essay, "Is Justified True Belief Knowledge?" first appeared in *Analysis* 23 (1963). For concerns about what counts

as a game, see Ludwig Wittgenstein's discussions about the definition of "game" in *Philosophical Investigations*. For results that at least partially challenge Wittgenstein's view, see various works of Alan Ross Anderson and Omar Khayam Moore—in particular their work on autotelic learning environments, in numerous publications.

5. An offered proof that 0.99999... equals 1.0:

  a. $1/3 = 0.33333...$
  b. $3/3 = 0.99999...$ Both sides of the previous equation were multiplied by 3.
  c. $1 = 0.99999... 3/3$ in the previous equation was reduced to 1.

The underlying assumptions here are that the fraction $1/3$ is equivalent to a never ending series of threes preceded by a decimal point and that the expression "$1/3$" and the expression ".33333..." are different names for the same number. The concern about equation *c* is that the contained expressions refer to different numbers—that there is a number between the numbers that each expression mentions.

6. If, for example, one wants to acquire an appreciation for what it is to be in a state of starvation, one cannot do so by merely coming to know what is meant by the word "starvation." One must have a sensitivity for what it is to be without food and to have no access to food for more than, say, a week. Fasting and starving are not the same.

7. In brief, under the guise of the audio industry standards for measuring the performance of amplifiers, two amplifiers can be said to have the same gain-bandwidth products when their output signals are equal for any input signal at any frequency. They can be said to have the same harmonic and intermodulation distortion characteristics when their distortion products are the same for all input signals at any continuous frequency or combination of continuous frequencies. Unless specified, when speaking about distortion, the reference is to total harmonic distortion, THD, or to intermodulation distortion, IMD.

8. I do not know whether a difference of less than 0.05% can be discerned by the human ear. It seems to me that it can when, for example, one amplifier has a distortion of, say, 0.09% and the other 0.045%.

9. The new method of measurement showed that the audible distortion characteristics of state-of-the-art audio devices cannot be reliably evaluated by using continuous or steady state signals (sine waves and square waves) as the source to be measured. Music, for the most part, is a series of pulses, and steady state measurements do not tell us much about how a device handles pulses.

10. Norwood R. Hanson, *Patterns of Discovery* (New York: Cambridge University Press, 1958); Thomas S. Kuhn, *The Structure of Scientific Revolutions* (Chicago: University of Chicago Press, 1962).

11. Michael Jackson and Ivan Karp, *Personhood and Agency: The Experience of Self and Other in African Cultures*, Uppsala Studies in Cultural Anthropology 14,

Uppsala University (Washington, D.C.: Smithsonian Institution Press, 1991); Kwasi Wiredu and Kwame Gyekye, *Person and Community* (Washington, D.C.: CRVP, 1992).

12. See Donald Davidson, "Radical Interpretation," in *Inquiries into Truth and Interpretation*, 2nd ed. (Oxford: Clarendon Press, 2001).

TWO

AKAN AND EURO-AMERICAN CONCEPTS OF THE PERSON

K. ANTHONY APPIAH

I propose to begin with a little analytical philosophical "apparatus," even though a hatred of—or at any rate a distaste for—such "technicality" may discourage some readers. So before getting down to the apparatus, I would like to say that I believe it is going to be helpful in addressing a question that is far from a technicality: namely, what is being lost when African conceptual languages are increasingly replaced with theoretical idioms from the West. I am going to suggest that it is far from obvious that this is a good thing: and not for nationalist reasons but for universalist ones.

Comparing Theories: Preliminaries

Sometimes we are faced with two ways of thinking that seem to be in competition with one another—I will call them theories—and we want to decide which we prefer. What it is for theories to be in competition can sometimes be straightforward: they may make predictions about the same sorts of things and those predictions may be different, and so they are about the same subject matter and they cannot both be right about it. It can be less than obvious, however, in real cases, in what sense two theories deal with the same subject matter. For the theories are likely to use different languages—they will have different theoretical vocabularies, different concepts—and some of what is said in the vocabulary of one theory, T, may be about things that, for example, T^1 does not refer to at all. Why do we think that Mendel's genes and our talk of sequences of nucleotides in DNA molecules deal with the same subject matter? For, as it happens, almost nothing that Mendel thought about genes is exactly true of DNA sequences. Why do we call some people in some societies "medicine men" or "witch doctors," which assumes that they are aiming to heal diseases, as opposed to say protecting your *mbisimo* (spirit) from the assaults of *mangu* (witchcraft); as was the case in Zandeland according to E. E. Evans-Pritchard?

Still, as I say, we can find ourselves in situations where we have to choose between two ways of thinking and talking about a situation, and, to put it at its most practical, we can judge that looked at in the T-way, we should do A, and looked at in the T^1-way, we should do A^1, *and we cannot do both*. And so, somehow, we go with T. Notice that this practical dilemma does not force us to choose between T and T^1 absolutely: for it may be that in other circumstances, where T recommends doing B and T^1 recommends doing B^1, we would go with T^1. And it might be that proceeding in this way, things turn out just as we wanted. (Thus, T might be the theory of our Western-trained allopathic doctor and T^1 might be the view of our herbalist: and when it is headaches we take aspirin and not herbs, and when it is infertility we take herbs and not surgery.) Still, practical dilemmas of this sort can lead one to reflect on the question whether one should prefer T to T^1 over all, or, more likely, whether there is not some new picture, $T^\star$, that explains why we should do A in one case and B^1 in the other. And such a question urges on us the ranking of theories overall: in this case a search for a $T^\star$ that ranks above both T and T^1.

Even when we are clear that two theories are about roughly the same things, we will usually need more than this to help us decide how to rank them. For usually it is hard to say exactly what it is for the theory to get things right because we use theories for so many different purposes. (Medical theories are used for everything from trying to understand what has happened to us, to deciding what therapies to use, to deciding whether we are in the right frame of mind to make a decision.)

If we knew what we wanted theories and their correlative concepts *for*, we could line them up against each other and compare their performances. There would still be no guarantee that we could rank any two theories that came along because the things we wanted them for—their uses, let us say—might be diverse and incommensurable. So one theory, T, might do very well on one criterion, C^1, and another, T^1, do much less well; but then with respect to some other criterion, C^2, T^1 might be the winner. If we did not know which of these criteria mattered most, this would leave us still unable to rank them. Even if we thought that, on balance, C^1 mattered more than C^2, there would still be the need to decide how to trade off a small win on C^1 against a big loss on C^2. And, once again, if we did not know how to do this, we would be left without a ranking again.

Some people think we do not need to worry about the problems created by multiple criteria because there is only one serious criterion for assessing theories and that is truth. One trouble with truth as a criterion is that it can be too undemanding. There are lots of little unimportant truths, vaguely stated, that are not worth collecting. Surely we want not just the truth but the truth about something that is worth having the truth about: and that takes us straight back to multiple criteria, since it is generally the case that what is important depends on many things.

Another trouble with truth is, it does not seem to come by degrees: most of our theories get some things right and some things wrong. Overall, then, they are wrong, since the only way to be right is to get *everything* right. (Well, not everything, exactly: a theory needs to get everything right that it says anything about at all. If a theory says nothing about apples, it cannot be the whole truth, but it could be the whole truth about oranges.) And once we grasp this, we see that, until a theory comes along that just gets the whole truth (about something interesting)—and this is an event for which I do not recommend holding your breath—what we need is some notion of closeness to the truth, verisimilitude. But now we are back with the problem of multiple criteria: for (once we have some sort of measure of distance from the truth) a theory can be close to the truth in some respects and far from it in others, and so we are going to have to trade off relative success in some areas against relative failure in others. (For it is not likely, in general, that T will get right everything that T^1 gets right and then get some things right that T^1 gets wrong. If that were the situation, the choice would, of course, be easy.)

The fact that what theories provide is verisimilitude (which is a favored way of not being strictly true) is already built into the ways we make and use them. Idealizations abound: and to say that a theory idealizes is to say either

1. that its claims are close to the truth or
2. that it ignores some factors that are, in fact, significant, at least sometimes, and would get things pretty much right if those factors were taken into account, or
3. both.

To suppose that an idealization is of type (1), you need to have a measure of distance from the truth, which is easy enough if what the theory predicts is some measurable quantity, like velocity or the proportion of offspring that will have black eyes and red fur; here you may say that a theory, T, is closer than a theory, T^1, in what it says about the measurable quantity if the value, $v(T)$, that T ascribes to it is close to the actual value, v, than the value, $v(T^1)$, that T^1 predicts. But lots of theories do not predict things of that sort: one predicts that A will happen, another that B will. C happens, which is neither A nor B, and there is no real sense in which A is closer to C than B is, or vice versa. (I predict your mother will buy the dahlias. You predict she will buy the roses. She buys the cactus. Who is closer to being right?) To suppose that an idealization is of type (2) is once again to face the question of what is significant, which will, once more, depend on what your aims are.

So, to summarize, here are some of the obstacles to deciding which of two theories is better.

1. They are about overlapping subject matters or it is hard to say whether they are about the same thing; that is, there is a problem about the sense in which they are in competition with each other.
2. We do not know what criteria to use in comparing them.
3. We do, but the criteria point in different directions and we do not know how to weigh their relative importance.
4. We have a criterion, verisimilitude, but one of the theories is closer in its predictions in some areas and the other is closer in others, and we do not know how to decide which area matters more (or by how much) and so we are back with problem 2.
5. We have a criterion, verisimilitude, but the theories differ in ways that mean the notion of relative distance from the truth is not applicable.

Let me mention one more problem that can arise because it will matter in what follows. That problem is:

6. that the two theories themselves play a role in our understanding of what their uses are: and so there may seem to be
no non–question-begging way of comparing them.

(So, to return to the debate between healers I mentioned earlier,
our herbalist might well tell us that the infusion we have been taking
every night has strengthened our *chi*, while the Western doctor says
that the antibiotics we did not take would have killed off the bugs by
now. If you are comparing these two points of view as views about
health, how can we find a way of saying what health consists in that
does not beg the question of who is right?)

Theories of the Person in Particular

Every society has at least one collection of ideas that I am going to call
a theory of the person. A theory of the person is a collection of views
about what makes human beings work. It will include views about
why people do things: in America we speak, for example, of fear,
hope, belief, intention, desire, envy, lust, and kindness when we are
trying to explain behavior. But it will also include views about what
people need for survival: food, for example, or air or light or family
and friends. And it will usually put all this together in a way that
involves some account of the relations between the events inside
people that make them act and the bodies that do the acting. Westerners currently do this in terms of talk about minds and brains; for we
think that fear and belief and hope and the like are largely housed in
people's brains (though we also think that some forms of excitement
have to do with hormones like adrenaline, which act not only on the
brain but also elsewhere in our bodies). But in other societies it has
been not the brain but the breast that has been thought of as the home
of many of the most important states that make people act—so it was,
for example, in the societies that produced the Homeric epics and the
Hebrew Bible; and breath was for both those societies the name of an
animating principle that explained why people's bodies sometimes
acted under the guidance of inner states and sometimes (when dead)
behave like other inanimate things.

A theory of the person is not something that the people in the
society will necessarily think of as separate from their views about
many other matters. For people interact, of course, not only with each
other, but also with a world, both social and natural, around them; and

are also widely believed to interact with the sorts of spirits, gods, and the like that we are inclined to call "supernatural." So, simply asking someone how they explain the things people do or what people need for survival is not generally guaranteed to produce a well-organized body of prepared doctrine.

Nevertheless, the readers of this book will be familiar with the assumptions about how people work that are among the shared operating assumptions of most people in Europe and North America; and they will also be aware, too, that there are in their own countries people whose theories of the person contain some less orthodox elements. (There are people around, for example, who think that the state of the heavens when we are born helps to explain why we do what we do or that some people are sometimes "taken over" by other [dead] people for whom they act as mediums.) But there will be no guarantee that you will know about a fully fledged account from an African culture; no guarantee, in particular, that you will know about the picture of persons that was the normal view a century ago in Asante—where I grew up—and is still strongly present in the Twi language that is spoken there.

So let me give you a brief sketch of that theory, that picture of how people work, before I turn to the question of how we might decide whether to prefer it to the sort of Western view with which you are probably familiar.

Asante Theories of the Person

Naturally, a theory of the person is hard to isolate from the general views of a people about the world—social, natural, and supernatural—in which they live. So it will help to have a broader context within which to place an Asante theory of the person. But in order to make any sense of Asante life, it is necessary to say a little about social organization. For, as we shall see, many ritual acts of a religious nature have components that appear to be modeled on other social acts and the conception of social relations amongst people informs the notions of relations with other sorts of beings.

As social anthropologists often discover, some of those things that we take most for granted within one culture cannot be assumed in another. And so it is when we come to consider the organization of the family in Asante. For Asante is a matrilineal culture: children belong to the families of their mothers. If we call a group of living

people who share common descent through the female line a matriclan, we can say that the Asante family is a subgroup of the matriclan,
usually consisting of a group with a common ancestress in their grandmother or great-grandmother. This group is what is usually referred to
as the "*abusua*."

The head of the family is typically a child's maternal uncle—his or
her mother's brother—but it may be a great-uncle, a nephew, or a
brother. For the senior male member of this group need not be the
eldest member. This head of the family holds property in trust for the
whole group and is responsible for the maintenance and the behavior
of its members. This property descends in the matriclan, again typically
from uncle to nephew (sister's son) though there are a number of
exceptions to this rule. (Thus, for example, jewelry passes from elder
to younger females in the matriclan and a hunter's gun may pass to
his son.)

Wider than the matrilineal family is the maternal clan, which is also
called the *abusua* or *nton*. There are seven or eight clans into which all
of Asante is divided: but the functioning group for most people
consists of fellow clansfolk who live in the same village or town.
Associated with the *nton* are a number of taboos: restrictions on food,
for example, or on the utterance of certain words. Membership of this
maternal group is held to flow from the fact that a person's body
(*nipadua*) is made from the blood of the mother (the *mogya*) hence
the *abusua* is sometimes called the *bogya*. The other two components of
a person are the *sunsum* (individual spirit) and the *okra* of which the
former—the *sunsum*—derives from the father at conception, and the
latter, a sort of life force, is sent to a person at birth from Nyame,
the high god, and departs the body only at the person's last breath (and
is sometimes, as with the Greeks and the Hebrews, identified with
breath). (The child also acquires at birth a "day-name," the name for a
male or female child born on that day of the week.) Despite the
primary descent group being matrilineal, Asante people also belong to
a paternal clan, called the *ntoro*, which also has its associated taboos.
These taboos are seen as arising out of the fact that the members of the
ntoro have souls that share a common source, and similarities of personality between father and son are held to derive from this inherited
sunsum.

Both *abusua* and *ntoro* were traditionally exogamous: that is, it was
incestuous to marry a member of the same matriclan or patriclan. Since,
therefore, my father's sister or brother is bound to marry someone
who belongs to a different *ntoro* (for I and my father's siblings are in

the same exogamous patriclan) and may quite possibly marry someone who is not in my mother's (and therefore my) matriclan, there is no barrier to my marrying my paternal cousin. To marry your mother's sister's child, however, would be incestuous: you belong to the same *abusua*. To someone who is used to seeing the children of the siblings of either parent as cousins, distinguishing between one group as being totally prohibited in marriage and another as not only not prohibited but also sometimes encouraged is no doubt confusing. But it must be remembered that a child's mother's brother is very often the head of his or her family. He or she may actually live in the maternal uncle's household and be brought up with the children of other maternal aunts. To marry within this group would, in effect, be like marrying a brother or sister—indeed my mother's sisters I call "mother" and their children I call by the same term I use to call my siblings.

In sum, then, according to Asante traditions, a person consists of a body (*nipadua*) made from the blood of the mother (the *mogya*); an individual spirit, the *sunsum*, which is the main bearer of one's personality; and a third entity, the *okra*. The *sunsum* derives from the father at conception. The *okra*, a sort of life force, departs the body only at the person's last breath; is sometimes, as with the Greeks and the Hebrews, identified with breath; and is often said to be sent to a person at birth, as the bearer of one *nkrabea*, or destiny, from Nyame. The *sunsum*, unlike the *okra*, may leave the body during life and does so, for example, in sleep, dreams being thought to be the perceptions of a person's *sunsum* on its nightly peregrinations. Since the *sunsum* is a real entity, dreaming that you have committed an offence is evidence that you have committed it, and, for example, a man who dreams that he has had sexual intercourse with another man's wife is liable for the adultery fees that are paid for daytime offenses.[1]

Comparing Asante Theories with "Western" Ones: Ramsey Sentences

Now it is very natural to contrast this theory of the person with another, broadly disseminated, one, much influenced by Western philosophy and science, in which a person is a body with a mind that resides in a brain. There are disputes about the exact relation of the mind to the brain and about whether the former is capable of disembodied existence. Many Europeans and Americans—and Africans— believe that the departure of the mind from the body is death; and that the mind, released from the body, renamed the "soul," survives somehow, perhaps even somewhere. This seems like a different theory—*sunsum* and *okra* are dual non-bodily entities, for example, while the mind is one—and so we are now faced concretely with one of those situations whose abstract characterization I began with, where we might want to make a choice. Let us call the broadly commonsense Western view, W, and Akan common sense about the person, A.

How are we to characterize what is at stake in the choice between A and W? I suggest we can adapt an approach developed by the British philosopher Frank Ramsey. The details do not much matter here, but the idea is straightforward enough. Take, first, A. Collect all the claims that A makes. Identify all the terms in it that aim to refer to entities—*sunsum*, *okra*, and so on—not recognized by W. (For the moment, I will put aside issues of translation: I assume that we can identify many terms in Asante Twi and English that have the same meanings.) For each such term introduce a distinct variable and replace that term with its variable. What you now have is something a bit like A, but without any of the words that are in dispute between it and W. So, for example, where you once had, as part of A, the claim that the *okra* leaves the body at death, you have the "claim" that x leaves the body at death; and for the claim that the *sunsum* travels during dreams, you have the "claim" that y travels during dreams. (I call these "claims," in scare quotes, because, since "x" does not yet have any function explained, saying that x does something, so far tells you nothing at all over and above that x does something.) Of course there are many, many such "claims" about x and about y. You can now capture the distinctive content of A by saying that it holds that there exists an x and a y such that...; and write down the conjunction of all the "claims." You have now constructed a Ramsey sentence of A, where all the terms in A that do not correspond to terms in W are treated as theoretical, and all other terms as observational. What that sentence says is, in essence, that there exists an entity that behaves in the way that Akan people believe the *sunsum* behaves, one that behaves in the way they think the *okra* behaves, and so on. Let us call the Ramsey version of W, W^R.

You can now do the same for W. If A does not recognize the word "mind," then replace it with a variable; if A does not believe in the "unconscious," replace it with another. And now we can make the Ramsey version of A, A^R.

What you have now is a couple of theories, A^R and W^R. Here are some important facts about the relations between them.

1. They share all the concepts that are shared between Akan and Western theories of the person.
2. They make different predictions about how people will behave: If I recall a dream of meeting you, then my *sunsum* met your *sunsum* last night, and you and I ought to recall the same dreams, for example; but that is not a consequence of W^R.
3. They entail the existence of different states and entities.

The first strategy I suggested in such a case would be to decide what the two theories are for and then to see if we can decide which of them does that thing better. Well, what are A and W for? One reasonable answer, as I also said, might be: many things. But of those potentially many things one in particular suggests itself as central, and that is understanding—and thus anticipating—how people will behave under the various circumstances that they encounter. If we could agree on a way of characterizing behavior—the things people do—and context (the circumstances they encounter), there is then an obvious way of comparing the two approaches, available in recent Anglo-American philosophical tradition.

So How Does the Comparison Go?

I argued at the start that there were half a dozen problems that might arise in the course of theory comparison. The first obstacle, I said, was that there might be a problem about the sense in which A^R and W^R were in competition with one other. But if we could see the two theories as attempts to explain and predict behavior, then we could compare them over that domain, provided we could describe (a good deal of) behavior in non–question-begging terms that did not commit in advance to one way of looking at things or the other. I do not think that most Asante people would think of talk of the interior states of people as simply a way of predicting and explaining behavior; that is not surprising, given that most Westerners would not think of their theory of the person that way either. After all, it seems more natural to describe much of what is going on here as attempts to describe the behavior of the *sunsum*, for example, which is not at all the same thing as describing the behavior of a person. And, similarly, most people in the United States do not think that references to, say, "love," are just ways of helping to explain and predict what their lovers will do. They care about whether they are loved, not just about whether their loved ones will behave like lovers. (I shall return to this point again later.)

But even though the users of A^R and W^R do not think of them behavioristically, *we* might be interested in the question of which did better by this criterion. It is, after all, an intrinsically interesting question who gets more of the behavior of more people right. Here we move out of the realm of conceptual into more obviously empirical matters. But I rather suspect the answer to the question who does better, will turn out to be something like this: people who use A^R are better at predicting the behavior of other users of A^R; and those who use W^R do better with other W^R users. There are at least two reasons why this is likely to be so. One is banal: people know more about the people in their own society than they do about people in others. The other is a little deeper. One of the reasons people act the way they do is because they have the theories of the person that they do. You are more likely to behave like a preference-maximizing utility consumer after doing an introduction to economics. Whereas, if you are an A^R-user, you are more likely to believe your *sunsum* met your boyfriend's last night, even if you do not remember it at first (especially if he gives you that flashing smile because, unlike you, he does remember his dreams). You may thus end up behaving as A^R predicts.

One consequence of these facts—neither of them, I think, very profound—is that the choice opting for A^R over W^R will have among its consequences that we come to think of ourselves and others differently and thus behave differently.

Now both of these theories get many, many things wrong from the point of view of behavior prediction. Both get many things right. And, of course, while the class of things that one gets right (like the class that it gets wrong) overlaps with the class that the other gets right (or wrong), they are not coextensive. Sometimes one does better, sometimes another. It is hard, I think, to make an overall comparison. Furthermore, if our criterion is truth, neither does very well, *even over the limited domain of behavior*. That makes the suggestion that we should base our decision on which one gets the most truth about behavior seem eccentric at best.

We have reached my second obstacle: not knowing what criteria to use. It is not that there are no standards (beyond truth) against which to test these pictures of the person, but that there are many.

One obvious further criterion is something like "truth to introspective experience." Do I sometimes feel as if someone else has taken control of my body?[2] If so, does W^R have anything to say about why I feel like this? If not, that suggests that, for these purposes, A^R does a better job.

Another is consilience with the rest of what we believe about the natural world. There is no doubt that contemporary natural science does a terrific job of managing, explaining, and predicting many things in our world; better, I think it will be acknowledged by most Asantes, than many of the older theories that were developed in Asante. To the extent that one of our theories of the person is easier to fit into that broader picture, that might be thought to weigh in its favor.

At this point, however, we have reached a situation (which I labeled obstacle 3 at the start) where we have a bunch of criteria that point in different directions and we do not know how to weigh their relative importance. And it is at this point that some will want to insist that the right thing to do is to turn to verisimilitude and ask, head on, which of the theories is closer to the truth.

Here we meet my obstacle 4. For, as we have seen, it is likely that one of the theories is closer in its predictions in some areas and the other is closer in others, and we do not know how to decide which area matters more (or by how much) and so we are back with trying to find criteria independent of verisimilitude. We also face obstacle 5: for the theories differ in ways that mean the notion of relative distance from the truth is not easy to apply.

How to Proceed?

I have not made a very serious effort actually to overcome my five obstacles because, as I said, the issues are heavily empirical (and, I should add, the tests have mostly not been done). But I have also not made much of an effort because, as I mentioned at the start, there is a sixth obstacle to theory comparison, which I put by saying: "The two theories themselves play a role in our understanding of what their uses are: and so there may seem to be no non–question-begging way of comparing them."

Now, here is the problem in the particular case of A^R and W^R. All my discussion so far, in terms of criteria for assessing the theories, has involved discussion of such matters as evidence, belief, and purposes. When you are trying to decide whether to adopt a theory, you are asking what grounds you will act on, for what purposes; what you will be willing to believe and the like. But purposes and beliefs are among the sorts of thing that theories of the person are about. In particular, to return to an earlier example, if my purpose is to discover whether you love me, the content of what matters to me is specified in part by the very theory that I am trying to evaluate.

In Conclusion

If I am right, it is not at all easy to see what non–question-begging arguments can be given for preferring A^R to W^R (or vice versa). As a result, giving up on our Asante concepts of the person is going to be premature, at best. Given that they have functioned successfully in the management of social relations for a long while, they are, at least, good for something. And, since social relations in Asante continue to strike both Asante and non-Asante people as having some attractive features, giving up on concepts that are clearly somehow partially constitutive of those relations needs to be justified by something better than the thought that our theories (like everybody else's) are incorrect. To give them up would be to give them up in exchange for something else. It is hard to see what argument could be made for such a wholesale substitution over the development of new insights within the existing framework. This will be worthwhile not only for us in Asante—improving theories in various respects is always desirable, by definition; the question is what counts as an improvement—but also for people generally. For, just as some useful discoveries—that you can make some sad people less sad with Prozac—developed within W^R, there is no reason to doubt that different useful discoveries could be made within A^R. In the long run, it will turn out, I am sure, that people will decide there is no *sunsum*; but I am equally convinced that eventually we shall lose our belief in the *mind*.

Notes

1. These notions are to be found in the writings of R. S. Rattray, who was the first ethnographer to give a written account of Asante ideology; and they can be confirmed by discussion with people in Asante today; see R. S. Rattray, *Ashanti* (London: Oxford University Press, 1955), 46. They are discussed also by Wiredu in Richard Wright, *African Philosophy: An Introduction*, 3rd ed. (Lanham, Md.: University Press of America, 1984), 141 and Kwame Gyekye in "Akan Language and the Materialism Thesis," *Studies in Language* 1.1 (1977):

237–44; and also in his *African Philosophical Thought* (Cambridge: Cambridge University Press, 1987).

2. In the epilog to *In My Father's House: Africa in the Philosophy of Culture* (New York: Oxford University Press, 1992), I described a moment when I certainly felt this way.

THREE

🙣

TRUTH AND AN AFRICAN
LANGUAGE

KWASI WIREDU

Since my thinking about the meaning of truth has been con-
ditioned by both a formal training in Western ideas and an
originally informal education in an African way of thinking, I would
like in this discussion to work my way through both environments. I
start from the Western angle.

We all, not unlike St. Augustine in the matter of *time*, understand
very well what truth is until we are asked for a philosophical elucidation. Trivially, truth is what is so. But what is the nature of the *what*
and of the *being so*? Thus interrogated, philosophers are quickly driven
to a Babel of theories.

Consider the first of these two enigmas. It is agreed on all hands that
it is an item of discourse rather than a slab of reality that may or may not
be so. The question is: "What exactly is the unit of discourse that is
susceptible of those characterizations?" Some say it is a sentence, others
that it is a proposition, and still others that it is a judgment, a claim, a
belief, or different from all these, that it is an idea. Frontal onslaughts on
this issue have seemed, traditionally, to get bogged down in logical and
ontological obscurities. Let us therefore try an indirect approach, uti-
lizing a thought of Tarski with what might, perhaps, be considered an
un-Tarskian intention. It was a basic part of Tarski's "semantic" theory
of truth that any definition of truth that had any pretense of material
adequacy must of necessity imply all equivalences of the form

"Snow is black" is true if and only if snow is black.

The *intuitive* persuasiveness of this suggestion consists in the fact that it depicts at once with clarity, simplicity, and concreteness the basic logical form of the idea of something being so. The semantic unit enclosed in quotes illustrates a *something* whose being so is exemplified by the second component of the equivalence. But to depict the logical form of an idea is not to explain it. And it may justly, therefore, be said that even with all the supplementary elaborations and refinements, Tarski's completed theory provides a rigorous depiction of the logical form of truth predication but not an elucidation of its philosophical import. (Actually, in at least some of his moods Tarski himself was not averse to this minimal, if not minimalist, construal of his construct.[1]) The logical depiction, to be sure, may be a tremendous achievement in itself. But if explanation is our objective, then it is obvious, by the same token, that what we need is some account of the epistemic status, or, if it comes to that, the ontological significance of the two sides of the equivalence.

In particular, it should be quite clear that some such account of the second component is necessary from our (premeditated) variation on the actual sentence employed by Tarski in his equivalence. As is well known, Tarski's equivalence in his 1944 article[2] was,

"Snow is white" is true if and only if snow is white.

Because readers are likely to think that snow is, *in fact*, white, they are likely to perceive the second component of the equivalence as having the status of a revelation rather than a judgment from some point of view or perspective. But there is nothing sacrosanct about Tarski's particular example, and our particular substitute example has the following significance. Since, by all appearances, snow is not black, the standing of the second component in our chosen instance of Tarski's equivalence is easily seen to be, not revelatory but, on the contrary, essentially perspectival. This is reinforced by a simple structural consideration: The equivalence ' "Snow is black" is true if and only if snow is black' logically implies the conditional 'If snow is black then "Snow is black" is true.' From this it is plain that the thought that snow is black, which held the position of a consequent in the equivalence and now serves as an antecedent, is just that, a *thought*. But it is a thought that stands in a certain relation with the thought that occurs in the other component (of the equivalence or the conditional, as the case may be). The nature of this relationship is the most important issue in the theory of truth. It turns out, not surprisingly, that the traditional theories of truth in Western philosophy may be seen as involving varying responses to this demand. To see the problem in this way is already to demystify it. Here are the resulting schemata of demystification.

(1) Correspondence theory:
a. "p" is true if and only if it is a fact that p.
b. Instance: "Snow is Black" is true if and only if it is a fact snow is black
(2) Coherence theory:
a. "p" is true if and only if it coheres with our *system* of beliefs that p.
b. Instance: "Snow is black" is true if and only if it coheres with our received *system* of beliefs to hold that snow is black.
(3) Pragmatic theory (in Dewey's formulation):
a. "p" is true if and only if it is warrantably assertible that p.
b. Instance: "Snow is white" is true if and only it is warrantably assertible that snow is white.

These proposals are, of course, merely, suggestive until explanations are supplied for the concepts of fact, correspondence, coherence, warranted assertibility, and "our" system of beliefs, an undertaking that, in each case, has proved to be studded with snares.

However, an interesting affinity between the coherence and pragmatic theories already leaps to the eye. In both theories, truth is a matter, not of the reference of a sentence, but of its logical and cognitive affiliations. In both theories, moreover, as I shall suggest later, the litmus test for truth amounts to the same thing, when properly conceived. By contrast, the correspondence theory, in so far as it goes beyond schema (1), seems to suggest that a true sentence is one that, by itself and as a whole, bears a certain relation to something non-cognitive. It is clear why a typical correspondence theorist will not be content with that schema. To take the given instance of the schema, both of its two components, namely, ' "Snow is black" is true' and 'It is a fact that snow is black' look, structurally, too much like claims, and would therefore be thought to be apt to communicate the impression that the correspondence relation is "merely" a relation between propositions. On the contrary, the message of the theory seems to be that the equivalence schema holds only because a true sentence *refers* to a "nonlinguistic" reality. More interestingly, the referring seems often to be thought of as isomorphic in the manner of a picture. A sentence is true if and only if it accurately pictures the given portion of reality, point for point. The Wittgenstein of the *Tractatus* is famous for the picture theory of propositions (among other things). In fact, it does not begin with him. It only reaches its *reductio ad absurdum* with him.

A veritably pictorial conception of the correspondence relation is already present in Russell's *Philosophical Essays*:

> When we judge that Charles I died on the scaffold, we have before us (not one object but) several objects, namely, Charles I and dying and the scaffold. Similarly, when we judge that Charles I died in his bed, we have before us Charles I, dying, and his bed. . . . Thus in this view, judgment is a relation of the mind to several other terms: when these other terms have *inter se* a 'corresponding' relation, the judgment is true; when not, it is false.[3]

In his later thinking, as in *Human Knowledge: Its Scope and Limits* and *My Philosophical Development*, Russell did not abide by the ontological literalness of this account, though he never abandoned the correspondence theory. He retained to the end the idea that truth has to do with the reference of our judgments to reality. The same idea is found in Austin's over-conventionalized formulation of the correspondence theory. According to him, "A statement is said to be true when the historic state of affairs to which it is correlated by the demonstrative conventions (*the one to which it 'refers'*) is of a type with which the sentence used in making it is correlated by the descriptive conventions" (my italics).[4] Reference, it seems fair to say, is the basic semantical idea of the correspondence theory. But it is also its basic defect. Pictorial reference merely aggravates the problem. So let us just consider reference. Quite evidently, reference is an indispensable category in the analysis of meaningful discourse. Our utterances, inscriptions, and gestures are, in themselves, merely physical occurrences. Their human interest is due to the fact that they frequently *signify* something. What they signify may direct our attention to objects or situations or to the products of abstraction or of the imagination. Involved here are the categories of sign, signification, and reference (objectual or otherwise). Thus, the sign "table" signifies a table. It does not, of course, signify a particular table, but rather the idea or concept of a table. It is this idea that refers to the particular table before which I am sitting. The association of the sign with the idea is a purely conventional relation. Languages other than English and its derivatives employ other signs for the same purpose. But, given this significational investiture, it is no longer a matter of convention whether in the present "historic state of affairs" I am sitting before a table or a rock. In other words, there is nothing conventional about whether the concept of a table applies or refers to the object before which I am sitting.

"Table" then, has signification and reference. Moreover, it has an objectual reference; that is, what it refers to is an object or something having to do with objects. By contrast, there are signs, such as "moral concepts" whose signification refers, not to objects, but to concepts.[5] In this case the referents are such concepts as 'honesty,' 'impartiality,' 'justice,' etc. By still another contrast, "unicorn" has signification but no reference, since (by all the zoological, as opposed to the mythological, reports) there are no such quadrupeds.

We will have occasion to recur later to the foregoing analysis of reference. But one thing to notice at once in all this is that what refers or fails to refer is the signification of a sign or concatenation of signs, not a statement. The signification of a sign is a meaning, an idea, a concept (simple or complex). We might therefore recast our previous statement by saying that it is a concept rather than a sentence or statement that may or may not refer. Consider the sentence, "The table in the room is brown." (For my purposes here, I will use "sentence," "proposition," "assertion," "statement," and "judgment" interchangeably.) It is clear, even pre-analytically, that the sentence makes the claim that the concept "brown" applies to, or refers to, the table in the room. It is clear, at the same level of reflection, moreover, that to say that the sentence itself refers to the brown table is to embark on an incoherent multiplication of words. For it would amount to saying that the claim that the concept "brown" refers to the table in the room refers to the table in the room. It makes sense to say that a concept refers to an object or situation; it does not make sense to say that the claim that the concept refers to the object or situation itself refers to the object or situation.

More technically, a declarative sentence, which is what "The table in the room is brown" syntactically is, typically contains some form of a finite verb that gives it the force of a declaration, a contention, a claim. This aspect of a sentence cannot *refer* to anything outside the sentence; it is what makes the mental process being symbolized a *declarative* propositional attitude. In our example it is equivalent to answering "Yes" to the question "Is the table in the room brown?" This "yes" element corresponds to what makes the difference between the idea of *the table in the room being brown* and "The table in the room is brown." The early twentieth-century English logician W. E. Johnson called it the assertive tie.[6] Let us just call it the assertive or declarative element. In inquiry the arrival of the assertive element indicates the concluding phase of the process. An inquiry, by the way, need not be a grand enterprise; just looking to see whether the table in the room is brown is as good an example of inquiry as any. Let us call the participial formulation that results from subtracting the assertive element from a sentence its *ideational content*.

Our point now is that it is the ideational content of a sentence that may or may not refer, not the sentence as a whole. The assertive element does not contribute to the referential relation; it merely declares it (positively or negatively). To suppose, as the correspondence theory does, that a sentence as a whole may refer is to mix the declarative function with the referential relation. This is the basic error of the correspondence theory of truth.

Let it be noted that the objection being urged against the correspondence theory (as commonly understood) is not that it wrongly talks of the correspondence of something linguistic to something nonlinguistic. The claim of correspondence, as should be clear from our discussion above, is a claim of reference. That it is possible for our linguistic formulations to refer to objects or situations or states of affairs is not only a presupposition of any theory of truth that is even slightly more perspicacious than utter madness, it is also the basis of any sort of meaningful discourse. Unless our thought and talk sometimes referred to objects and situations—let us call these collectively *reality*—the least of our infelicities would be an enforced inability to communicate. More ominously, we would not even survive as human beings. Transitions from the linguistic to the nonlinguistic and also from the linguistic to the linguistic are the commonest thing in discourse. The second type of transition is apt to escape too referential an approach to the concept of truth, such as is encouraged by the correspondence theory. That kind of transition is exemplified in our discussion of reference given above by the transition from the notion of *moral concepts* (as signification) to specific moral concepts such as honesty, impartiality, and justice (as referents). I will return to that second transition in due course. But it is important to be clear about the importance of the first type of transition. The concern for truth is, in many spheres of cognition, a concern with the reference of our thought to reality. The correspondence theory is not at fault in insisting on this. The problem with that theory consists in misconceiving the nature of the structures of thought involved in the referring relation; which is what we have explained above.

In terms of the explanation just alluded to, it would be recalled, it is the ideational content of a sentence, not the sentence itself, that may or may not refer to reality. It might be thought that this is semantical caviling. After all, so might go the reasoning, we could establish the convention that a sentence refers to reality if and only if its ideational content refers to reality. This is actually close to some ways of talking about reference in ordinary discourse. But, philosophically, this could be seriously misleading, unless it is borne in mind that while it would be only by convention that a sentence may be said to refer, it is not by any manner of convention that the ideational content of a sentence may be said to refer. It is by the very nature of thought and things that this latter is so.

But a much graver consequence can flow from speaking incautiously of the reference of sentences. One is led in that way to suppose that what we do in inquiry is to try to figure out whether sentences or statements, antecedently available to us, refer to reality or not. The model of inquiry operative here is what I have previously called the shopper's model of belief-formation.[7] It is as if beliefs were displayed on hangers in a belief store and epistemic customers just needed to select ones with suitable truth attributes.

In fact, however, we do not always start an inquiry with a sentence proposed for our consideration. And even when such a sentence is to hand, it does not, for the given inquirer, have the force of a commitment. This is something that fixation on Tarski-type equivalences has helped to conceal from many philosophical seekers after *truth*. In the equivalence ' "Snow is white" is true if and only if snow is white,' we seem to be supplied with a sentence due for truth inspection. But, actually, the quotation marks around it eliminate its assertive force, which is only restored by the "is true" attached to it. This process of restoration, hypothetical in the context of the equivalence, standardly, marks the conclusion of the given inquiry. Tarski and his followers and even non-followers in many cases did not notice all this. Consequently, it has seemed as if in asking the question of truth we are always in possession of a sentence corresponding to the first component of a Tarski equivalence.

On the contrary, a little attention to the conditions of inquiry should make it clear that frequently we start inquiry without an antecedent suggestion. Often inquiry is provoked by a question, a problem, a puzzle, and we are thrown upon our own imaginative resources in generating competing ideas out of a sense of the given situation. That idea which, of all those to hand, leads to a solution of the problem is the one that brings us to truth. To obtain a solution is simply to be able to conclude an inquiry with a warranted judgment, by the lights, of course, of the given inquirer.

But notice that the logical syntax of that prosperous outcome of inquiry is not that of ordinary truth predication but of judgment construction. (The significance of the word "ordinary" here will emerge later.) In other words, the result attained is most naturally formulated not as "P is true," since, by hypothesis, there was no "P" to be evaluated, but simply as "P." Such a "P" is, however, structurally more laden with information than the "p"s and "q"s of truth-functional logic. These range over functions, not judgments, and I adopt here the convention of representing them by small letters. As a variable, "p" is merely a function. It is the function that takes the values "truth" when "truth" is assigned to it and "falsity" when "falsity" is assigned to it. In itself it is value-free, incomplete, in the language of Frege, unsaturated. Accordingly, in prose it can only, as the Frege of the *Begriffsschrift* indicated, stand for a participial phrase, such as "The circumstance that unlike magnetic poles attract one another" (Frege's example). In the early Frege, and rightly so, the function "p" does not stand for a declarative sentence, such as "Unlike magnetic poles attract one another." Such a semantic unit is only obtained by assigning the value "truth" to the function.[8] Thus P = df. Tp, which in our present symbolism is the result of assigning the truth-value "T" to the function "p." Note, therefore, that the function is of a *participial* character. Syntactically, exactly the same is the case with the *ideas* that propel inquiry, as noted earlier; they are participial explorations of relevant possibilities. For example, in a particular inquiry, the idea of *unlike magnetic forces attracting each other* may be the driving force. Hence, the assignment of a truth-value to a function corresponds, intuitively, to the construction of a warranted judgment from an *idea* in the process of successful inquiry.

Dewey called truth in this sense warranted assertibility. In essence, if not in idiom, this conception of truth is basic also to the pragmatism of Pierce and of James (in his fleeting moments of rigor). Truth in this sense is internal to the constitution of warranted judgment. It may be called truth in the *primary* sense. Given a truth determination in this sense, a corresponding truth predication is automatic when the appropriate judgment is proposed for consideration. That is, if our inquiry has already warranted the truth-value assignment that converts the *idea* of *unlike magnetic forces attracting each other* into the judgment "Unlike magnetic forces attract each other," then we are automatically in a position to greet this sentence with the comment "It is true." It is at this level that truth discourse takes the form 'P is true.' Since there is a comparison of judgments in the picture, we may speak here of a comparative concept of truth. This is the nature of truth in its ordinary, garden variety, though without the primary variety it will not exist.

In the primary sense truth, for any judicious pragmatism, is the 'idea,' that works (i.e., that leads to the solution of the problem under investigation), not the *belief* that works, which latter, if it were proposed, would be but a recipe for wishful thinking. Studying the "consequences" (Dewey's word) of an idea, for example, of Smith having stolen the missing eggs, for the investigation of the matter of some stolen eggs may enable us to crack the mystery. In that case, we are brought to the position of being able to assert warrantably, "Smith stole the eggs." The idea, in this instance, has *worked*, and the "working" was a cognitive process. On the other hand, whether the belief that Smith stole the eggs will work for (the happiness) of Smith's grandmother, for example, is of no cognitive interest for the inquiry concerning the eggs, though it could have quite ramifying psychological consequences. Truth, then, has to do with the cognitive utility of ideas in inquiry (ideas being understood in the technical sense explained earlier), not with the impact of specific beliefs on human fortunes. This was one of the most important points made by Dewey in his magisterial review of James's *Pragmatism*.[9]

Another point that has needed to be made is that to be warranted is not necessarily to be true except from an identical point of view. This rider disables an objection treasured by critics of the Deweyan theory of truth.[10] It is often pointed out that a proposition warrantably assertible at its time of birth may be conclusively shown to be false at a later time. Even so, we still can, at that latter vantage point, recognize the statement to have been warrantably assertible. From this it is thought to follow that a statement can be both warrantably assertible and false, contrary to Dewey and followers. But here there is a *non sequitur*, which thrives on inattention to a subtlety about tenses. No statement has been shown to be both warranted and false. The warrant belongs to a past point of view, the falsity to a present one. The statement was warranted but is now no longer so. We can, indeed, from our vantage point say that the statement was false even though it was warranted. But to say that a statement was warranted does not necessarily commit one to it.

Truth, however, entails commitment. Thus, commitment is what truth has over and above warrant. To say that something is (or was) true is to assert not only that it is or was warranted but also that one is committed to it. Tense then makes a difference. "Was warranted" does not imply "is warranted," but "was true" implies "is true" (provided, of course, that we are dealing with complete statements). This excess of meaning that *truth* has over *warrant* consists in nothing more mysterious than commitment. This element of commitment is what the rider just mentioned adds to the idea of warrant in the pragmatic equation. Thus, the definition is not " 'p' is true = df. 'p' is warrantably assertible" but rather "('p' is true)$_{s1}$ = df. ('p' is warrantably assertible)$_{s1}$" where the identical subscript indicates an identical point of view. I have used 's' to stand for "standpoint " or "point of view." This is a subtlety that Dewey does not discuss, leaving room for cavils.

The objection to the pragmatic theory on the grounds that a proposition can be warrantably assertible without being true is also encouraged by a well-entrenched tendency for people to elevate their own current perspectives into Olympian truths. Thus, a Deweyan pragmatist will be informed that a belief such as that the world is flat may have been warrantably assertible in the long past but is now known not to be true. The lesson hereby offered is that truth is distinct from warranted assertibility, since some warrantably assertible propositions are, on this showing, false. Apart from obliviousness to the requirement of the identity of point of view discussed in the previous paragraph, it is clear that such criticism fails to notice that the statement that the earth is not flat is simply our current perspective. It is warranted by the best scientific thinking of our time, but it is not categorically different from a belief. So, if it is a truth, then that "truth" is, in actual constitution, a belief; and like all human cognition fallible. Proper epistemological modesty, accordingly, would enjoin the recognition that just as the best accredited beliefs of an earlier time may become refuted errors of our time, our own best beliefs may be similarly overtaken by advancing time. If this is so, then we can say that the time will, to be sure, can, never come when we shall be in possession of truths, as distinct from warranted beliefs. Either, then, truth is warranted assertibility or it is a certified impossibility. On the other hand, such fallibilism seems frequently to be eclipsed in the human consciousness when the occasion is the contrasting of our "truths" with the false opinions of earlier epochs.

The same tendency to privilege our own opinions lies behind the contention that some propositions can be true while not being warrantably assertible. What would a concrete instantiation of this alleged possibility look like? If we bear in mind the requirement of the identity of point of view, implicit in Dewey's pragmatism and explicit in mine, then our task would be to imagine a situation in which one and the same proposition is held, from one and the same point of view to be true and yet not warrantably assertible. Since " 'p' is true" implies 'p,' what we have here is somebody asserting 'p' and avowing also that the assertion of 'p' is not warranted. But if it is not warranted, why assert it? No account seems available except in terms of pure arbitrariness. The arbitrariness here consists in seeking to insulate one's belief from all scrutiny. The strategy seems to be that if it can be made out that the belief is true independently of any basis or warrant then no questions of justification would be admissible. The plan, however, carries its inconsistency on its face. At least the legitimacy of the strategy itself is unprotected against inquiry. It is perhaps out of some manner of recognition of this that even those who claim to know that God exists without any sort of rational reflection, nevertheless, claim to know "by faith." Their belief is thus, allegedly, not unwarranted, being "based" on faith. Their belief, in other words, is supposed to be warranted by faith. The examination of this kind of warrant, however, does not belong here.

Before leaving the question of true propositions not warrantably assertible, it should be observed that warranted assertibility is not the same as provability. If it were, truth would be scarce in empirical life. The stuff of rational discourse is made of experiential and experimental reasoning as well as deductive ratiocinations.

The foregoing account suggests the following dual resolution of our first enigma, which concerned the nature of that of which truth (or falsity) may be predicated. If the subject is truth in the *primary* sense, our earlier discussion indicates that what is susceptible to it is an *idea* in the sense of the ideational content of a given judgment. On the other hand, if the concern is with truth in the *comparative* sense, the object of truth predication is an antecedent statement or judgment. But it is one not initially emanating from the point of view of the inquirer of the given moment but from that of the instigator of the given inquiry. (This point of view, by the way, may be of the same person, at an earlier time.) This resolution of the first enigma also delivers us from the second, which is about the notion of *being so*. It is easy to see, in light of that resolution, that *being so* consists, in regard to the primary concept of truth, in an *idea's* being warranted in rational inquiry, and, in the comparative sense, in a judgment under review being found to be similarly warranted.

This discussion carries the seeds of a possible unification in the three contending theories of truth noted above. Revisit the coherence theory for a moment. It cannot be pretended that coherentists, historical or contemporary, have been irresistibly persuasive in explaining what coherence is. Yet the coherence that conformity to the canons of rational inquiry confers on the cognitions of a rational person may be all the coherence needed. If so, the coherence theory coheres nicely with the pragmatic one. Both theories are founded on the notion of rational inquiry. But rational inquiry is in large part an interaction with the world, external or internal, and a principal aim of thought is to attain satisfactory reference to it. It can never be overemphasized that in our referential inquiries our aim is to gain, for our thought, reference to reality. Attaining truth means that the appropriate conceptual constructs in our thinking have reference to reality. The feeling that the coherence or the pragmatic theory construes truth as a relation between "mere" propositions betrays a severe misapprehension about the nature of inquiry. Inquiry is not or, at any rate, need not be the arbitrary spinning of "propositions," unconnected with those proddings of experience called problems. A proposition warranted in rational inquiry is frequently the result of the observation of nature and experimentation upon it. Talking, then, of the coherence of a proposition with our system of beliefs or of its warranted assertibility is often talking of what actually obtains out there in the world.

Thus, suppose that, for example, "Kaunda is an African" is a warranted judgment. Even by a basic analysis of predicative language, the sentence might be interpreted as saying that the object named by the word "Kaunda" satisfies the sentential function "x is an African" (shades of Tarski). Following Frege,[11] we may call 'x is an African' a concept and read the sentence under discussion as saying that the concept of being an African applies or refers or *corresponds* to the object named. This secures for us, when generalized, a basic elucidation of referential sentences, which must account for a very large percentage of the sentences we live by. The thought here is that to say that a sentence of this kind is warranted is to say that its conceptual content applies or refers to a portion of reality. This reference relation is the legitimate meaning of *correspondence*. It may be all the correspondence we need in truth here.

However, not all judgments are referential. Nor are all referential judgments objectual. Both points are evident in the analysis of reference given earlier. To take the second first, consider the statement "All moral principles are universalizable." This is referential, even if hypothetically. But it does not envisage reference to any object or objects out there. Its possible referents are conceptual. Consequently, the veritable fixation on the transition from the linguistic to the non-linguistic endemic to the correspondence theory ill coheres with examples of this kind. The situation is even worse when we come to statements that are not referential at all. Take a sentence like "Out of nothing comes nothing" and try to apply Austin's correspondence definition of truth to it.[12] The incongruities involved in the exercise are, evidently, due to the inapplicability of notions like "historic state of affairs" and "demonstrative conventions" to such an example. Not surprisingly, Austin was uncomfortable with examples of this kind.

The reader might want at this stage to ask, "If the correspondence theory suffers from this and all the other defects alleged in this discussion, then why is it so plausible on the face of it?" Any answer must start with an acknowledgment of the plausibility of the correspondence theory. This plausibility is due partly to a misconception, partly to a misidentification, and partly to a linguistic peculiarity of English and kindred languages. The misconception consists in construing the frequent need for our concepts to refer to reality as the need for our sentences to fulfill the same function. This misconception contributes to the apparent plausibility of the correspondence theory because the need itself for some reference to reality in our thought is genuine. This matter has been already discussed above at some length.

The misidentification in question consists in the precipitous identification of the correspondence theory with the Tarski-type formula " 'p' is true if an only if p." In fact, that is contrary to Tarski's own view of the equivalence. As far as he was concerned, this equivalence with, indeed, his entire *semantic* theory of truth was neutral with respect to the various *epistemological* theories of truth. Tarski was right, for, as seen early on in this discussion, the equivalence is common to all the three theories of truth to which reference has been made above. This is why it is not quite correct to say that Tarski's theory is an attempt to provide a logically rigorous reconstruction of the correspondence theory. All three theories are, in effect, interpretations of the equivalence. The plausibility of that equivalence, therefore, cannot rightly be attributed to the correspondence theory in any proprietary way.

One step in the interpretation of the equivalence in the direction of the correspondence theory is represented by the formula ' "p" is true if and only if it is a fact that p.' As I noted earlier on, this particular equivalence is likely to be thought by many correspondence theorists to be in need of supplementation. Historically, the supplementation supplied has invoked the idea of a referential relation between a true proposition and a fact. At peak, this relation metamorphoses into one of picturization. Nevertheless, the leaner formulation seems frequently to do duty for the correspondence theory as a whole. In that scenario the correspondence theory acquires considerable plausibility. But that plausibility, as will be shown later, lacks universality. It depends on the peculiarity of the English language and its cognates.

Thus, we have the following interesting situation. The formula under discussion certainly expresses an undeniable semantic relationship between the notions of truth and fact, even if its epistemological and ontological reaches are shrouded in controversy. Certainly, nobody moderately instructed in English will be tempted to deny it. Besides, it is conceptually informative in a philosophical way, since it elucidates the connection between two notions very fundamental to communicative discourse. Yet, when the formula is translated into a radically different language, such as my own mother tongue, namely, the Akan language spoken in parts of Ghana and the Ivory Coast, it reduces to an uninformative tautology, sans all philosophical pretences. This trivialization of the formula arises from the fact that in Akan the notions of truth and fact may be rendered by means of one notion, namely, the notion of what is so, *nea ete saa*. The sentence ' "p" is true' may be expressed as ' "p" *te saa*' and "It is a fact that p" as *Nea ete ne se* p. The expressions *(e)te saa* and *nea ete ne se* are just grammatical variants for rendering the idea of being so.[13] In the upshot, the Akan version of the formula amounts, roughly, to saying something like ' "p" is so if and only if what is so is that p,' which is an unconcealed tautology. To be sure, all tautologies are splendid truths. But some are conceptually informative, and others are not; and certainly this one is not. From it therefore, no philosophical enlightenment can be anticipated.

What the foregoing shows is that, although the equivalence " 'p' is true if and only it is a fact that p" is correct and philosophically interesting in English, it is truistic in Akan but of no philosophical interest. One might seek to evade this conclusion by suggesting that if the Akans do not have different verbal formulations for *fact* and *truth*, all that this may mean is that the Akan language is not expressively adequate to the task of rendering these concepts. The following is a simple reason why this will not do. If the equivalence being discussed holds in English, then whatever can be expressed in English in terms of "is true" can be expressed in terms of "is a fact." Since at least, by hypothesis, one of these expressions can be rendered in Akan, it follows that whatever can be expressed in English by any one of these two concepts can be expressed in Akan. An even more substantive conclusion follows: If one of the two notions can express every thought that can be expressed by anyone of them, then, beyond grammatical niceties, what we have is a duality without a difference. If so, the particular form of the correspondence theory represented by the equivalence under examination is not an option in the theory of truth in any language like Akan.

This brings us to an interesting intercultural fact about philosophical problems and theses: Some of these are culture relative, or more specifically, language relative; their existence depends on the peculiarities of some culture or cultures. When the determining factor is language, I have called this dependency *tongue-dependency*.[14] Of such a nature is the equivalence thesis relating truth to fact, and the language involved is English. Probably, all languages generate some tongue-dependent problems and theses. It therefore behooves every philosopher, whatever his or her language, to watch and pray lest he or she confuse tongue-dependent issues with universal ones.

The foregoing is not an advocacy of relativism. Tongue-dependent issues do have a universal intelligibility with respect to their home languages. Moreover, some may be important in their native environments. When that is the case, this fact can be appreciated by not only native speakers but also non-native ones. Moreover, any philosopher working in a second language is well advised to apprise him- or herself of the provenance of those problems in relation to that language. Although, both tongue-dependent and universal problems require the attention of all concerned, the latter are of more importance from a transcultural standpoint.[15] Because of the historical influence of Western languages and philosophies in Africa, African philosophers have a special need of the intellectual circumspection just mentioned. With respect to the correspondence theory, this discussion shows that this circumspection can only come of careful attention to our various vernaculars in philosophical reflection.

Notes

1. Alfred Tarski, "The Semantic Conception of Truth and the Foundations of Semantics," *Philosophy and Phenomenological Research* (1944). Reprinted in H. Feigl and W. Sellars, eds., *Readings in Philosophical Analysis* (New York: Appleton-Century-Crofts, Inc., 1949) and in many other anthologies.

2. Ibid.

3. Bertrand Russell, *Philosophical Essays* (London: Allen and Unwin, 1966), 153. I have quoted and commented on this formulation in "Truth in the Akan Language" in my *Cultural Universals and Particulars: An African Perspective* (Bloomington: Indiana University Press, 1996).

4. J. L. Austin, "Truth," *Proceedings of the Aristotelian Society* Suppl. 24 (1950). Reprinted in George Pitcher, *Truth* (Englewood Cliffs, N.J.: Prentice-Hall, 1964).

5. It is usual to speak of the reference of a sign rather than the reference of the signification of a sign. However, this seems to encourage some people to proceed as if signs in themselves can refer. The artificiality of our diction is motivated by premonition of such an error.

6. W. E. Johnson, *Logic* (New York: Dover, 1964). First edition 1921.

7. Kwasi Wiredu, *Philosophy and an African Culture* (Cambridge: Cambridge University Press, 1980), 213.

8. Gottlob Frege, *Translations from the Philosophical Writings of Gottlob Frege*, trans. Peter Geach and Max Black (Oxford: Basil Blackwell, 1960).

9. John Dewey, "What Pragmatism Means by Practical," in *Essays in Experimental Logic* (New York: Dover, 1916).

10. Another objection, even more prestigious than this, was urged by Rudolf Carnap in his "Truth and Confirmation." (See H. Feigl and W. Sellars, *Readings in Philosophical Analysis* [New York: Appleton-Century-Croft, 1949].) The argument is this. By the law of excluded middle, every proposition is either true or false. If "'p' is true" means "'p' is warrantably assertible," then, given any proposition, either it or its negation is warrantably assertible. But this is incorrect, since there are propositions whose truth or falsity we do not know. In fact, a decade before Carnap wrote, Dewey, in effect, forestalled this objection in his *Logic: The Theory of Inquiry* (New York: Holt, Rinehart and Winston, 1938), by pointing out that the logic of inquiry is three- rather than two-valued. There is the true, the false, and the problematic.

11. Frege, *Translations from the Philosophical Writings*, chap. 2 "Function and Concept."

12. If this example is too metaphysical for you, take "Two plus two equals four."

13. I have discussed this translation in "The Concept of Truth in the Akan Language" in *Cultural Universals and Particulars*. The Akan classicist and philosopher J. T. Bedu-Addo does not accept it, but his own translation of "It is a fact that" supports my claim that in Akan both "It is a fact that" and "It is true that" are rendered in terms of the same notion. According to him, "the best translation of the English sentence ['It is a fact that it is raining'] is: *Eye nokware se nsu reto*. (Literally, 'it is true that it is raining')." See "On the Concept of Truth in Akan," in *Philosophy in Africa: Trends and Perspectives*, ed. P. O. Bodunrin (Ile-Ife, Nigeria: University of Ife Press, 1985), 76. Notice that in this translation the same phrase *Eye nokware se* translates both "It is a fact that" and "It is true that."

14. See, e.g., my *Cultural Universals and Particulars*, chap. 7, p. 101ff.

15. That there are universal problems is easily understood (ibid.).

FOUR

AN OUTLINE OF A THEORY
OF DESTINY

SEGUN GBADEGESIN

In "Destiny, Personality, and the Ultimate Reality of Human Existence: A Yoruba Perspective," "God, Destiny and Social Injustice: A Critique of a Yoruba *Ifa* Belief," and *African Philosophy: Traditional Yoruba Philosophy and Contemporary African Realities*, I grappled with the concept of destiny as it features in Yoruba philosophical discourse.[1] My approach in those essays has been to situate the concept in the contexts in which it gets applied and to draw the philosophical implications of its usage in such contexts. In this regard, one cannot shy away from its ethnological foundation, its religious-spiritual dimensions, and its socio-political consequences. In this essay, I will pursue the discussion further, paying particular attention to some objections that have been raised since the appearance of the first two essays.

My contention is the following: The Yoruba concept of destiny is a complex one. It may be suggested, as some have, that this complexity is probably the source of the problems that scholars have identified with it. If we are able to understand its complexity, the argument may proceed, the problems might dissolve, and the objections that have been raised against it may turn out to be unwarranted. While I agree with the first part of this observation, regarding the complexity of the concept, I do not share the optimism of the latter part. It is simple-minded enthusiasm and unnecessary nationalistic fervor to try to patch up problems that are quite obvious from the vantage point of philosophy. At least, so I will argue.

Odu Corpus and Two Stories

In the *Odu Corpus*, there are at least two references to the concept of destiny as it features in traditional Yoruba philosophy, and I do not think one needs a serious argument to support the claim that there is no better starting point for this discussion than the literature of Ifa. The concept of destiny has its raison d'être in Ifa. But, of course, the clarity of its treatment of the concept is another matter.

In *Ogbegunda*, the story of how *ori* is chosen in *orun* (heaven), and its irrevocability once chosen, is told. It is the story of three friends— Oriseeku (the son of Ogun), Orileemere (the son of Ija), and Afuwape (the son of Orunmila). Obatala had finished molding their physical bodies, and they were ready to go to the house of Ajala, the heavenly potter of *ori*, to choose their *ori*. The three friends were warned by their friends to go directly to the house of Ajala and not to break their journey for any reason. While the other two friends took this advice seriously, and went straight to the house of Ajala, the third, Afuwape, decided to first see his father before going to choose his *ori*. Oriseeku and Orileemere got to the house of Ajala first and picked the *ori* of their choice, and proceeded straight to the earth. Afuwape got to his father and met with a group of divination priests, divining for his father. These diviners advised Afuwape to perform some sacrifice so that he would choose a good *ori*. He did, and he went his way to the house of Ajala. Though he met some obstacles on the way, he overcame them all, apparently due to the sacrifice he had performed. He chose a good *ori*, with the help of Ajala, and he was able to succeed in life. His two friends, Oriseeku and Orileemere, did not make a good choice and were never successful in life. The choice of each was a burden to the end of their lives.

The second reference is in *Ogunda Meji*, an *Odu*, which confirms the importance of *ori* to a person. In the story each of the gods (major and minor) is asked if he or she is willing to follow his or her devotee to the grave, to literally die with his or her devotee. None of them is willing, not even Orunmila, who then concludes that it is only a person's *ori* that can go with him or her to the grave. Literally, "*ori*" means head, and the conclusion is therefore literally true: The head of a dead person is never cut off before the person is buried. But it is also meant to be an idiomatic truth: Ori is a god, just as Ogun or Oya. But more than this too, the Yoruba believe that a person's *ori* is his or her paramount god. Therefore the story concludes that no *orisa* blesses a person without the consent of the person's *ori*; and we should therefore leave other *orisa* alone and worship only our *ori*.

In these two stories, we have the conundrum of the concept of destiny. I can identify at least seven fundamental questions that have to be addressed to make sense of the concept. First, is the choice of *ori*, the same as the choice of destiny? Second, is there really a choice involved? Third, does the concept of responsibility have a role in the explication of the concept? Fourth, does the concept allow for connection between destinies, for instance, between mother and daughter? If so, does this happen by accident or by design? Fifth, how does the belief in reincarnation affect the concept of destiny? Sixth, is there only personal destiny or is there also communal destiny? Seventh, what is the significance of destiny, and is the belief in destiny rational? I will address each of these questions as a basis for a coherent theory of destiny.

Ori and Destiny

Ori, in Yoruba language, means head. What has it then to do with destiny? *Ori* is an important part in the makeup of the human person. *Emi* and *okan* are the others. *Ori*, like *okan*, has a dual character. It refers to the physical head, which is considered vital to the physical status of a person. It is, for instance, the seat of the brain. But when a typical Yoruba person talks about *ori*, he or she is more often than not, making reference to a non-physical component of his or her person. For there is a conception of an *ori*, in which it is believed to be the bearer of a person's destiny as well as the determinant of personality. How does this element come into the picture?

There is a common agreement in the tradition and in its literature about the makeup of the human being. According to this tradition, the human being is made (created?) by the combined effort of Obatala, the maker of the physical body, and Olodumare, the Supreme Being, who gives *emi*, the life force or soul. *Emi* is a nonmaterial force responsible for life. Its presence ensures life and its absence means death. But the *emi* is itself immortal, and it may reincarnate in another body. The problem this belief raises for the concept of destiny will be discussed later. *Okan*, the other component of the human person, also has a dual nature. It is at times material and at others nonmaterial. In its former nature, it is the heart; in its latter nature, it is the mind, as a center of consciousness responsible for thinking, desiring, wishing, deliberating, etc. As such, its contents include *ero* (thought), *ife-okan* (desire), *eru* (fear), etc.[2]

After Olodumare has put the *emi* in place, the newly created body-plus-*emi* proceeds to the house of Ajala, the potter of *ori*, to acquire an *ori*, as in the case of the three friends referred to earlier. (Figuratively, we may imagine Ajala's house as a compound in the palatial block of Olodumare and the fashioning of persons as a division of labor between the three: Obatala, Olodumare, and Ajala). It is not without reason that Obatala is referred to as *eleda* (maker) and Ajala is referred to as *alamo ti n mori* (the potter who makes the *ori*). *Ori* is the bearer of each person's destiny. This is not the same as the physical head; though, for a reason that has to do with the important role of the latter in the life of a person, it is taken as a symbolic representation of an inner head, which is then taken to be the bearer of destiny. This inner head is *ori-inu*, or simply *ori*. Therefore, though *ori* is not identical with destiny, it is its bearer, and as such, the remote controller of a person's life.

Destiny is the preordained set of outcomes of life, wound and sealed up in the *ori*. Every human being is believed to have an allotment, and it determines what they will be in life. It determines the general course of life. *Ori* is its bearer and receptacle, and therefore its controller, hence the rationale for the claim in the second story that no *orisa* blesses a person without the consent of his or her *ori*. For since *ori* controls destiny, and since destiny is the allotment of a person in life, even if one performs sacrifice to the *orisa*, there is no guarantee unless one's requests are compatible with one's destiny.

An objection has been raised against treating *ori* as an entity by itself. It is suggested that *ori* is merely another term for destiny, and that, as such, it "means quite little more than that some things are unavoidable by virtue of our birth and circumstances of life."[3] The problem with this way of interpreting the concept is that it abandons the structure of the belief in favor of a "contemporary" account. This is clear from his argument that "as classical responses to the need to account for personhood, these explanations (from Yoruba *Ifa* verses) cannot be foisted on contemporary Yoruba thought as changes have been necessitated by new experiences."[4] What Bewaji seems to be missing is this: If we are reviewing a traditional account, we must state the belief as it features in the system before we attempt any credible critique in light of "new experience." Or must we impose our own belief on the traditional belief system even when we resist "foisting" a traditional account on contemporary thought? But this is what he has done, especially in his accounts of *ori*, *emi*, and destiny. For him, *ori* is destiny. But *ori* is not a spiritual entity. Therefore *ori* is not the bearer of destiny, and the embodied *emi* is the chooser of destiny. But if *ori* is destiny, then *emi* is the chooser of *ori*. Now, Bewaji also argues that a person could not have had *emi* or life or soul prior to conception. And since *emi* (in his account) chooses destiny, it follows that no destiny could have been determined prior to conception. Finally, for Bewaji, *emi* cannot survive the demise of the body. Therefore no one can have a built-in destiny to join any ancestors after death.[5] Obviously, this interpretation is an attempt to modernize the concept of destiny. Even as such it fails, because Bewaji has to be able to locate *emi* in the makeup of a fetus for his account to make "modern" sense. And of course, to be consistently modern, he has to provide an account of how, where, and when this *emi* "chooses" destiny.

I find Bewaji's position puzzling, to say the least. On the one hand, he objects to my interpretation of the traditional belief because he thinks that I accept the mythical account of tradition. Yet he wants to impose a "modern" account on the traditional source of the belief—to give it a modern twist. On the other hand, however, when I criticize the belief in its traditional form in my "God, Destiny, and Social Injustice," Bewaji also has problems with my critique because, according to him, it is from a modern liberal perspective, while he would rather take into account "the religious-pragmatic alternatives" in Yoruba thought. Well, I find it interesting that one can coherently reject a "mythical account" and at the same time take seriously a "religious-pragmatic" account.

Ori, Destiny, and the Problem of Choice

How does a person get his or her destiny? Is it by choice? Or is it by imposition? There are various conflicting accounts in the interpretive literature, due largely to the existence of numerous accounts in the traditional literature, including the literature of Ifa itself. One has to pay attention to all in the interest of full understanding, even if it leaves the puzzle largely unsolved. Three accounts stand out: *ayanmo*, *akunleyan*, and *akunlegba*. Others are either variants of these three or synonyms for destiny. Thus, *ipin* and *kadara* are synonyms for *ori*. They are not alternative ways of getting destiny as Bewaji appears to think. So I shall argue.

Ayanmo

Literally, *ayanmo* means "that which is chosen and affixed to one." Here we have an idea that destiny is chosen and affixed. We do not, however, have an idea of who does the choosing. It is either the deity or the human. If it is the deity, then the problem of choice does not arise. But the problem of responsibility arises. For, if I do not myself choose my destiny, and it is chosen for me, what right does anyone have to blame me for being what I have been predestined to be without any input from me? If I do the choosing, the problem arises about what kind of choice it is that an unconscious entity makes. I will go into this momentarily.

Akunlegba

Akunlegba literally means "that which is received while kneeling." Here, destiny is conceived as the portion that is imposed on one, most likely by the deity. One just receives it, and one has no choice in what it turns out to be. In this conception of destiny, the problem of choice does not arise, but the problem of responsibility can be raised.

Akunleyan

Akunleyan means "that which one kneels down to choose." Here it is the human entity that makes a choice of a particular destiny. In the first story, this is the model of destiny that is used. Afuwape and the others make their choices. One could picture the procedure this way. The body-plus-*emi* entity goes to the house of Ajala. There are numerous *ori-inu* (inner heads) with various destinies sealed up in them. The body-plus-*emi* entity looks around the room before making a choice of one. In the Afuwape story, we are told that Afuwape was looking for one that is beautiful on the outside. But Ajala helped him to pick a good one. This is the consequence of his having performed the sacrifice as recommended by the divination priests. In any case, the emphasis here is on choice, and this is what creates the problem of choice. How so?

Choice presupposes freedom and the availability of genuine alternatives. None of these conditions is present in the case of the "choice" of destiny. The body-plus-*emi* entity is unfree, since he or she has to have a destiny. So he or she cannot avoid making a "choice" and cannot walk away. Second, this entity is unfree to choose in the sense that the entity has no personality, without which it is impossible to have preferences of life patterns. Destiny is what confers personality; for it is what confers tastes and preferences, important elements of personality. But without a specific personality, one has no basis for choice. Third, this being has no full information to make a choice. There is no recitation of what is in each of the *ori*. So this being has no basis for comparison between them, without which it is impossible to make a real choice. Finally, there are no genuine alternatives, since there is no way of differentiating in any intelligent way between the *ori*, at least as far as their real essence is concerned. On the outside, each *ori* looks exactly like the other. With all these observations, it appears clear that the concept of choice is problematic when applied to the choice of destiny.[6]

Another objection has been raised against this interpretive analysis of the problem of choice. While many scholars have identified this as a problem for the concept, Bewaji sees it as a "straw-man argument." For he thinks that we see it as a problem because we have not focused on all the available alternative accounts. One such available account, according to him, is *adayeba*, which does not presuppose choice, because it focuses on "the material conditions of existence." He actually thinks that this is what I mean when I spoke about the existential situation, "the reality of existence." According to Bewaji, "*Adayeba* indicates that you have no control over where you are borne [*sic*], whether your parents are Hausa, Ibo, Nupe, or Yoruba . . . whether you are born into wealth or poverty."[7] Obviously, there is a confusion here. This is not what *adayeba* means in the context of destiny. *Adayeba* is no more amenable to study than *akunleyan*, which is its first half, and it is unforgivably mistaken to suggest that *adayeba* "discusses the material conditions of birth, parentage, socio-economic and political relations of persons . . . to forge a destiny."[8] There is simply no notion of *adayeba* isolated from *akunleyan*. Therefore, if the latter is a failure, as Bewaji suggests,[9] so must be the former.

Indeed, Bewaji himself later confirms that *adayeba* is never used in isolation. It is always used as a precis for a longer statement: *akunleyan, oun l'adayeba; a daye tan, oju nkan gbogbo wa* (what we chose kneeling is what we come to meet in the world. But when we arrive in the world, we become impatient with our lot). What this means is simply that the destiny that one chooses before coming into this world is what becomes one's lot in the real world. Therefore, the reality of existence cannot be isolated from the previously chosen destiny. Though he comes close to this understanding of the full statement, Bewaji does not appreciate its full significance. That is, it only confirms the problem of choice as a real one. This is why he could go on to suggest that *adayeba* can be "empirically analyzed to see how much one has made of one's circumstances" but that it "has failed to feature in philosophical discussions by African scholars" with "a liberalist background or pretensions to democratic attitude."[10] What exactly does this mean? A liberal scholar will be interested in a defense of free choice and suspicious of imposition of lots as it is in the case of *akunlegba* (received while kneeling). But it does not then mean that such a scholar will ignore *akunlegba*, since it can help focus the problem of responsibility. This has been my own focus in treating this account of how destiny is received, and it is only appropriate to turn to it now.

Ori, Destiny, and Responsibility

If destiny is really not a product of a genuine choice, as must be the case when we look at *akunlegba* (received while kneeling) as the source of destiny, the question arises as to the appropriateness of praise or blame. Is a person responsible for what he or she has not really chosen? Yet, the traditional Yoruba do not shy away from praising and/or blaming people for their actions. How then does one reconcile the apparent inconsistency? It should be easy if individuals are truly responsible for the choice of destiny. Then it would make sense to praise them or blame them. Thus, it may be argued that the car-jacker chose his punishment along with his choice of his car-jacking profession. But if the choice was not his, and it was imposed on him (through *akunlegba*), then there is a problem that cannot be brushed aside. There are two approaches to the issue.

From one perspective, destiny is not a cut-and-dried phenomenon, and it is alterable. Indeed the average Yoruba acts as if destiny is alterable. Therefore, even if a bad destiny has been imposed on one, one has a responsibility to try to change it for better. Divination for a newly born baby about its future prospects is the direct means of doing this. The rationale is that the diviner has the power to discern the destiny of everyone, and to do something about an unfavorable destiny. Since the procedure is available to everyone, the argument is that whoever does not take advantage of it is to blame for any problem he or she may have in life, not the initial destiny. Yet this conclusion does not take into consideration the fact that even after all is said and done, an unfavorable destiny may not go away, or at least so does the belief go. For is it not true, in the language of tradition, that *ayanmo ko gboogun?* That is, destiny does not succumb to medicine. The question then must be faced: Why do the typical Yoruba refuse to accept an unfavorable destiny only to end up accepting the fact that a bad destiny cannot be altered? Second, why do the typical Yoruba proceed on the assumption that a good destiny may be negatively altered by the machinations of others, and never give up this assumption, but continue to arm themselves against evil doers? The answers to these questions are at the heart of Yoruba philosophical thought. As a prelude to an answer to the first question, we have to note the following. A typical Yoruba has an optimistic attitude towards life. He or she is born into a family that is loving and caring. He or she also knows that the gods are there for protecting and prospering the individual. Therefore, the first attitude to life is one of optimism.

Secondly, the divination process never comes up with a purely negative prediction for a client. The logic of divination is to predict in such a way that the goodness of life's prospects is not permanently blocked out. Thus, even if a diviner "sees" a problem, he puts it in positive light and may recommend sacrifice. For instance, the diviner is not expected to say: "You are destined to die." Rather he would say, "You are advised to perform xyz sacrifice to avert an untimely death" or "you are advised to avoid going on a long journey for xyz number of days to avoid an accident." These examples show that even the diviner brings forth the optimistic aspect of the belief in destiny. It is therefore this attitude that informs the behavior of the people, and why they proceed on the assumption that all is well. However, suppose that even after the sacrifice against untimely death, the client still dies in a mysterious circumstance. Here the recourse is made to the fact that it has always been his or her destiny, and it cannot be avoided. Yes, it does not in practice lend itself to resignation, but if one puts together the two phases of the process: the first initial optimism and the second hands up recourse to helplessness, it would appear that an uncharitable critic may sense an inconsistency, where a sympathizer senses pragmatism.

A second approach is even more problematic, since it proceeds on the assumption that a bad destiny may be the result of the individual's own character subsequent to the imposition of an otherwise good destiny. Thus, a person destined to be a successful surgeon may turn out a failure because of his or her laziness and fraudulent activities, and a case like that deserves blame. In other words, destiny only guarantees the potentials, not the actualization of a life prospect. The latter depends on the efforts of the individuals, hence the emphasis on *ese* (leg) and *owo* (hand) in the elaboration of the concept. The leg and the hand are the symbols of hard work without which a good destiny cannot come to fruition. Yet the problem is only partially resolved by this approach. For if one can make sense of destiny as it pertains to success or failure in respect of career or wealth, it does not appear that the same answer will do for misfortunes that have no noticeable source in a person's character. This is the case with an innocent victim of earthquake or flood, and one cannot blame such a bad destiny on the character of the victim without further assumptions about an earlier life.

The Interconnectedness of Destinies

The very idea of destiny suggests that there must be some connection between the destinies of various peoples: mother and child, spouses, friends and relations. For the child whose destiny is to die at infancy is born to a family whose destiny it is to mourn its child. Therefore, one can assume that each of the parents must also have chosen (or received) a related destiny. And by extension, could it also mean that every member of a particular community chose related destinies, at least to the extent that significant events in the lives of each would have impact on others. For one thing, the queen's destiny is to rule her people, whose destinies include being ruled by this particular queen. Could it also not mean that the car-jacker's destiny includes the choice of his victim whose destiny then is to be robbed and perhaps killed by this particular person? This insight about the interconnectedness of destinies may be a reflection on the traditional communal mode of living among the Yoruba and may provide an intellectual rationale for the political appeal to the notion of a common destiny when it suits political leaders.

Individual and Communal Destinies

Individual destinies determine the outcome of individual lives. Destiny is the meaning of a person's existence—the purpose of existence. However, this personal life purpose cannot be separated from the communal reality of which the individual is only a part. This is due in part to the interconnectedness of destiny discussed above. However, it is also due to the fact that the purpose of individual existence is intricately linked with the purpose of social existence and cannot be adequately grasped outside it. While confirming the personality of an individual, destiny also joins each one to the community, and personality becomes meaningful by appeal to destiny and community. In any case, destiny is itself a community concept, a means for the community to provide its members with meaning. In the final analysis, a person is what she is in virtue of her destiny, her character, and the communal influence on her.

But what does it mean to say that destiny is the purpose of existence? Simply put, an individual's destiny is what he or she is supposed to live for. I have argued elsewhere that destiny is like a message to be delivered. The deity sends the message through each person, and it is the person's own contribution to the totality of the good in the community in particular, but also in the universe. Conceived in this way, there is bound to be raised the problem of apparently bad or even wicked destiny, for example, the car-jacker's destiny. How is that supposed to promote the totality of the good in the universe? It appears that one cannot consistently maintain the view that destiny is to promote the good, and acknowledge the fact that some destinies are clearly evil.

The Akan view, as interpreted by Kwame Gyekye, avoids this dilemma. For according to that view, God imposes destiny, and it is always good. The occurrence of evil in the world is then attributed to the existence of wicked people. However, as I argued in *African Philosophy*, the problem here is that the three theses by Gyekye cannot be consistently maintained. The three theses are: God imposes destiny; destiny is always good; destiny is unalterable. If we add to these theses the obvious fact that there is evil in the Akan community—people die prematurely; natural disasters are real forces that the people contend with—then it becomes clear that one of the three theses must be false. Gyekye admits that the path of a person may be "strewn with failures, either because his or her own actions, desires, decisions, and intentions or because of the activities of some supposed evil forces."[11] If these evil forces are human, then their own apportioned destiny must be bad, which means there is bad destiny. Or if they originally have good destiny, which was changed, then it means that destiny is alterable. If they are natural forces, then again, there is bad destiny.

Destiny and Reincarnation

Two other important related beliefs of the Yoruba are the beliefs in immortality of the soul and reincarnation, and it is necessary to clarify how the belief in destiny fits into these two. The Yoruba seek three goods in the world: *ire owo, ire omo, ire aikupari iwa* —the good of wealth, the good of children, and the good of immortality. The latter is, for them, the most important, because it is the crown of existence (*iwa*). *Aiku* is immortality. The belief is that bodily death is not the end of one's life, for the soul lives on in a different plane of existence. This soul (*emi*) may then reincarnate in a different form of existence at a later time. Thus, a dead parent may reincarnate in the form of a child to her daughter or granddaughter. With respect to the belief in destiny, this belief in immortality and reincarnation raises a number of questions. First, how does one conceptualize the connection between the original destiny allotted to the original person in her first life and the new destiny in her second life? Is it the same destiny that is only temporarily suspended at death, or indeed is this death one phase of the entire long destiny that has to be "lived" out. Or does the first destiny lapse at the first death, and a new destiny chosen at each reincarnation? It does not appear that much thought is given to this puzzle in the traditional philosophical speculation about destiny.

We could try to see how the various options fare. First suppose it is the same first destiny that extends over all the "lives" of the person. It would follow that one is not really dead until all the details of one's destiny are worked out in the various lives. Indeed, some of the mythical stories, which illustrate the belief, suggest something to this effect. There is, for instance, the story of the young man. As he was about to go into the world for the first time, he recited his destiny for the sealed approval of Olodumare, the Supreme Being. His destiny was to go into the world, live to a youthful age, have a girlfriend, fix a date for the wedding, and on the wedding day, he would go into the bush to ease himself and would be bitten by a snake. Then, as he put it, "I would come back." In other words, he would end his life in this way. In this account of the matter, reincarnation is just the continuation of the same life. But if so, there would be no need for the choice of a new destiny. "I would come back" would then have to be followed by a further narrative on what will happen next. Perhaps "then, I would stay a little bit and go back to be born into my original father's family again." This would account for the phenomenon of *abiku*, born to die children.

But suppose the person has a different allotment of destiny at each reincarnation. Then can it be said that the same person is reincarnating after each death? This would raise a serious problem regarding the meaning of being the same person. For if it is true that one's personality is really determined by the kind of destiny one has, then each new round of destiny chosen by the *emi* would appear to turn out a different person provided the destiny chosen is not identical. So even if this time around, this new being were brought into the world through the same mother as before, it would not mean that it is the same person. It all boils down to what a person is, and in the tradition, a person is a combination of *ara* (body), *emi* (soul or life force), and destiny (*kadara* or *ipin*).

The Significance of Destiny: Addressing the Question of Rationality

The belief in destiny has a special place in the worldview of the Yoruba. Like the conception of cause and chance in terms of personal idioms about the activities of gods and spiritual entities, the belief in destiny fits perfectly well into the traditional system of belief. Furthermore, if one explores it carefully, one would discover the rationale for the belief. There is no doubt that the belief serves a purpose, to assure human beings that they have a role to play in the world (even if it is an assigned role), that they are not by themselves (because their role has been endorsed by the deity), and that the meaning of their lives is encoded in the message of destiny. Therefore, people should not worry unduly about failure; but since destiny is an indication of potentiality, they should also not be complacent. The belief also suggests to us that the Yoruba have some anxiety about situations beyond the control of anyone and are keen to provide some cushion for the rough and tumble of life.

From the foregoing paragraph, one may conclude that the belief in destiny has its rationale. But a further question is in order: Is the belief rational? This is the question posed by the late Peter Bodunrin in his classic "The Question of African Philosophy."[12] As he puts his argument:

> showing why a people hold a particular belief is not sufficient to show that the belief is rational. Given any social practice one can always find a reason for it. An explanation of an event in terms of the motives of a person or a god is rational only if evidence is given for the existence of the person or god, or sufficient reasons given why their existence must be assumed and arguments adduced as to why the person or god should

be supposed to be implicated in the particular event. Surely, to show that a belief arises from emotional needs, if this is in fact true, can hardly be construed as having shown it to be rational.[13]

Bodunrin's point is that a traditional belief, like any other belief, must be evaluated from a philosophical point of view. No one can fault this demand. All that we have said about destiny providing meaning for people's life may be true, the question must still be posed, how rational is the belief? This may be addressed from various perspectives. I will identify three: First, is the belief coherent? That is, are its internal components consistent with one another? Second, is the belief consistent with other beliefs the people hold about the world? Third, is the belief (theory) compatible with reality (practice), as we experience it?

To the first issue, from the earlier discussions, it seems obvious that there is a tension between the various components of the belief in destiny. On the one hand, there is a tension between the idea of a predestined life and the idea of an individual having responsibility for his actions. It is similar to the belief in determinism and free will. If we assume a changeable destiny, then we may draw an analogy between destiny and weak determinism, which is consistent with free will. One may then suggest that destiny is also compatible with responsibility. But this only moves the problem of incoherence to another arena. Here it is instructive to quote from Barry Hallen:

> A Yoruba will say that once destiny is "fixed" by *Olorun* it cannot be changed. It must take place. Nevertheless on other occasions the same person will say that it is possible to "miss" the destiny one has been apportioned, in the sense of becoming confused and lost during one's lifetime and doing things for which one is not at all suited. Or an external force can interfere with one's destiny. Neither of these is entirely consistent with the belief that once destiny is fixed, it is unalterable and must take place.[14]

This surely appears to be an example of inconsistently held beliefs within a single structure of belief, and as far as Bodunrin is concerned, it must be seen and evaluated as such. But Hallen does not; hence Bodunrin's objection to Hallen. For Hallen, the inconsistency is only there if we look at the Yoruba belief from the perspective of a Westerner. He sees the various beliefs that may be called upon when an explanation is required as comparable to

> the various partitions that are ranged along the wings of a stage and may be swung into position depending upon the demands of the next

scene. Each partition corresponds to a certain belief. There are other belief-panels in the wings that would be inconsistent with it if they were brought into play simultaneously. But this does not happen (except in very exceptional circumstances) because when a certain kind of problem occupies stage centre the same partition is always moved out to serve as its explanatory background.[15]

Bodunrin is not pleased with this approach, which he sees as "a good account of why the Yorubas do not find it odd to live with inconsistent beliefs." But, as he puts it, "Hallen's account can hardly be construed as showing that the Yorubas hold consistent views on destiny as expressed in their concept of *ori*; rather his account explains why the Yorubas do not see any inconsistencies in their belief system. But this does not remove the inconsistency."[16] On this issue, I think Bodunrin is right. This is the position I argued for in "God, Destiny and Social Injustice," which Bewaji characterizes as a liberal position. But it does not require an ideological orientation to identify a logical flaw in a belief system. Of course, I am not implying that one cannot find arguments to remove the inconsistency.

The question is what kind of argument is there to remove the apparent inconsistency? The question of the belief in the alterability of destiny is fundamental to the theory. The issue we have raised with it is whether this belief is compatible with the idea of a fixed and unalterable destiny. Now, one way out of the apparent dilemma is to see the belief in an unalterable destiny as fatalism and to argue that this is not the Yoruba position. Many scholars have argued this way. Thus, Moses Makinde has drawn a distinction between strong destiny, which he identifies as fatalism, and weak destiny, which he identifies as the Yoruba concept of *ori*.[17] If fatalism is unalterable, weak destiny, as in *ori*, is not. Therefore, the argument goes, there is no inconsistency in the belief. Another argument is that even the strong notion of destiny is open to alteration as far as the Yoruba are concerned. According to this interpretation, the concept of *ase* (special divine words) is superior to that of *ori* or *ayanmo* (destiny) because it issues from Olodumare. The point here then is that Olodumare can effect a change through *ase* once a supplication is made and accepted. The fact that the Yoruba act as if they believe that destiny is alterable would seem to support this interpretation.

The second issue has to do with whether the belief is consistent with other beliefs people hold about the world. A list of major Yoruba beliefs about the world will include at least the following: There is God; there are *orisas*; death is inevitable; work is the cure for poverty; character is beauty; character is the king of all talismans; moderation is the source of honor and respect, and so on. From this list of beliefs, can it be said that there is one that is inconsistent with the belief in destiny? Again it would appear at first that the belief that *orisas* is the determinant of success or failure is inconsistent with the belief that work is the cure for poverty. However, as observed above, the Yoruba acknowledge the importance of hard work in the realization of a good destiny. This is why *ese* (leg) and *owo* (hand) are brought into the picture. The meaning of this is that both the hand and the leg are important instruments in the realization of one's destiny. Therefore it would not appear that there is a conflict between the two beliefs. With respect to character, it has also been observed earlier that one of the ways in which one's destiny may be altered is through one's own character. Of course, one may raise the question, as in other cases, how is it that one's character would contribute to the altering of one's destiny, since it is supposed to have been a component of the destiny in the first place. I do not myself see an adequate answer for this in the structure of the belief.

The third issue is whether the belief (theory) is compatible with reality (practice) as we experience it. For instance, since the theory (of destiny) suggests that one has a preordained allotment before coming into this world, one possible practical implication is resignation. Yet in practice, no one adopts a philosophy of resignation. Does this suggest then that the theory is incompatible with our practice? Again, one way of addressing this issue may be to call attention to the complexity of the theory of destiny with its in-built correctives. Destiny does not even in theory imply resignation, one might argue, because there is the notion of potentiality built into it. Therefore, destiny must be seen as a potential that still has to be fulfilled. Second, one may argue that since destiny is only a potential, even in theory, one cannot consistently adopt a philosophy of resignation until one has made the strenuous effort without success. But, of course, there are other beliefs in the system, which reject measuring success in terms of wealth or position. Third, as discussed previously, it may also be pointed out that the theory of destiny allows for the concept of *ase* with the consequence that even a strong notion of destiny is liable to alteration with the involvement of Olodumare. Therefore, since the theory allows for this, it is apparently not inconsistent with the practical efforts to avert failure. What is needed is a thorough analysis of the full logic of the theory. Then one can expect a better fit between the theory and practice of destiny.

Conclusion

From the foregoing, it seems clear that the concept of destiny as it features in Yoruba philosophical discourse has good potentials for a rewarding philosophical investigation. I have only attempted to raise some of the issues that call for further analyses and investigation. I am sure that there is a lot more, and that even on those that I have tried to address here, there is a lot more to be said and not a few objections to be raised. But I think it is clear that one cannot dismiss the concept as irrational without further argument. It seems also clear that one cannot drive a wedge between the theory and the practice of destiny without further argument. Finally, since the belief in destiny continues to feature prominently in the social lives of the people, serious philosophical efforts will continue to be required to deal with the various issues that need to be resolved to move us towards the formulation of an adequate theory.

Notes

1. Segun Gbadegesin, "Destiny, Personality and the Ultimate Reality of Human Existence: A Yoruba Perspective," *Ultimate Reality and Meaning* 7.3 (1984): 173–88; "God, Destiny and Social Injustice: A Critique of a Yoruba *Ifa* Belief," in *The Search for Faith and Justice in the Twentieth Century*, ed. Gene James (New York: Paragon Press, 1987), 52–68; *African Philosophy: Traditional Yoruba Philosophy and Contemporary African Realities* (New York: Lang, 1991).

2. For an extensive discussion and defense of my account of *okan*, see my *African Philosophy*, chap. 2.

3. J. A. I. Bewaji, "Yoruba Concept of Human Destiny: Demystifying a Theory," unpublished paper, n.d.: 28.

4. Ibid. 18.

5. Ibid. 21.

6. Gbadegesin, *African Philosophy*.

7. Bewaji, "Yoruba Concept of Human Destiny," 28.

8. Ibid. 33.

9. Ibid.

10. Ibid. 29.

11. Kwame Gyekye, An Essay on African Philosophical Thought: The Akan Conceptual Scheme (New York: Cambridge University Press, 1987), 116.

12. Peter Bodunrin, "The Question of African Philosophy," *Philosophy* 56 (1981): 161–81. Reprinted in Richard Wright, *African Philosophy: An Introduction*, 3rd ed. (Lanham, Md.: University Press of America, 1984), 1–23. Page reference is to Wright.

13. Wright, *African Philosophy*, 15.

14. Barry Hallen, "A Philosopher's Approach to Traditional Culture," *Theoria to Theory* 9.4 (1975): 259–72. Cited in Wright, *African Philosophy*, 16.

15. Ibid. 17.

16. Ibid.

17. Moses Makinde, "A Philosophical Analysis of the Yoruba Concept of Ori and Human Destiny," *International Studies in Philosophy* 17.1 (1985): 53–69.

FIVE

PERSONAL IDENTITY IN AFRICAN METAPHYSICS

LEKE ADEOFE

Pre-theoretic concerns about personal identity challenge us to provide a coherent and unified response to the following questions: What is a person? What is it for a person to be the same persisting entity across time (or at a time)? How many ontologically distinct entities constitute a person? What relationship, if any, exists between an individual's first-person, subjective experiences and our objective, third person's perspective? African philosophy takes the challenge much more seriously than Western philosophy.[1] In the former, unlike in the latter, plausible responses to one question are routinely informed by plausible responses to others. In this essay, I explore the extent to which an African theory of reality has provided integrated responses to the personal identity questions and build on those responses. My approach, partly descriptive and partly imaginative, ought to be familiar; it has been borrowed from a tradition that dates back at least to John Locke.[2] What emerges is a tested conception of human existence that is formidable enough to be explanatorily useful vis-à-vis personal identity questions.

The Ontological Distinction

A tripartite conception of a person characterizes the African thought system.[3] A person is conceived to be the union of his or her *ara* (body), *emi* (mind/soul), and *ori* ('inner head'). Unlike *ara*, which is physical, both the *emi* and *ori* are mental (or spiritual). This dichotomy might induce us to think of the African view as dualistic. But it would be a mistake to do so, since *ori* is conceived ontologically independent of the other two elements. Thus, the African view is properly thought of as triadic.[4] It is philosophically interesting that a person is a creation of different deities. *Ara*, the body, is constructed by Orisa-nla, the arch deity; Olodumare (God or 'Supreme Deity') brings forth the *emi*; while another deity, Ajala, is responsible for creating *ori*. *Ara* is the corporeal entity from head to toe, including internal and external organs, and it becomes conscious with *emi*, which, apart from its life-giving capacity, is conceived as immortal and transmigratory. The inner or metaphysical head, *ori*, the other non-corporeal entity, is the bearer of destiny and, hence, constitutive of personality.

Understanding the Distinction

Thus, within the purview of African metaphysics, a person is made up three elements, *ara*, *emi*, and *ori*. Since their ontologies are logically independent of each other, the three elements are ontologically distinct and properly conceived as a triadic view of persons. *Ara* refers not only to the whole body, but also its various parts. However, the metaphysics does not make clear how much of a body is minimally needed for sameness (or continuity) of body. Presumably, our nontheoretical assumptions about what sameness or continuity of body amounts to will suffice for our discussions. However, those nontheoretical assumptions may include those that are peculiarly African, for example, the *abiku* or *ogbanje* syndrome, in which some children are believed to continuously repeat life cycles. As evidence for this syndrome, Africans point to similarities of bodies involved to posit bodily continuity between them. What is not clear is whether in these special cases, similarities in bodies are constitutive of, not merely evidence for, bodily continuity. *Emi* is the mind/soul. Its presence is indicated by phenomenal consciousness, an effect of divine breath that manifests (sort of) in breathing. We may note parenthetically that nonhuman creatures and plants have *emi*. Injunctions are usually made not to maltreat *nnkan-elemi*, things "inhabited" by *emi*. This attitude, however, has not led to Jainism. *Emi* is taken to be essential to having ratiocinative activities, but it is not endowed with person-like characteristics as in certain Western traditions, for example, Descartes's.[5] Indeed, the Western view that where the soul goes, there goes the person is not African, not at first blush anyway. Some African philosophers, however, have described *emi* as "the most enduring and most important characteristic of a person," but there is no support within the African system of thoughts to understand this in a Platonic or Cartesian sense.[6] That *emi* is considered most enduring might tempt us to think that for Africans ensoulment embodies personhood much like in Western thought systems. But this temptation should be resisted for they also contend that *emi* has no variable qualities, that is, *emi* has no distinguishing characteristics.[7] What *emi* does, it seems, is help ground consciousness. Thus, while *emi* is most enduring and perhaps the most important element of a person, it is arguable that it encapsulates personhood. *Ori* refers to both the physical head and the inner/metaphysical head, and the latter is sometimes referred to as *ori-inu* to avoid ambiguity. Notice that Africans seem to think that there are metaphysical components of several body parts, most notably, the head, the heart, and the intestines. But the metaphysical components of the latter two serve largely the semantic function of conveying the roles of the relevant body parts in the proper bodily and psychic functioning of a person.[8] One philosophically interesting question then is why only *ori* has been elevated into an ontologically constitutive element of a person. A plausible response is that *ori*, unlike other metaphysical components, is a deity in that, among other things, it is considered worthy of worship and appeasement.[9] But this response is not satisfying: Why has *ori*, and not any other metaphysical body part, been deified? Why is deification of *ori* not due to its ontological status rather than the other way around? These are attractive quasi-logical inquiries, but I strongly doubt that they are promising enough for follow up. A more promising and fundamental issue to pursue is whether *ori* is a deity as it is generally claimed. A useful distinction to explore here is between an entity that is a deity and an entity towards which we only maintain what I will call a 'deity stance.'[10] Some substantial considerations make it plausible to think that *ori* belongs to the latter category. Consider, first, the following. Suppose *ori* is really a deity. That everyone has *ori* makes each person a deity or possessor of one. But neither view adequately represents the African view. The view that each person is a deity is attractive, but not African. It conflicts with the African view that some individuals become deities on becoming ancestors; you cannot be becoming what you already are. Second, the view of *ori* as both a deity and an ontological constituent of a person makes supplications by the person to Ori supplications to him- or herself. This would be odd unless supplications in this context are taken as metaphorical expressions of good wishes about oneself. Indeed, on this view of *ori*, it would be difficult to understand deferential attitudes to *ori* as both a deity and an ontological constituent of a person. And since we are all agreed that *ori* is ontologically constitutive of a person, it is more plausible to reject the view that Ori is a deity. Against the first consideration, an objector might argue that Africans as a matter of practice posit a hierarchy of deities, and that Ori is a deity in and of itself does not conflict with the belief that individuals become deities on becoming ancestors. That Africans posit a hierarchy of deities is true, but the transition from one deity to another is alien to the African view.

The Thought Experiment

What is a person in the African view? This question is ambiguous between two different but related questions: What are the constitutive elements of a person? What makes a person the same persisting entity across time? In response to the first question, the constitutive elements are *ara*, *emi*, and *ori*. The task is to determine the extent to which this response would help with the second but interrelated question about persistence. Suppose we become Cartesian, and conceive of the soul of one person, Adler's, transferred to the soulless body of another. If ensoulment embodies personhood, Adler now has a different body. (Locke, who does not think that the soul is immortal, would want Adler's brain transferred instead.) But do we have any reason to think of the issue this way rather than a case of mental derangement or clairvoyance? This is the personal identity issue in Western metaphysics. In reidentifying a person, do we trace the body or the mind? Generally, the mental (or psychological) continuity theorists think that we are to trace the mind because the mind encapsulates all that is really important: our hopes, fears, beliefs, and values. And if our mental life were to cease, we would have ceased to live. For them, we are defined by the mental. Bodily continuity theorists, on the other hand, think that we are to trace the body. That way, they reason, we respect the biological fact that we are basically organic beings, no matter what else we happen to be. Underlying the issue here is the distinction between a person and a human being. 'Person' refers to the fact that we are social entities, 'human being' to the fact that we are organic entities. The mental theorist emphasizes the first fact, the bodily theorist, the second. Thus, John Locke, a mental theorist, assumes that if we successfully transfer, say, Adler's brain into John's brainless body, the John-bodied person is now Adler. For the John-bodied person now exhibits the mental life of Adler. (Of course, there are serious difficulties in imagining this kind of exchange, but let us put them aside till much later.) Lockean followers, for example, Derek Parfit, have gone further by claiming that transfer of the brain is not necessary; what is important is securing Adler's mental life in John's body no matter how that comes about.[11] What is important in these transactions, they argue, is that relevant mental lives continue irrespective of how this is done.

Defending Continuity Theories

The mental continuity theory and the bodily continuity theory are the two main competing views, though some variants of the former, and hybrid views of both, are sometimes considered interesting enough to merit separate discussions.[12] But, in general, alternative views to the main ones are not encouraging. Suppose, for instance, the John-bodied person (after the transfer of Adler's brain) is considered a new person altogether, that is, he is neither John nor Adler. The problem with this view is that it is totally inconsistent with our understanding of human origins; new humans cannot, in our view of the world, come to exist as described. To illustrate, suppose that two qualitatively identical pieces of paper are ostensibly turned into a slice of cheese and a baby. Which transformation would we accept as real? Some might be inclined to claim that neither is real, but if we must choose, it seems a lot more plausible to accept the paper–cheese transformation than to accept the paper–baby transformation. This is because our metaphysical intuitions about human origins are so firm that we are prepared to discount what would ordinarily count as empirical evidence to the contrary. Some objectors might argue that the John-bodied person is better considered a new person, rather than a new human being. Their objection would be that our strong metaphysical intuitions are about human beings, not human persons. Indeed, given our willingness to consider some nonhuman species persons, our philosophical imagination is not stretched to consider the John-bodied person neither John nor Adler but a new person, though not a new human being. The problem with this view is that the John-bodied person is peculiarly capable of performing any of the roles formerly associated with Adler, the physical circumstances permitting. In particular, the John-bodied person is willing to be held liable for promises, obligations, and duties formerly defining of Adler's personhood. More perplexing would be the willingness of the John-bodied person to follow up on the promises, obligations, and duties of Adler in accordance with Adler's own life plans. There is thus no serious justification for claiming that the John-bodied person is a new person. The distinction between 'person' and 'human being' is meant just for this: to preserve the practical value of our life plans and projects. Since Adler's life plans and projects are successfully pursued by the John-bodied person, it seems more plausible to consider the John-bodied person Adler than a new person, which is what the psychological continuity theorist claims.[13]

The Soul

There are good reasons, then, for the Western metaphysician to consider the psychological continuity theory and the bodily continuity theory as the main competing theories of persistence of persons. The next task for the Western metaphysician as he or she sees it is to determine which continuity theory is more plausible, and which variant of that is most explanatorily useful. Some useful philosophical insights have emerged in that determination, and I will touch on the most promising, but, first, a discussion of some tensions that undermine the whole issue of persistence in Western philosophy. Consider the Cartesian dualist concerned about persistence. The Cartesian dualist claims that body and soul are the two ontologically irreducible constituents of a person, with the soul being the essence of the person. Since for the dualist the soul is the person, the issue of persistence is concerned with tracing the soul. Where the soul is, there goes the person. But surprisingly, neither of the two main theories of persistence expresses this dominant view of most people. The more plausible the Cartesian theory seems, the less plausible either theory of persistence. Notwithstanding degrees of psychological and physical continuities involved, if persons are ensouled, it is the soul that underlies persistence. The soul by itself escapes tracing, but so much the worse for personal identity theories, the dualist would claim. 'Scientifically minded' philosophers, as most Western philosophers are in their professional lives, would claim that the Cartesian notion is not as plausible as its competing materialist views. What Descartes teaches, they will argue, is the importance of our occurrent and dispositional mentation in personhood, which is encapsulated in the various psychological continuity theories. Materialists are right that psychological continuity theories make clear our inclination and willingness to define ourselves by our mental lives. In that sense, then, the theories encapsulate the Cartesian insight that a person is a thinking thing that, *inter alia*, doubts, understands, and denies. Of course, materialists are not all agreed on what psychological continuity theories consist in. Some, for example, Derek Parfit, claim that the informational content of our mentation is all that matters, irrespective of how that sameness of information is secured, either by the brain, computer chips, or whatever. Some others, for example, Sydney Shoemaker, argue that sameness of information is valuable in persistence to the extent that there is sameness of brain or a functionally analogous entity.[14] There is disagreement as to how much information needs to be preserved for sameness of persons, but we may put all that aside here. Yet other materialists, for example, Bernard Williams, would argue for a physical continuity theory: sameness of the body (with or without the brain, but preferably with the brain) is necessary in preserving identity.[15] Apart from the most obvious cases, these three 'scientifically minded' approaches deliver different judgments on issues of persistence, and there is considerable disagreement on which approach is most plausible. Indeed, most of the discussions about persistence in analytic Western metaphysics turn on determining which approach best reconciles our deeply rooted intuitions about the nature of persons with certain thought experiments about persistence, though it is not always understood that way. In any event, all this, I hope to show, is much ado about nothing.

Persistence and the Nature of Persons

Consider again the Cartesian solution. Whatever else we might think about the solution, we must concede that it has two main advantages over the continuity theories. First, it links its ontology of persons with its view of persistence. The soul is an ontological constituent of a person and, on its view, sameness of the soul constitutes sameness of person. Psychological continuity theorists are right in thinking that part of the attraction of same soul criterion is that it *ceteris paribus* preserves sameness of mentation. But this is not all—its linkage between *what* we are, our *whatness*, and our persistence is important, however difficult determination of the latter is. Without the linkage, what we are is one thing, our persistence, another. But whatever disagreements we may have about persistence, there is a pre-theoretic supposition that our persistence is about *us* and ought to preserve our *whatness*.[16] Sameness of mentation does not provide the link; it perhaps constitutes evidence for our persistence, but it is silent on what we are. Different but inconsistent ontological assumptions about us are possible with sameness of mentation criterion. This partly explains the disagreement among psychological continuity theorists, hence, the desire of some of them to also emphasize sameness of brain. But we are not our brains, however important that organ is in our proper functioning. Thus, in securing Adler's occurrent and dispositional mentation in the John-bodied person, the latter does not then become Adler. Or, to put the same point differently, that the John-bodied person is Adler violates our ontology, and the violation is not mediated by transfer of the brain. Notice that I am neither claiming nor suggesting that we *are* organic entities. We are not our bodies, and in general, I consider physical continuity theories much weaker than their psychological counterparts for the simple reason that they uniformly fail to consider the practical importance we attach to personal identity.

The second main advantage of the soul is the apparent integrated unity that it provides our mental lives. Mental characteristics over time, however similar and overlapping, would not by themselves constitute the mental life of an individual. Some psychological theorists realize this, but apparently think that the brain could provide the cement. Although sameness of brain provides evidence for psychic unity, it does not constitute it. David Hume, after first claiming that our identity is *ersatz*, realized this when he lamented in the appendix of the *Treatise* that he could not find what binds the constant flux of consciousness and sensations.[17] Hume finds it difficult to reconcile his atomistic principle that our perceptions are distinct and separate with the psychic unity that seems to characterize us. The usual Humean relations of contiguity in time and space, and causality, would not do here, since they are neither necessary nor sufficient for psychic unity. Hume's own radical empiricism prevents any appeal to the soul, but Hume's failure as confessed to in the appendix is a failure of continuity theories.

First-Person vs. Third-Person Perspectives

Another tension that threatens discussions about persistence in Western metaphysics is the third-person perspective of those discussions. Formulations of schemata for continuity theories, bodily or psychological, neglect the first-person perspective: Adler is the same person as John if Adler is bodily or psychologically continuous with John. The underlying assumption is that the continuities and, supposedly, personal identity, are objectively and, hence, third-person verifiable. Yet concerns about, say, *my* personal identity, are about *me*, and one would expect personal identity discussions to reflect this subjective aspect of the issue. The question then is what it is for a third-person, objectively determinate entity (or cluster of entities or aggregate of parts or whatever) to nevertheless be me, and not someone else. For continuity theorists, the challenge would be to identify what it is about my intentions, beliefs, desires, and other psychological phenomena that make them mine. One possible solution is that all the psychological phenomena "supervene" on the workings of my central nervous system, not someone else's. But this is not satisfactory enough, for we might ask what it is in particular about my central nervous system that makes it mine. Another alternative route to generating the same issue is to posit a distinction between my psychological phenomena and central nervous system, on the one hand, and between the central nervous system and me, on the other. My psychological life, it seems, could have been sustained with a different but perhaps structurally similar central nervous system. Moreover, we understand the claim that I could have had a different psychological life (or body) and a different nervous system and still be me. That is, we understand what it is for me to be a subject undergoing radical psychological changes and still be me: "Help! I am undergoing these terrible changes in my psychology." Language use is hardly decisive in these matters, but it seems reasonable to claim that the cry for help here is not tautological: My psychology is undergoing these terrible changes in my psychology. Thus, focusing on psychological phenomena is, in general, mistaken. Also, we understand that my complete physical and mental surrogate, capable of a life third-person qualitatively indistinguishable from mine, would not be me. No amount of Parfitean intuitions about what presumably really matters "in survival" will change these bare facts about me and my persistence. It is easy to determine how our intuitions might have gone wrong. With Adler's brain successfully transferred into John's brainless body, we intuit that the John-bodied person is now Adler. In this case though, the John-bodied person, too, thinks that he is Adler. That is, judgments from both the first-person and third-person perspectives agree with each other. We assume that our objective, third-person judgment is correct, and that the subjective, first-person judgment is correct to the extent that it concurs with the former. We think of situations, say, hypnosis and false memory, in which the first-person's judgments are not reliable, and become further convinced that subjective judgments by themselves are untrustworthy. But our assumption here is mistaken. There is nothing personal about personal identity without the person. If there is no epistemic gap, so to speak, between a first-person judgment and the person, then the judgment is the correct determination of identity, irrespective of any contradicting third-person judgment. Thus, we cannot neglect the first-person perspective; it is central to personal identity.

Applying the Concept of *Ori*

My concern with personal identity is concern with my psychic unity, not my soul—unless I am worried about the possibility of life after death. Concern with psychic unity is concern with the extent to which activities in my life fulfill a purpose. The purpose in turn provides meaning to my life, and it is that meaning that evidences to me psychic unity, that my life is on track. Now, we do impose purpose on ourselves. For example, I may decide to spend the rest of my life feeding the homeless. But this kind of purpose and attendant psychic unity are second best. Notice that I could have made my purpose the harassment or killing of the elderly, and my psychic unity could have been derived from this. Thus, self-imposed purpose and psychic unity may help to calm the nerves, but what is needed is the purpose that emerges from a quasi-historical self-actualization. Self-actualization here depends on our state of being and on the state of being we are yet to become, albeit with a *ceteris paribus* become. A life lived consciously or otherwise in conformity with this state of becoming is a life on course, and the purpose that emerges from it provides genuine psychic unity to the individual. *Ori*, understood as destiny, embodies the quasi-historical self-actualization. Trees do not have *ori*, and neither do cats, dogs, and dolphins. My concern with my identity is with whether my life is on track. It helps if my physical and psychological lives are not radically discontinuous, but this requirement is neither necessary nor sufficient for my identity.

For greater perspicuity of issues involved, imagine a transfer of Adler's *ori* to John's physical head—without his *ori*, of course. Since *ori* embodies personality, the moderating characteristics underlying an individual's social relations, John's new life should now resemble Adler's former life. But what does 'resemble' mean in this context?

Two pictures suggest themselves. First is the Lockean picture: John is now capable of fulfilling the social roles of Adler, for he now exhibits Adler's former mental life. Second is what I will call Abel's picture: John now has the characteristic fortunes (or misfortunes) defining Adler's former life. The second picture is closer to the African view; the first would make *ori* functionally isomorphic with the brain (or soul) in Western metaphysics, thereby undermining the philosophical basis for *ori*.

To sharpen the example, assume the following: Adler's former life had been enviable. His desires were nicely moderated. He was successful in friendships, business, health, and in his communal relations. He could hardly do anything wrong. John's former life was the exact opposite. He failed consistently in his endeavors. His sincere and worthy efforts to succeed and be perceived differently came to naught. Indeed, John was not doing anything substantially different from what Adler was doing, but the outcome for John had been consistently bad, and for Adler consistently good. Africans would ascribe the disparities in results to their choices of *ori*. If we now suppose an exchange of *ori* between Adler and John, we would expect John's life to be consistently worthwhile and admirable, and Adler's life consistently the opposite. The supposed exchange between Adler and John exemplifies what we might call, broadly speaking, an exchange of personalities. With changes in a person's personality, there are likely to be corresponding changes in the person's social roles; and with new social roles come new social identities. This explains the motivation of the mental theorist in Western metaphysics in assuming there had been an exchange of persons in cases involving an exchange of social roles. Notice that the main objection to the mental theorist is that his or her solution violates our organic nature. The African solution appears not to have done this. Human identity is preserved in the union of the body and the soul (*emi*). In *ori* resides personality. A tripartite conception of a person allows for transferring the latter without violating 'human beingness,' at least not in the way the bodily theorist finds objectionable.

A possible objection might be that an exchange of *ori* might not lead to an exchange of social roles, and that there would be no basis then for thinking people have exchanged anything. To illustrate the objection, consider again the Lockean mentalist approach. In transferring a brain from one body to another, our intuition that personhood is transferred in the exchange of brains is based partly on the assumption that such a transfer would lead to exchange of social roles. But with an exchange of *ori*, we need not assume an exchange of social roles. What an exchange of *ori* secures is a change in fortunes and self-realization. A change in fortunes might lead to a change in social roles, but this need not be so. Thus, with the exchange of *ori* a person may be suitable to perform only his or her former roles and tasks. The question then is why we must think personhood has been transferred with the exchange of *ori* when there is no noticeable change in social roles.

The objector here incorrectly assumes that our concern with specific social roles underlies our concern with personal identity. To be sure, our view of ourselves is to some extent manifested in the social roles we perform. This explains why social roles may help to flesh out our intuitions about personal identity. Social roles help to make clear what is personal about personal identity. However, our concern is not with specific social roles but with whatever roles we are involved in to be as enhanced as possible. No specific social roles are constitutive of anyone's identity. Mental theorists are confused about this. They correctly notice that we care about the continuity of *our* intentions, beliefs, and memories. They correctly assume that the reason for this is because we care about the success of our projects. And since our intentions, beliefs, and memories are particularly suited for our projects, they wrongly elevate the projects into the criterion of personal identity. They reason that our projects define us and we are whatever can fulfill the projects under consideration. But if, as African metaphysics suggests, our concern with personal identity is that whatever projects we are engaged in are to be fulfilled as well as possible, then it is a mistake to elevate these projects into a criterion of personal identity as the mental theorists have done. The concern with the continuity of our intentions, beliefs, and memories is a concern not with specific projects but with the successful completion of whatever projects there are, as long as they contribute to our self-actualization. Thus, the mentalist intuition about the defining role of projects in a person's identity cannot be used to undermine the view of *ori* as a constitutive element of a person.

Conclusion

Any credible theory of personal identity must be metaphysically and socially stable, and the two forms of stability must be interconnected. By "stability," I simply mean the ability to deliver consistent judgments. Metaphysical stability helps to explain the unity of the self, so to speak, that makes personal identity possible. Social stability helps to explain our socialized existence—our belief systems, social character, and projects of value that seem to make our lives meaningful. A theory of personal identity is likely to be stable in some form or another, but the challenge is to be stable in both forms in the same context at the same time with respect to the same determinations. Continuity theories dating back to Locke's—including Hume's—are socially, but not metaphysically, stable. Hence, their general inclination, despite varied reasons, is to think of the concept of a person as a "forensic" notion. However, both forms of stability are linked in the concept of *ori*. *Ori* provides the needed metaphysical support to our social existence; it helps to make our beliefs, character, and social projects really ours. With *ori*, our social existence exemplifies a self-actualization process. That is, we know that the social projects we care about are those we ought to care about, not just ones we fortuitously care about. The same with our beliefs, desires, and social existence in general; things are the way they ought to be. Notice that the ability to engage in self-evaluation is worthy on its own, but it is a poor substitute for self-actualization.[18] Being able to reflect and self-determine which social existence we want for ourselves is not as desirable as knowing which social existence we ought to want. Indeed, what is attractive about being able to determine for ourselves is that such a process promises to give us what we ought to want for ourselves.

The self-actualization process allows me to recognize a social life as mine, not my surrogate's. Notice that the recognition is not dependent on the particular contents of the social life. The explanatory insight we gain through the concept of *ori* is demonstrated when we consider the quagmire in folk wisdom about what makes an individual flourish. Most people concede that material wealth does not make an individual "happy." The same can be said for having a good job, friends, intelligence, and an admirable character. We might be tempted to think that a life with *all* the characteristics is a "happy" one. Not necessarily so. A moment's reflection shows that such a requirement is neither necessary nor sufficient for the individual to be "happy." I want to suggest that a "happy" life is one that is in sync with the individual's self-actualization process. The quagmire is due to not having the concept of *ori* (or its functional analogue) as a mode of explanation in the cultural repertoire of the perplexed. *Ori* provides an individual with a stable, truly integrated identity that is also first-person perspectival and self-concerned. And it is this kind of identity that is able to provide unified responses to the identity issues with which I started the essay.[19]

Notes

Many of the ideas contained herein were first presented in Boston at the 1994 APA Eastern Division Meeting under the auspices of the APA Committee for International Co-operation. A subsequent refinement was presented in Kingston, Jamaica, at the 1995 Annual Conference of the International Society for African and African Diaspora Philosophy and Studies.

1. Amelie Rorty, "Introduction," in *The Identities of Persons* (Berkeley: University of California Press, 1976).

2. John Locke, *An Essay Concerning Human Understanding*, ed. P. H. Nidditch (Oxford: Oxford University Press, 1975), iii. 27.

3. My focus is on the Yoruba, an ancient traditional people of Nigeria. The Yoruba, perhaps more than any other African group, have contributed greatly to the culture of the Americas. Their influence, in religious and metaphysical terms, extends to Brazil, Argentina, Cuba, Jamaica, and the United States. But there are similarities between their metaphysical system and that of the Akan of Ghana. For an excellent but general discussion of the Yoruba concept of a person, see Segun Gbadegesin, *African Philosophy: Traditional Yoruba Philosophy and Contemporary African Realities* (New York: Peter Lang, 1991), 27–59. For a brief look at the Akan system, see Kwasi Wiredu, "African Philosophical Tradition: A Case Study of the Akan," *Philosophical Forum* 24.1–3 (1992–93): 48–51.

4. As Gbadegesin duly points out, another term for *ori* is *enikeji*, which roughly translates "partner" or "surrogate." He quotes, with approval, Wande Abimbola's claim that *ori* is a divinity. I argue later in the essay that it is perhaps more accurate to claim that the Yoruba maintain a "divinity stance" toward *ori*. That is, they only relate to *ori as if* it is a divinity.

5. Rene Descartes, *Meditations on First Philosophy*, trans. John Cottingham (New York: Cambridge University Press, 1986), 16–23. See M. A. Makinde, "An African Concept of Human Personality: The Yoruba Example," *Ultimate Reality and Meaning* 7.3 (1985):195.

6. Ibid. 196.

7. Ibid. 198.

8. This is one approach. Another is to think of the Yoruba as being in an objective-subjective participatory mode with the body. Since she is not her body, a Yoruba 'sees' her body as an object, so to speak. But she also 'sees' her body as intrinsically hers. The synthesis is a system that posits metaphysical components of bodily parts. For now, I choose the former approach.

9. After all, the Yoruba do literally say that if we must choose between the *orisa* and *ori*, we are better off with the support of *ori*.

10. Similar to Daniel Dennett's notion of intentional stance. See his *The Intentional Stance* (Cambridge, Mass.: MIT/Bradford Books, 1987).

11. Derek Parfit, *Reasons and Persons* (Oxford: Oxford University Press, 1984), Part 3.

12. See, e.g., Robert Nozick, *Philosophical Explanations* (Cambridge, Mass.: Harvard University Press, 1981), 29–70. Nozick calls his the closest continuer theory.

13. For a strong opposing viewpoint, see Marya Schechtman, "The Same and the Same: Two Views of Psychological Continuity," *American Philosophical Quarterly* 31.3 (July 1994).

14. Sydney Shoemaker, "Persons and their Pasts," *Identity, Cause, and Mind* (New York: Cambridge University Press, 1984), 19–48.

15. Bernard Williams, *Problems of the Self* (Cambridge: Cambridge University Press, 1973).

16. This is probably the point Marya Schechtman is making but within the Lockean tradition. Her acrobatic effort to save the Lockean intuition fails. She guesses right that she needs a "substance-self," but without *ori* (or a functional analogue) to work with, her reading of Locke is too forced. See Schechtman, "The Same and the Same," 202, 206ff.

17. David Hume, *A Treatise of Human Nature*, ed. P. H. Nidditch, 2nd ed. (Oxford: Clarendon Press, 1978), 633–36.

18. H. Frankfurt, "Freedom of the Will and the Concept of a Person," *Journal of Philosophy* 68 (1971).

19. A word on thought experiments. Since the publication of Kathleen Wilkes's *Real People: Personal Identity without Thought Experiments* (New York: Oxford University Press, 1988), it has become fashionable to be unduly skeptical about the power of thought experiments to deliver reliable judgments about personal identity. For me, it is precisely because the notion of a person is ordinarily too vague that we need thought experiments to make more precise the real issues. Understandably, the more a thought experiment subsists on our background knowledge, the more we are likely to consider its judgments firm and reliable. But that is the nature of the beast here and in many other things, too.

SIX

THE CONCEPT OF THE PERSON
IN LUO MODES OF THOUGHT

D. A. MASOLO

A careful reading of the debates on the concept of *juok* reveals the heavy burden of colonial influence in our ways of thinking about the world since the arrival of colonial institutions. *Juok* is a Luo concept, and it is usually translated as "soul" or "spirit." Some African philosophers have taken note and rightly warn against the failure on the part of African philosophers to critically clean African thought of colonial superimpositions. Among such avant-garde thinkers is the Ghanaian philosopher Kwasi Wiredu. He decries the colonial legacy evident in representations of African thought as the function of "the historical imposition of foreign categories of thought on African thought systems through the avenue of language, religion, and politics."[1] In his now classic text *The Invention of Africa*, V. Y. Mudimbe clearly charted the historical drama of the European construction of the idea of Africa through the triple discursive enterprises in anthropology, mission work, and political domination.[2] It was constructed under the shadow of the Christian paradigm. The early works of the first generation of African intellectuals reflect this legacy in their use of the categories of European thought to explain and analyze African thought. It is to this mold of African thought that Okot p'Bitek's and Bethwell Ogot's debates on the concept of *juok* clearly belong.

Concerning Okot p'Bitek, he is not the typical disciple of Western thought, yet he is neither a disciple of Mbiti nor Idowu.[3] Much of his scholarship was dedicated to drawing sharp opposition between African and Western thought and value systems. By many measures he was an uncompromising cultural nationalist, a characterization to which, I believe, both his scholarly and poetry works attest. His famous satirical poems *Song of Lawino* and *Song of Ocol* are a scathing derision of Western cultures and of Africans who have been blinded by them into rejecting their own heritage. But there is an irony to the significance of the intervention of such critics like Okot p'Bitek: they double simultaneously as both insiders and rebels in the practice of postcolonial theory and critique. It is not their mistake. It is the nature of the dialectic in the history of colonialism and its negating aftermath.

It is within this paradoxical standing of postcolonial theory that one finds elements of Western thought firmly rooted in Okot p'Bitek's works, even as he viciously critiques the imposition of Western categories on African thought systems. P'Bitek's critique focuses especially on the study of African religions and, by extension, on the entire discipline of social and cultural anthropology. In *African Religions in Western Scholarship*, p'Bitek criticizes social anthropology as a typical colonial discipline that was created as an appendage and justification of European expansionism. He characterized it as specializing in the study of the "problems related to the culture and welfare of the less advanced peoples of [the] Empire." Throughout imperial Europe, programs for the study of the colonized peoples were hosted in the Royal Institutes, either of Anthropology, as in Britain, or of Overseas Studies, as in Belgium. P'Bitek contends that anthropology was a colonial discipline and that its language and conceptual framework were the representational tools of the colonizer and were irrelevant in independent African institutions. According to p'Bitek, "Western scholars have never been genuinely interested in African religions *per se*. Their works have all been part and parcel of some controversy or debate in the Western world."[4] Similar sentiments recently have been restated by a new generation of Western anthropologists, who view the old anthropological tradition as largely a European self-projection through representing others as "that which the European self was not." The works of Clifford Geertz, James Clifford, Marcus and Clifford, Marcus and Fischer, and Johannes Fabian echo p'Bitek's contempt for cultural anthropology.[5] Within the context of postcolonial theory, p'Bitek's critique aptly foreshadowed both the idea of the European invention of Africa[6] and the calls for the decolonization of the mind such as one finds in the work of the novelist Ngugi wa Thiong'o and of Wiredu.[7] Along with this general project, adds Rosalind Shaw, was the invention of "African traditional religions" as the more "primitive" genre of religion as perceived through Judeo-Christian categories of the West.[8] According to Shaw, "'Invention' critiques such as Mudimbe's would seem to apply with particular force to the study of religion, given that the term 'religion' itself is absent from the languages of many of the peoples whose practices and understandings we describe as their 'religion.' "[9] Shaw's argument is not so much that terminologies cannot be adapted across cultures to stand in for ideas similar to those for which a term may refer in its linguistic origin. Her objection is to the "invention" of previously inexistent realities through the uncritical transfer of terms between possibly unrelated sets of categories of thought and practice. In other words, the taxonomic archive of anthropology, by which we know and identify various aspects of non-Western cultures, acquire their significance only from their comparative and derivative status vis-à-vis their Western springs. Thus, she argues, "if we examine those traditions usually selected as 'world religions', we find that even if they have little else in common, they have written texts, explicit doctrines, and a center or centers of authority, all of which have characterized those religious forms which have been dominant in the West."[10] Similarly, the so-called African traditional religions were created, with the collaboration of Christian-trained African theologians, through the authorized translation of Christian concepts and doctrines into indigenous African languages. That this practice took place and continues in a controlled manner is evidenced by the controversies frequently precipitated by African clerics, like the former Zambian Bishop Emmanuel Milingo. They were considered wayward when they proposed to incorporate "rejected" African concepts and practices (like the acceptance of the idea of the existence of ghosts and the practice of their exorcism) into mainstream Christian liturgy.

The Status of Dualism in the Luo Conceptual Scheme

P'Bitek remains one of the sharpest critics of Western anthropology in Africa, especially of the Christian missionaries' use of its conceptual categorization of African thought. In this p'Bitek sharply differed from B. A. Ogot who appeared to have been enamored to Tempels's idea of an "African philosophy." Like Tempels, Ogot sought to study *jok* as a key theoretical (conceptual) linkage between, on the one hand, "African customary practices and institutions" and, on the other, "African ideas of the universe, of existence, and of destiny—particularly important if world religions such as Christianity and Islam are to have their roots in the African soil."[11] According to Ogot, there were "old" and "new" African beliefs and practices, the former "pagan," and the latter owing their nature to the process of Christianization and Islamization. Furthermore, he confided in the Western anthropologists to show "us [Africans] what can be done with some of these concepts," just like "Evans-Pritchard has recently shown in his analysis of the term *kwoth* which, as I hope to show, is similar to *jok* in many respects."[12]

Both Ogot and p'Bitek concur that the concept of *jok* or *juok* could not simply be wished away, since it occupied a central place in the Nilotic people's languages and conceptions of the universe. However, the two differed fundamentally in regard to the meaning or conceptual nature of the term. Ogot first: in his view, which concurs totally with those of the anthropologists who have studied the concept as it occurs in the languages, beliefs, and practices of several other Nilotic groups, "The term *jok* or *juok* usually means God, spirit, witchcraft, ghost or some form of spiritual power."[13] It is quite apparent from Ogot's discussion of Lienhardt's, Howell's, and Thomson's studies of the Shilluk and of Evans-Pritchard's *The Nuer* that the translations were significantly influenced by Christian categories.[14] The characterization of the Shilluk's senses of *juok* into two levels of spirit (*wei*) and body (*del*) as the Shilluk version of the "trinity" is interesting if not altogether suspect of imposition on them of non-useful foreign categories with new meanings. Lienhardt must have relied on the frequent and dispersed uses of the term in Shilluk language to infer that *juok* was in everything and so must have been for the Shilluk the first principle, the ultimate explanation for everything, and the necessary logical concept.[15] Lienhardt indicates further that the Shilluk distinguish the *jok mal* (the *jok* up high, allegedly the heavenly *jok* or spirits) from the *jok piny* (the *jok* below or worldly spirits). The distinction is attributed to Nyikang, the founder of the Shilluk nation according to Shilluk legend. Nyikang is also characterized as their first ancestor. According to Lienhardt, this distinction indicated quite clearly that the Shilluk hierarchize the *jok* powers into divine ones and worldly ones that derive from the former. Thus, he deliberates, the *jok mal* refers to the creative powers of God, while the *jok piny* refers to the orderliness of the Shilluk world, especially their socio-political organization that Nyikang oversees on behalf of the divine.

But the heaven–earth distinction alleged by Lienhardt and his fellow scholars is hardly a Luo conceptual distinction. The Luo speak of *mal* or *malo* in purely spatio-physical senses. *Polo malo* is where the clouds gather and birds fly. It is the "location" of the stars, the most prominent among which is the sun, *chieng'*. Due to their relative size from the human position, other spatial bodies only twinkle (*mil*) like fireflies in the night; they are twinklers, *otide* (plural for *otit*), but the sun, *chieng'*, glares (*chieng' rieny*). Although the Luo attach great importance to the sun, it is unlikely that they think of it as a deity or of its position as the abode of supernatural entities. *Polo malo* merely means "up in the air" as opposed to on the ground *piny*. The sense "identified" by Lienhardt appears newly introduced into Luo reference to indicate something close to the Christian "heaven" as the binary opposite of "earth" in the Christian sense of "worldliness." Thus rather than "identifying" in the Luo languages the Luo use of the term "*mal*," Lienhardt and his fellow European scholars were in fact imposing on Dholuo a new use of the term. This imposition had some fundamental conceptual problems as the analysis of p'Bitek's notion of *jok* later will show. The Luo think of entities in physical or "quasi-physical" terms, as occupying space from where they can be summoned or related to in several other ways indicating their proximity in nature to the physical reality of the living who communicate with them or to the world in which such communication occurs. Due to this understanding of the nature of reality, the Luo speak of *piny* in ways that demand some explanation, however brief.

The term *piny* has both physical and quasi-physical senses. In its purely physical sense, "*piny*" means "earth," "the ground," or "territory," all signifying occupied or occupyable space. At other times the term *piny* is used to refer to the spatio-temporal category in which existence takes place. "*Ru piny*" refers to duration or, rather literally, transcendental time within which the reality of objects is determined. The Luo speak of *ru piny* as transcendental time because *piny*, viewed as reality in general rather than merely as physical space, is regarded to be greater than the possible cumulative life span of humans. For them, then, that greater reality is unthinkable except in terms of its own duration, which must also be greater than the duration of the possible cumulative life of humans. This is why the Luo speak of *ru piny* as wearing down even the stubbornly slow-maturing *Apindi* (Rubiaceae) until its fruits ripen (*aming'a piny ne ochiego Apindi e thim*). It is also said of *piny* that it is *piny nang'o*, it outlasts (licks, swallows) everything. Because "*ru*" indicates time, as inferable from the alternation of day and night (the visibility and invisibility of the sun and the twinklers), it appears that when used in this (*ru piny*) sense the term *piny* refers to the entire universe and not just the earth or world. *Ru piny* is therefore an abstract phrase depicting the category of space-and-time, almost always conceived together.[16] Also, the saying "*piny nang'o*" is used to indicate that the dead go to *piny*, not to *polo* or *malo*, "above," as in the Christian sense of "heaven above." Rather, for the Luo, the dead become *jo-piny* (*jok-piny* in Central and Northern Luo variations). To talk with the dead is to talk with those from *piny*, which the Luo regard as symptomatic of mental troubles. Indeed, curiously, missionaries referred to non-converts as *jo-piny*, those who remained traditional. So there are *piny* names, like Masolo, and Christian ones like George, Thomas, and such others that people acquired through Christian baptismal renaming. Since these separations, categorizing some names as of *piny* has come to indicate that they are from the traditional ancestral archive, precisely those that the missionaries had intended to obliterate through replacement with those from European and Jewish ancestry. As a result, *piny* came to signify "evil" for the missionaries, who quickly gave it an opposition in the form of "up" or "heaven," the firmament, for which they used the term *polo*.

The Concept of *Jok* in p'Bitek's Work

What, then, is or are *jok*? In tackling this question, the legendary Ugandan Luo scholar Okot p'Bitek arrived at answers slightly different from those presented earlier. He starts by unquestionably accepting the category of religion as a helpful tool for analyzing and organizing Acoli thought, despite disagreements with the earlier missionary and anthropological positions of Driberg, Lienhardt, Hayley, and as supported later by Ogot under the influence of Tempels.[17] The English term "religion" may be extended to refer to a variety of beliefs and practices not found in many recent Western cultures since the dawn of Christianity and Islam. But this extension, as Shaw argues in the work I cited earlier, happens alongside the translation of elements of non-Western cultures into Western categories that continue to serve as the measuring standard. Hence, she concludes, "African religions" are the creation, not just victim, of Western scholarship. So how does the concept of *jok* fare in this new world? P'Bitek himself appears to be aware of the varying Christian attitudes toward non-Western conceptualizations of the inhabitants of the spiritual world.[18] Depending on how conservative a Christian scholar was, non-Christian deities were classified as either "ghosts," "devils," or "pagan deities." The latter characterization, p'Bitek notes, was first introduced by a German missionary, Max F. Muller, and came to permeate the work and efforts of anthropologists and missionaries, including those who did not share in his evolutionist view of "paganism." Quite arbitrarily, the missionaries selected the local term that they thought was closest to their Christian idea of God. In some cases, like among the Acoli, they experimented with different terms before settling on one. In others they introduced new words from either their own vernaculars or Kiswahili, neither of which was less foreign to the target community. Committed to prove the universality of the experience of the one supreme god, which p'Bitek denies, and making Christianity appear locally grown and adaptable to indigenous languages, which is the focus of his critique, the missionaries not only reverted to awkward methods for their task, they often also chose quite the wrong local terms for the idea of the Christian god. While the missionaries were eager to overlook the roots of the local words lest it deviated from their goals, p'Bitek remarks that "of course, the original etymological sense of the word matters a great deal to someone who is primarily interested in the conception of gods as Africans see them, rather than in the *christianized* conceptions of these deities, the result of many years of preaching and teaching."[19] In other words, p'Bitek views conversion as highly doubtful, especially to such an extent that would make Christianity a local experience. As for African scholars' reasons for their discipleship to the project of Christianizing African religious conceptions, p'Bitek thought of the urge in them to counter the disparaging Western scholars' and missionaries' assertions.

After an eloquent critique of Western misinterpretations of African ideas and concepts in the service of Christianity and other aspects of Western cultures, p'Bitek settles down to his own rendition of the concept of *jok*.[20] How, then, to ask a lead question in p'Bitek's discussion, does one escape the Christian influence in regard to the notion of *jok* without rejecting the dualist Christian influence of the two realms of reality, viz., the physical and the spiritual? As I have argued above, the oppositional dualism of worldly–heavenly separation was introduced, rather arbitrarily, by the missionary zeal intent on splitting Africans' worldviews into two, separate, mutually independent and unequal spheres to provide abode for a new deity.

According to p'Bitek, the missionaries developed a high god for the Acoli and Lango and gave him the name Lubanga, which they borrowed from Bunyoro where they had earlier worked, because they believed that the word *jok* did not seem to have a precise significance in Acoli language. The idea of a high god among the Central Luo, p'Bitek writes, "was a creation of the missionaries."[21] The *jok* are "spirits," yet they are not completely nonphysical either, since Acoli do not believe in a spiritual entity, *à la* Descartes, which is independent and separable from the body. *Jok* are "members" of society (clan, family, lineage, community, etc.). There are shrines (*abila*) erected for them at different social (chiefdom, family, and individual) levels. Some *jok* originate from within the clan, others are encountered in new settlements once inhabited by other groups, and they are usually recognized and can interact with their new neighbors. The Luo, including Acoli and Lango, distinguish foreign *jok* from their own familiar ones. The former tend to be violent and more demanding. Owuor Anyumba, writing as a young undergraduate researcher at Makerere in 1954, has to date given the clearest analysis of the concept of *juok/juogi*.[22] He argued, correctly, that analysis of the concept reveals the reasonably acceptable belief that once people inhabit a place long enough to have called it home and buried their dead there, they leave there a sense of their influence on the environment. They give it a sense of their identity. So, with time, the Luo regarded some places as theirs by identifying those of their ancestors (*juogi*) who had given these places their identity, just as much as they recognized the *juogi* of those groups who earlier had occupied the new places they settled, hence the appearance of the ferocious *juogi* of Lango, since the migratory Luo arrived on the shores of Lake Lolwe (Victoria to the British). Historians tell us that probably this place once was inhabited by the Nandi, Kipsigis, Maasai, and other Nilo-Hamitic groups, either contemporaneously in different parts, or successively prior to the arrival there of the Luo from around 1750.[23] In Luo, *juogi mag Lango*, also called *sewe*, referred to the various groups of the Kalenjin and Maasai peoples. This was due to their "wild" war cries and behavior as if out of control of their minds.

If Anyumba is right, then p'Bitek's categories of *jok*[24] are understandable as part of the historical topography of the Acoli landscape. The various chiefdom *jok* name the various ancestors with whom members of some chiefly lineages identify. Their *jok* status is associated with mass deaths resulting from either war or other collective calamities. To these one can add the *jok nam* (the *jok* of the river or lake), *jok kulo* (the *jok* of the pond), *jok thim* (the *jok* of the wilderness), and so on. These refer to the lingering identities of those who may have met their deaths in these places, some by accident, others as a result of war or sometimes suicide, and whose bodies remained unrecovered for proper rituals and burial. The Luo believe that people who take their lives in anger or as victims of mistreatment by family "conceal" their remains from recovery but can be heard singing their lamentations when people visit or pass by the places where they had died. They become *jok* or *juogi* of those locations. When they avenge their unfair death on the living they become *chien* and torment the conscience of the culprits.

The categories of *jok* suggest that all *jok* were *jok piny*, as *piny* is the only place where they abide. Also, it appears from the categories, that the *jok* were not deities and were not worshiped as suggested by the European (Driberg, Hayley, and Lienhardt) studies of the Shilluk, Acoli, and other Luo groups. As p'Bitek tells us, European scholars of "African religions" were eager to find a pagan construct on which to build a conversion to Christianity. Where there was none, they readily invented one. *Malo* (above or heaven) appears to have been newly introduced to pave the way for the construction of a dualist worldview that would facilitate the teaching of the Christian one.

Furthermore, according to p'Bitek,[25] the *jok* are always particular; they are referred to by both their "proper" names and the specific category to which they belong. "When the Nilotes encounter *jok*," he writes, "it is with a specific and named or easily definable *jok*, and not some vague 'power' that they communicate with."[26] The *jogi* are individualized and concrete; "they can also be, as it were, known [apprehended] through the senses."[27]

Piny as the Center of the Luo Universe

There are other senses of *piny*. One is political. The Luo speak of *piny* as ultimate authority, especially when or where the idea of authoritativeness is implied. Both among the living and in reference to key regulations of society as defined by ancestors, the Luo regard the word of *Jo-piny* as ultimate. In the former sense *jo-piny*, as opposed to *jo-dak* (resident aliens, usually a few families from a different clan and one or more of whom may be related to the locals by marriage), are the indigenous local people whose customs and laws rule supreme and define the judicial territory of those who call them their own. Hence to attribute a required action or behavior to the demand of *jo-piny* is to claim the unquestionable status of the requirement. "*Piny owacho*" (literally "the land has spoken"), used in the present tense and without the prefix "*jo-*," refers to directives from a higher office of government or civil society. But when used with the prefix, and in the past tense, as in "*jo-piny nene owacho*" (literally, "as it was said by those who now have gone into the earth [ancestors]"), it refers to the authority of tradition as set by the wise ancestors. In both cases, the phrases are used to claim unquestionability of the dictum at the center of the discourse.

It is clear from these accounts of the meanings of the concept *piny* that the Luo did not think of it as being lower or less than anything else. Rather, it was the only way they thought of the universe or reality in general. It is also clear from the account that the dualism of which the anthropologists and missionaries spoke, and which Ogot sought to defend and legitimate, is not only absent from the analysis of the concept *piny*, supposedly in oppositional relation to *mal* or *malo*, it also is not inferable from the Luo worldview as outlined previously.

The Tempels Factor

Ogot's analysis of the concept of *juok* in terms of the vital force is historically explainable. Writing only two or so years after the English translation of Tempels's book, *Bantu Philosophy*, Ogot was understandably a victim of the sweeping influence that Tempels's work had on a wide range of his readers. Ogot's endorsement of Tempels's idea of the vital force as present in all things, and its hierarchization among beings of forces explains Ogot's accord with Lienhardt's invented distinction between *jok mal* and *jok piny* as "higher" and "lower" *jok*, respectively.[28] But here too, there probably is an overzealous interpretation of the term *jok*. Among its many meanings, *jok* (or *juok*) is a term with several shades of interrelated meanings at the center of social and moral thought. First among these is the use of the term for the ancestral name(s) (singl. *juok*, pl. *juogi*) given to individuals as their "official" or rightful family names, often from either maternal or paternal sides of one's ancestry. When a child is named after such an ancestor, the individual becomes a special point for re-grounding memory of the ancestor, and members of her or his family relate to her or him with such respect and fondness befitting the social status of the ancestor for which the child is named. The Luo believe that the dead continue to linger on "somewhere" after death and continue to interact with family. It is believed that they "demand," through diviners, to be named. An ancestor can demand to be named in several descendants. This is the way the Luo define the extent of the social network of their ancestry and keep track of their relatives. This must have been a socially and morally useful practice because it made the ancestry of individuals evident through their names, thus helping to prevent in-breeding by incest: people are not allowed to marry or have sexual relations with anyone known or suspected to share with them even the faintest shade of ancestry. Christian missionaries classified these *jougi* as *piny* names and condemned them as signs of pagan ancestor-worship. Surprisingly, on the other hand, the names of European and Jewish ancestry were regarded as godly and were imposed on African converts. Until today African converts are encouraged, even by their fellow African churchmen and church-women, to pray to the European and Jewish dead whose names they bear to intercede for them when they want favors from God. The Kenyan theologian John Mbiti wrote eloquently about Africans forming a community that includes not only the living but significantly also the living dead as he called them.[29] Perhaps the idea of the living carrying the names of their ancestors as their *juogi* is a good example of Mbiti's point. The best known Kenyan case of rebellion against the missionaries' war against African names is what the late Kenyan politician Oginga Odinga recorded in his political autobiography, *Not yet Uhuru*.[30] Although it was fashionable for converts to take on new names for themselves, Odinga was indifferent to the usefulness of baptism and to the significance of adopting new names. Despite his opposition, he accepted the names Obadiah Adonijah to be imposed on him as a condition to attend school. He never used them. For a while, Odinga even appeared to like the Europeans' religion, until, he says, "it dawned on me that I had listened to many preachers and they seemed, all of them, to preach one thing in common—the suppression of African customs . . . they tried to use the word of God to judge African traditions."[31] In later years, Odinga raised much controversy when he insisted on baptizing his children with African names. Ironically, it was a European missionary, not African padre, who agreed to baptize his children with African names, a practice that became fashionable thereafter for both its elegance and political significance. Says Odinga: "I was delighted: I had lived up to one of my strongest convictions. But the stories went about that I was abnormal, and strange."[32]

There have been few Africans to actually reinstate the dignity of African ancestral names within Christian discourse like Odinga did, thus often lending the impression that conversion to Christianity is possible only upon negation of African identity. This schism, obviously, reflects the oppositional dichotomy created by scholars like Lienhardt and Driberg among others. What is not clear from Odinga's story is how he and his wife chose their children's names. They (Ng'ong'a, Molo, Oburu, Rayila, Amolo, and Odinga) all appear to be ancestral names, but the divinatory method of *juok*—(*juogi*)—name identification is neither discussed nor mentioned.

P'Bitek's analysis of *jok* reveals that there is not just one way to understand the term. He maintains that *jok* are perceived as physical or quasi-physical in nature, and they act as good or bad moral agents. People believe that some *jok* can prevent personal or collective misfortune like illness, a plague, or failure of crops, while others are blamed for misfortune. There are morally good and bad *jok*, an idea that seems to concur with the Southern Luo idea of *juogi* in the possession sense discussed by Anyumba. For the latter, the good *juogi* are usually a source of medicinal knowledge, which they are believed to reveal to those they possess. The bad *juogi* demand and torment for sacrifice more than they are helpful. The *juogi* of Lango—more precisely, of the Nandi, Kipsigis, and Maasai[33]—or *sewe* are usually identified with the latter character. They are generally hostile. According to p'Bitek, the bad *jok* can be hunted down, captured, and killed, suggesting that *juok* is a mode of being that merely conceals but does not transform or transubstantiate the physical mode.[34]

Juok as the Moral Quality of Practice

In the social and moral senses, *juok* means an anti-social attitude and character. Intentionally harmful behavior is usually referred to as *juok*. To qualify as *juok*, a behavior must be determined to have been well calculated to cause any form of harm to other persons, and is usually carried out in concealment, even when it involves some form of violence. Thus, killing another person in a physical fight does not qualify as *juok* if the protagonists see and recognize each other openly. The protagonist who is practicing *juok* may well know his or her victim, but typically conceals his identity when he attacks. A *jajuok*, as the practitioner of *juok* is called, waylays his or her victim at conveniently isolated or bushy places or either stalks or trails them to such preferred spots before making moves and throwing objects to frighten them. But a *jajuok* does not always kill. In fact, it is rare that a *jajuok* kills anyone, unless the habit of *juok* of this kind becomes for them a convenient cover for committing a premeditated crime. Sometimes, and indeed most frequently, they simply terrify others, causing fear in them by frightening them under the concealment of night, or frightening them by sneaking into their homes and throwing objects on the roofs of their houses as they sleep. Also, they may simply run up and down or around other people's compounds in the night, thus frightening the owners and their animals if they keep any. The intentional act is called *yido*, and the habitual practice which forms into character is known as *juok yido*. It is said that the "power" of this *juok*, actually an intense urge like a drive out of obsessive compulsion, can overwhelm its practitioner so much that they may feel like "running" in daylight or it can push them into wanting to play "*juok* games (usually dirty tricks)" on others. But, unlike the obsession of Freud's theory, in which the individual is actually a victim of the drive, *juog yido* id is acquired; it is learned and one can decide of his or her own free will not to take part in the practice. *Juok* is kept within families and can be brought to a man and his future children by a wife who was born into or brought up by a practicing family. Similarly, a woman from an innocent family can learn *juok* after marriage from the practicing family of her husband. But due to its social stigma *juok* is not publicly admitted, and a dissenting initiate or importer could be killed for fear that they would reveal the family secret or for fear they would spread the unwanted behavior to a non-practicing family or clan. It is said that a *jajuok* lacks moral restraint (*wang'e tek*) and shame. Toward others they lack compassion except perhaps for their own with whom they share habits and therefore mutual sympathy.

Because of these habits, this type of *juok* is practiced strictly in the night, which makes a *jajuok* a master of the nocturnal world. Scanty evidence suggests that people who practice this type of *juok* tame nocturnal wild animals, like leopards or snakes, which become their accompanying pets in rendezvous. If true, such company would certainly and greatly enhance their capacity to terrify their victims, while in most cases avoiding doing physical harm to them. The best known account of this type of *juok* is Onyango-Abuje's novel *Fire and Vengeance*, a curiously detailed step-by-step description of the demeanor and mental state of a *jajuok* during the act.[35]

Another form of behavioral *juok* is believed to be practiced by individuals who use magic or witchcraft to cause harm to persons or to their property. The *jajuok* of this category can be a *janawi*, *jandagla*, or *jatung'*. The "medicine" of the former two kills instantly while that of the latter kills its victim after a prolonged and often emaciating illness. The *jabilo*, whose practice is grouped with the latter two, is believed to cause harm by making the efforts of their victims to be punctuated by failures especially in those domains where they have been known to be successful. Thus, the *jabilo* is driven by competitive jealousy, either their own or of those who hire their services against a third party who they envy or are in competition. He overpowers and checks the performative capacities of a real or perceived rival for the benefit of self or client.

To claim that *juok* is a kind of "force" in Tempels's sense is tantamount to claiming that all the uses of the term (as ancestral names, as the mischievous actions of the night-runner or *juog yido*, and as the magical powers of the *janawi, jandagla, jabilo*, and *jatung'*) as identified earlier have the same meaning. Such a position would further claim that *juok* is a "power" that enables people who act in those capacities to do so. Perhaps this would not be a problem if the claim did not have the implication of widening the meaning of "power to do" to the metaphysical domain. We have seen above that this extension of the meaning of *juok* is owed to the influence of Tempels's idea of the "vital force" and claims that all existents, humans, spirits, animals, plants, inanimate objects, and ideas, all share the common property called *juok*. But if indeed it were the case that *juok* was a property of the inanimate world, objects would, at least at times, be referred to in Dholuo as *juok*, like is done for humans. Yet even a simple examination of the use of the term *juok* reveals that this is not so. One does not refer to a stone in Dholuo as *juok*, but, in the appropriate circumstances, only as *gir juok* (an object or tool of *juok*). To say of something, or sometimes of an animal, that it is *gir juok* is to claim, not that it has a property called *juok*, but only that it is an object that belongs to someone who uses it in their practice of some kind of *juok*. It may be a chip of rock or stone, or a collection of a variety of different objects together. Sometimes it is the strange nature of where they happen to be at a particular time when someone else finds them, or the unusual collection of the objects together, that bring to the mind of the finder the thought that there must be some deliberate action behind the finding. Such deliberate action is obviously strange, for one usually does not find, for example, a piece of mirror, pieces of grass, a few insects, and such things, tied together neatly in a handkerchief, and lying behind their house where they are most likely to walk first thing in the morning, unless they had been placed there by someone known to be out of their mind. In such circumstances the mind behind the finding is probed and may be regarded as either "functionally twisted" like in the case of someone out of their mind, or "functionally immature and playful," like in the case of children, or "morally twisted," "calculatively up to some trick," like in the case of a *janawi*, *jatung'*, *jandagla*, etc. If the former two possibilities are established, that is, that the objects were the collection of someone functionally out of their mind or of children at play, the charge of *juok* is usually invalidated, but is seriously sustained in the latter case. It is the moral agency of the perpetrator that prompts charges of *juok* because their behavior is in discord with the expected norm. But the object(s) is/are referred to only as *gir juok* (pl. *gik juok*), "the artifacts of someone with *juok* (evil) intentions." It is thus clear that in such a case *juok* is not being attributed to the objects but to the suspected human action behind the objects. The tamed leopard that the night-runner takes with him or her on the nocturnal rendezvous is their "*juok* thing" (*gire mar juok*), and so is the fire they carry to flash around as they dash through the dark night.

In these action-oriented senses the term *juok* appears to be used to judge the moral nature of public behavior of persons. Hence, in this particular sense, not everyone can be referred to as a *jajuok*, but anyone can be referred to as so if they behave in manners suggesting ill intentions for their actions. Thus, a person can be called *jajuok* if, when swimming with others, he or she tried to play games that mimic, or are perceptible as betraying intentions of drowning someone else in their company. And a person is also said to behave in a *juok* manner if he or she intentionally suggests to others to engage in harmful actions like jumping from a cliff or breaking a taboo. The harmful nature of the action needs to have been known to the perpetrator but unknown to the victim of the urging. A *jajuok* is, by and large, a person who is publicly regarded as having a propensity to behave in morally unacceptable manners. Thus, the practical sense of *juok* is a characterization no one accepts upon themselves. Rather, it is imposed on them by the judgment of others. *Juok* is the daring and unrestrained moral capacity to commit evil.

Related to the connotations of *juok* is its derivative sense, *ajuoga*, usually used for a diviner. The diviner is the person who unravels the hand of a *janawi*, *jatung'*, *jandagla*, or even *jajuog yido* in the misfortune of others. She or he is also the "medicine person" who gives the curative antidotes against the *juok* deeds of the aforementioned. Sometimes an *ajuoga* can double as a *jachieth*, usually an herbalist whose expertise is purely pharmacological, but she or he will mainly be known for their divining as the basis of their practice. Also, on occasions, an *ajuoga* can double in one of the negative roles because they have the diagnostic knowledge of the powers of a *janawi, jatung'*, or a *jandagla*. Whether or not there is any thread of truth to the claim is questionable. Claiming that all these people derive their descriptions from sharing in some common capacity is like claiming that physicians, pharmacists, and other medical technicians share a definition because they work in the health sector. We use the term "medic" for the physician, and the adjective "medical" for others in the wide field of health-related practices without claiming that "the adjective "medical" when used to refer to the functions of the person in the MRI laboratory is synonymous with "medic" when used for the woman who serves as my family physician. Similarly, I submit, the fact that there is a common root *juok* linked to the many words used for the people whose practices and behaviors we have described does not imply that the root is connotative of a shared metaphysical essence about who they are or what they do. If the root word indicated a metaphysical essence shared among them, then what about you or I who do not fit into any of the previously mentioned functional or behavioral categories?

However poor Dholuo may be, I submit that we face a difficult problem trying to determine whether there is anything conceptually common to the various uses of the term *juok* as we have analyzed it above. If there is, then the conceptual analysis we have given above has not helped, and perhaps further assistance from linguistic analysis would be of greater benefit than a philosophical one has been able to give.

It is hard, in the face of all these incompatible senses of the term, to suggest that *juok* has just one underriding meaning common to everything in nature. If it were so, then *juok* would have to be an entity or object, or some property, like mass, that is shared by all things of which it is attributable. This would further imply that at least some members of one category of material things, like stones, have it in the same proportion. But we have just seen that people do not speak of the ancestral *juogi* of stones, nor of beasts, nor do they refer to present (as opposed to dead) humans and beasts as *juok*. We have also seen that among humans, some individuals are said to have *juok* (bad moral character) in them while others do not. Furthermore, the *juok* of the night-runner (*juog yido*) and also of the *janawi, jandagla*, and *jatung'* is the moral nature of their acquired behavior and not some material quality present in them by some intrinsic endowment.

Juok and the "Soul"

Like "evil," *juok* is neither an independent substance nor a substantive quality like mass or shape, color or smell, but a moral quality of action that is attributable on the basis of an action's effect on idealized quality of life, particularly happiness. Thus, contrary to what Hayley says of the Lango idea of *juok*,[36] it is neither "power" nor "soul," unless the latter terms are used strictly in the context of moral agency or capacity for action. To say that "there is evil in the world" does not mean "evil" is a substance or entity that exists either by itself or inside some other entity. It supposedly implies only that from our (human or rational) point of view there are bad and unpleasant experiences that different people encounter from different causes. Similarly, Luo-speaking people talk of *juok* as a behavioral tendency that anyone is susceptible to if they are not steadfast in their pursuit of moral uprightness. But *juok* is neither an object nor any other form of entity like substance.[37]

The Luo attribute the sustenance of life to *chuny*, the kernel of biological life. Every organic thing has *chuny*. It makes plants germinate and grow, and it enables the organic functioning in animals, including humans. *Chuny* is responsible for the pulse, as it is for growth and use of limbs and other biologically supportive organs. Thus, a living cockroach has no less *chuny* than a living dog or living human and no more than a living plant. They wither when their *chuny* begins to wane, and they die when their *chuny* "gets disconnected (*chot*)." A person, plant, or beast is pronounced dead when their *chuny* is said to be "gone" (no more). There is no more life in them. In these senses, *chuny* has a purely material or organic meaning. *Chuny* is thus separate from and is what enables *adundo* (heart) to function. It is also not identical with *chuny* (liver) for which the same word is used. In other brain functional-related senses, *chuny* also means emotional and cognitive capacities: the emotional acts of liking, desiring, and willing, and the cognitive acts of believing, doubting, and conviction. Thus, one says *chunya dwaro* or *chunya gombo* (I would like to...I desire...I wish I could...), or *chunya onge* (I don't feel like...I have no desire to...or for...), or that *chunye rach* (she or he is angry, in a foul mood or, when it is habitual, she or he is ill-tempered). Yet, despite these uses of the term, it is not very clear that we can infer from such analysis that *chuny* is equivalent to what is connoted by the English term "substance" in the sense of entity.

In nonorganic terms, one says of another that *chunye ber* (she or he is pleasant or kind), or *chunye ler* (does not get revolted by nasty situations) to express the various emotional attitudes toward other people and things. In cognitive terms, one says *chunya oyie* (I am convinced, I am in agreement, I accept, or I believe), *chunya ok-oyie* (I am not convinced, I don't believe), or simply *ayie* (I agree, I accept, I believe [it]).

Since the arrival of the missionaries, *chuny* has been restricted to apply to something called "soul," something for which the Luo appear not to have had a clear or separate concept or term to refer to it. The point we want to make, however, is that as helpful as these conceptual delineations may be, they do not point, and are not related, to the idea of *juok* as the central idea in Luo conception of reality. Related to these concepts is the Luo idea of what happens to personhood when one dies. In a general way, the Luo appear to believe that something in the nature of persons survives the death of the body. Whatever it is that survives, the Luo appear not to have a term for it that signifies its nature. We have seen earlier that the name of an ancestor becomes a *juok* for a living descendant given the same name. We have also seen that this element cannot be the material *chuny*, nor is it the emotional or cognitive *chuny*, as the dead are never said to exercise these capacities at all. This ambiguity has led people in the missionary era to claim that *tipo* is it. But a careful consideration reveals that this term is used only analogically and not as a substantive noun. *Tipo* means shadow, in the literal sense of the term, like *tipo yath*, the shadow of a tree or anything else as cast by light's impenetrability of its body. Shadows are physical occurrences. Because shadows are physical occurrences and bear the general shape image of the real object from which they are cast, the Luo talk of whatever survives the physical death of a person as their shadow, meaning that it bears the likeness of the real person. Hence the saying *tipo ng'ane neno e wang'a* (the image of so and so appears to me vividly). Although the imagery of sight is used to express the idea of appearance, it is clearly understood in Dholuo that the appearance of the *tipo* of those not physically present does not involve direct sensory experience but only memory. In terms reminiscent of the Humean idea of impressions, the Luo describe the vividness of memory by saying they "come to the eyes" (*biro e wang'* or *neno e wang'*), reduced to the crude visual impressions, but in truth they are only being clear and distinct to the mind. Christian converts have now been made to say that *tipo*, and sometimes *chuny*, rise to heaven, which does not make much sense in Dholuo.[38] Indeed, the Luo legends of Luanda Magere, the indomitable hero who could not be killed except by spearing his shadow, was told to emphasize the extraordinary quality of heroism. The Luo believe that leadership and heroism are unique qualities that the ordinary person does not possess. The story of Luanda Magere describes him as "*ng'ato magalagala*" (a mysterious person). Hence the concealment of his prowess in his *tipo* (shadow) could not have been an ordinary way of understanding personhood and its structure.

How People Know

It appears inevitable, in pursuit of the nature of personhood in the Luo scheme of thought, to outline how consciousness and selfhood are related and what further light they may shed on the idea of the person. Of the things we become aware of, the most intimate and immediate one is the reflexive awareness of being aware. The British philosopher Bertrand Russell called this acquaintance by introspection, saying that "We are not only aware of things, but we are often aware of being aware of them."[39] When we have a sensory experience, we are aware of having the experience, thus making the experience itself, like feeling warm or seeing a goat, an object with which we are acquainted. The Luo call such intimate awareness (by introspection) *ng'eyo i chuny* or *ng'eyo gi chuny*, which is "getting into the act of knowing itself." Thinking, or thought, is called *paro*, which is carried out in two different ways, *paro gi chuny* (thinking inside or to oneself) and *paro gi wich* (thinking in the head). *Aparo* (I am thinking, I think so), as a one-word sentence, is usually taken to mean the latter, thought to have an object outside thought itself, as in the English "I am thinking about or of something," the "something" being the object outside thought at which thought aims. This type of thinking is calculative and involves analysis. Solution of mathematical and logical problems is done in the head (*goyo kwan e wich*, or *goyo kwan gi wich*, and *pimo wach gi wich*). The latter translates literally as "determining the nature of speech" and focuses on truth, *adiera mar wach*, meaning, *ngech wach* or *tiend wach*, and sense, *donjo wach e wach moro*. People who are good (fast) at math and at the solution of logical problems are said to have "light heads" (*wich ma yot*), while people who are slow at these mental exercises are said to have "heavy heads" (*wich ma pek*). Thinking inside (*paro gi chuny*), on the other hand, is to turn inside into one's own conscience, to sort one's awareness. When someone sorts their *chuny* (*nono chuny*), they are said to examine the seat of their believing as opposed to the nature of the belief. The latter would be the same as carrying out an epistemological or logical analysis (*nono tiend wach*). Thus, people are asked to probe their *chuny* if they are suspected of telling a lie. *Chuny* is said to be a person's best friend (*dhano osiep chunye*), they can never lie to it. To examine one's *chuny* is thus to confront oneself to determine that that which is inside them is indeed what they are also projecting to the outside, reporting or stating. It is obvious that the examination of *chuny*, acquaintance with own acquaintance, or to know that one knows reveals a self (*an awuon ei chunya*). But it is a gross mistake to take *chuny* as a substance that is independent of the act *nono* (examining), because *chuny* does not become identical with the *an* (*awuon*), which is roughly translatable into English as the "I-self." In fact, *an awuon ei chunya* translates as "I-self inside my *chuny* (self-awareness)," a rather cumbersome expression. Also, although it is said at death that someone's *chuny* is "disconnected," this does not imply the heaving off of something or part thereof from another. It simply means life has stopped, like the flow of electric energy stops when there is a disconnection; the energy is not "separated," in the sense of being carried away, from the wires that carried it when it was present.

Conclusion

The foregoing analysis is based on an old approach to understanding personhood, one that tried to trace, by responding to earlier suppositions, elements of "essence" or "identity" of persons. It assumed that such "core" features of self can be identified from the analysis of cognitive and moral actions of persons. What this analysis has yielded is that the substantive concept of personhood seems not to have been a focus of Luo conceptualization of the nature of the person, and that focus on it is not an adequate means for grasping the full range of the expression of personhood. The expression of personhood results from the interplay between the culturally objectified perceptions of persons and the subjectively apprehended aspects of social life through which individuals express their subjectivity in opposition or resistance to the conventionally defined roles, rules, and regulations of the *habitus*. This, I hope, will be another part in the development of what we now have grounded here as inquiry. For now, let it suffice to say that contrary to earlier claims, the term *juok* does not appear to have one meaning among the Luo-speaking peoples, nor does it fit into the Judeo-Christian dualist scheme. As p'Bitek remarked, the Luo appear to have placed focus not on a world defined by static ontological categories, but by the agency of persons and the impact of their actions on the world as a complex of social categories. The self or person-hood is revealed through the cognitive and moral actions that persons perform and through the emotions that they express. Role playing involves responding to objectified expectations like participating in furthering one's lineage by passing on names (*juogi*), by recognizing the spirits (*juogi*) of the departed, both foreigners and kin, but also by negotiating one's self-knowledge against the perceptions of them by the community when they are categorized one way or the other within the moral value system in which they abide. In other words, person-hood is not a passive "dress" that people acquire. Thus, one may ask, how do persons labeled as *jajuog yido*, *jajuog nawi*, *jajuog ndagla*, *jajuog tung'* respond to such labels? That is for a future work.

Notes

1. Kwasi Wiredu, *Cultural Universals and Particulars: An African Perspective* (Bloomington: Indiana University Press, 1996), 136.

2. See V. Y. Mudimbe, *The Invention of Africa* (Bloomington: Indiana University Press, 1988).

3. See Bolaji E. Idowu, *African Traditional Religion: A Definition* (London: SCM Press Ltd., 1973).

4. Okot p'Bitek, *African Religions in Western Scholarship* (Nairobi: Kenya Literature Bureau, 1979), p. viii.

5. See Clifford Geertz, *The Interpretation of Cultures* (New York: Basic Books, 1973). See James Clifford, *The Predicament of Culture: Twentieth-Century Ethnography, Literature, and Art* (Cambridge, Mass.: Harvard University Press, 1988). See George Marcus and James Clifford, eds., *Writing Culture: The Poetics and Politics of Ethnography* (Berkeley: University of California Press, 1986). See George Marcus and Michael M. J. Fischer, *Anthropology as Cultural Critique* (Chicago: University of Chicago Press, 1986). See Johannes Fabian, *Time and the Other: How Anthropology Makes Its Object* (New York: Columbia University Press, 1983).

6. See Mudimbe, *Invention of Africa* and Kwame Anthony Appiah, *In My Father's House: Africa in the Philosophy of Culture* (Oxford: Oxford University Press, 1992).

7. See also Ngugi wa Thiong'o, *Decolonizing the Mind: The Politics of Language in African Literature* (London: James Currey, 1986) and Wiredu, *Cultural Universals and Particulars*.

8. See Rosalind Shaw, "The Invention of 'African Traditional Religion,'" *Religion* 20 (1990): 339–53.

9. Ibid. 339.

10. Ibid. 340.

11. Ogot, "The Concept of Jok," 123. Full citation needed here.

12. Ibid.

13. Ibid.

14. See G. R. Lienhardt, "The Shilluk of the Upper Nile," in *African Worlds: Studies in the Cosmological Ideas and Social Values of African Peoples*, ed. Daryll Ford, International African Institute (London: Oxford University Press, 1954), 138–63. See Godfrey R. Lienhardt, *Divinity and Experience: The Religion of the Dinka* (Oxford: Clarendon Press, 1961). See P. P. Howell and W. P. G. Thomson, "The Death of a Reth of the Shilluk and the Installation of His Successor" *Sudan Notes and Records*, 1946. See E. E. Evans-Pritchard, *The Nuer: A Description of the Modes of Livelihood and Political Institutions of a Nilotic People* (Oxford: Clarendon Press, 1940).

15. Lienhardt, "Shilluk of the Upper Nile," 155.

16. Sometimes the Luo say "*Oru wuod Aming'a*," a tautological phrase that tries to combine two different expressions of the same meaning, *ru piny* and *aming'a piny*—both of which mean "the (relative) eternity of the universe"— by separating and converting the prefixes *ru* (which means long duration in terms of days and nights—many days and nights) and *aming'a* (which, also, means long duration in terms of a temporal stretch—a long stretch of time) into personal subjects related by descent in which *Oru* becomes the "son of" *Aming'a*. The Luo use this tautology to claim that eternity (*aming'a*) and the countable duration of days and nights are closely related. This *piny* is the center of the universe and of human experience, there is no rival other. For other references to other ideas associated with the concept of *piny*, see E. S. Atieno Odhiambo, "A World-View of the Nilotes? The Luo Concept of Piny," in *African Historians and African Voices: Essays Presented to Professor Bethwell Allan Ogot*,. ed. E. S. Atieno Odhiambo (Basel, Switzerland: Schlettwein Publishing, 2001), 57–67.

17. See J. H. Driberg, *The Lango* (London: Unwin, 1923). See G. R. Lienhardt, "The Shilluk of the Upper Nile.," *African Worlds*, ed. G. Lienhardt (Oxford University Press, 1954). See T. T. S. Hayley, "The Power Concept in Lango Religion," *Uganda Journal* 7 (1940), and *Anatomy of Lango Religion and Groups* (Cambridge: Cambridge University Press, 1947). P'Bitek's critique of these early and Christocentric studies of the concept of *jok* is in his 1963 essay "The Concept of Jok among the Acholi and Lango," in *Uganda Journal* 27.1 (1963): 15–29. His critique of Tempels and Ogot is in a brief 1964 review of Tempels's book. See Okot p'Bitek, "Fr. Tempels' Bantu Philosophy," *Transition* 13 (1964): 15–17.

18. See p'Bitek, *African Religions in Western Scholarship*, 59.

19. See ibid. 65 (emphasis in the original).

20. See Okot p'Bitek, *Religion of the Central Luo* (Nairobi: East African Literature Bureau, 1971), 40–43.

21. See ibid. 50.

22. See H. Owuor Anyumba, "Spirit Possession among the Luo of Central Nyanza, Kenya," *Occasional Papers in East African Traditional Religion*,

Department of Religious Studies and Philosophy (Kampala: Makerere University (unpublished monograph), 1954), 1–46. See also, by him, "The Historical Dimensions of Life-Crisis Rituals: Some Factors in the Dissemination of Juogi Beliefs among the Luo of Kenya up to 1962" (unpublished conference paper), June 1974.

23. See Bethwell A. Ogot, *History of the Southern Luo* (Nairobi: East African Publishing House, 1967). This excellent text remains the most detailed and authoritative history of the Padhola and Kenya Luo to date.

24. See p'Bitek, *Religion of the Central Luo*, 59–120 and *African Religions in Western Scholarship*, 70–79.

25. P'Bitek, *African Religions in Western Scholarship*, 70.

26. Ibid. 71.

27. Ibid.

28. Ogot, "The Concept of Jok," 124.

29. John Mbiti, *African Religions and Philosophy* (London: Heinemann, 1969).

30. See Oginga Odinga, *Not yet Uhuru: An Autobiography* (New York: Hill and Wang, 1967).

31. Ibid. 42.

32. Ibid. 55.

33. The Luo refer to the various Kalenjin groups collectively as "Lango," as distinct from their (Luo's) own kin, the Lango of Eastern Uganda of whom Okot and Ogot write in their studies of the Luo.

34. P'Bitek, *African Religions in Western Scholarship*, 73.

35. See John C. Onyango-Abuje, *Fire and Vengeance* (Nairobi: East African Publishing House, 1975).

36. See Hayley, "The Power Concept in Lango Religion." See also his *Anatomy of Lango Religion and Groups*.

37. In his 1964 review of Tempels's *Bantu Philosophy*, p'Bitek was very critical of attempts to follow Tempels by trying to explain *juok* as the most general attribute of all things (Being).

38. Incidentally, the Luo have great stories about Tanzanian medicine men and women who are said to be capable of calling the shadows of absent people to appear in a basin of water so they can "slaughter" them by imitating the act on their shadows. Commentaries falsely assume that the Luo believe in the mechanism of the calling as the reason they fear Tanzanian witchcraft. But actually the reason for their fear is their awe for the absurdity of the claim that someone's *tipo* can actually appear at a place they are not. For that to happen the responsible medicine people must be extraordinary or unusual humans, and it is this imagination that causes fear in them. Anyone would feel a little funny when they hear that someone they thought was ordinary was actually not.

39. See Bertrand Russell, *The Problems of Philosophy* (1912; Indianapolis: Hackett, 1990), 49.

SEVEN

PHYSICAL AND METAPHYSICAL UNDERSTANDING

Nature, Agency, and Causation in African Traditional Thought

I. A. MENKITI

Because metaphysical discourse is several steps removed from the original core of understandings that define the common sense of things, a question often occurs in philosophy that has to do with the way and manner in which the gap that exists between the common and metaphysical construction of things is to be filled out. A philosopher, having put on one side common sense, the sense that is held in common regarding the things that are in the world, and having put on the other side metaphysics, whose understanding is also about the things in the world, soon notices a dilemma crashing in on him. The dilemma has to do with the gap, the discontinuity in the discourse issuing from the two types of understanding. Focusing in on himself, the philosopher could come to the conclusion, after a process of inference, that he is, deep down, a thinking substance, that the mind is more real than the body; or that the self is a bundle of perceptions and that causation is nothing but constant conjunction; or that the material world is illusory and only spirits exist; or that God and nature are identical, one and the same thing; or that the world is made up of monads, nothing else; perhaps that tomorrow is tomorrow and does not have the same relationship to today as today has to yesterday; and so on.

The one thing about all of the different metaphysical positions stated here is that they all succeed in leaving the metaphysician with an empty feeling inside, insofar as he, the metaphysician, still intends on being a regular part of the ordinary world. In this ordinary world he believes he knows that, though he thinks, he also has a body and if this body be crushed by an automobile, his mind, wherever it hides, will surely be finished; he believes he knows that cause and effect are related in an intrinsic way, not just as constant conjuncts; he believes he knows that the physical pavement on which he sometimes stubs his toes surely exists and is ever ready to remind him of the durability of the physical world should he pretend otherwise; and he believes he knows that the God of his worship is not the Nature of the mountain spaces or of the free-running wilderness streams.

Faced with this cognitive war inside, the metaphysician can make one of the following decisions: (1) reject the claims of common sense, arguing that it, not metaphysics, stands in need of correction; that just as appearance does not always reflect reality (for example, a straight stick in water looking bent or a mirage in the desert indicating a body of water where none exists), so likewise we cannot count on the unmediated perceptions of common sense to deliver the goods of knowledge; (2) decide to jettison metaphysics on the grounds that being a late arrival, a secondary attachment parasitic on the more fundamental common sense, if choose we must, then surely metaphysics is what has to go; (3) opt for a third position, recognizing that a wholesale rejection of metaphysics is not feasible, given that some form of metaphysical discourse is unavoidable and perhaps indeed necessary in the regimentation of our lives. Nevertheless, we insist that metaphysics has to discipline itself, and this it can do by seeking continuity with the world of common sense, so that whenever the question arises, its validation can always be secured within the frame of the same ongoing common task of getting to know the world as adequately as we can, given the limitations of our human situation.

This third approach, I believe, is worth pursuing, since, as observed earlier, if completeness of understanding is our goal, then there is really no way to purge ourselves completely of metaphysical thinking. Metaphysics is guaranteed by the very fact of common sense itself, by ordinary language, both of which are already philosophically impregnated and not as innocent as at first glance meets the eye.[1]

This brings me straight to the world of African philosophy and the way in which the problematic stated here is handled within the frame of traditional thought. It is my aim to argue in this essay that metaphysical understanding in traditional African thought so neatly dovetails with the regular understanding of physical nature that the two understandings ought to be seen as forming one continuous order of understanding. The understanding of the human person, in a naturalistic setting, is a good illustration of the flow between these two types of understanding. The relative absence of cant and of assorted forms of supernaturalism in the area of African morality is a direct consequence of this empirical persuasion in the grounding of metaphysics. And in the area of religion, the absence of a belief in heaven and hell, or in a day of final judgment at some detached point in an unrealized future, is also a consequence of such grounding. Finally, political authority did not see the sources of its validation in a Creator outside of time and space, but in the here and now, and what could be gleaned down below as pertaining to the will of humans, including ancestors also understood as being agents in the here and now.

Given all of this, it behooves us to investigate more thoroughly the way and manner in which traditional African metaphysics is grounded, since so much of what we want to say in the crucial areas of ethics, religion, and political governance, turns on the question.

Let us begin by going straight to some observations made by Okot p'Bitek, who, in his book, *African Religions in Western Scholarship*, remarks:

> When students of African religions describe African deities as eternal, omnipotent, omniscient, etc., they intimate that African deities have identical attributes with those of the Christian God. In other words, they suggest that Africans Hellenized their deities, but before coming into contact with Greek metaphysical thinking.[2]

However, this is not the case, and nothing is lost in its not being the case. For in p'Bitek's view, Africans "do not think metaphysically" — a conclusion that he sees as being borne out by a straightforward look at African languages. He writes, "The Luo language bears testimony to the fact that the Nilotes, like the early Jews, do not think metaphysically. The concept of Logos does not exist in Nilotic thinking; so the word *Word* was translated into *Lok*, as in the greeting 'Lok ango?', 'What is the news?' "[3] It is evident from the passage that p'Bitek casts himself squarely in the ranks of those who look askance at metaphysics, believing that metaphysics, in refusing to play by the rules set by the deliverances of common sense, should not expect ordinary people to take seriously what it says.

But then the point, as against p'Bitek, is not that Africans do not think metaphysically. Rather, one notes, or ought to note, that Africans do not engage in the kind of metaphysical thinking that he has just shown. For in heeding his caution about an undisciplined deployment of Western metaphysical schemas on African worlds, one does not, it seems to me, have to concede the blanket claim that

Africans do not think metaphysically. If he is right to complain about what appears to him to be an untenable metaphysics coming down on Africa on a Western wind, it does not therefore follow that a complete rejection of metaphysics is called for, since such a conclusion would wind up denying Africans the right, the space, to claim a different kind of metaphysics.

In general, it is granted that certain approaches to metaphysics make sense only against the ideational background that provides them their ancestry and simply will not do if transported, without qualification, to other ideational settings. Leaving aside for a moment the question of whether Africans think or do not think metaphysically, that is, the whole question of ethnophilosophy and the debates that it has generated regarding untenable animist claims, failed attributions, canonical texts that are not there, oratory that is not literature, a tribe named Africa that we cannot find, sages and philosophers who remain hidden in an impenetrable collective mist and refuse to show us the *individual* records of their mental deliberations, leaving aside all of these questions or considerations, let us proceed to examine the bases for the claim that while certain forms of metaphysics may be found alien in an African setting, there are other understandings, properly describable as metaphysical, that can be shown faithful to the African material.

William Abraham once remarked in his book *The Mind of Africa* that in the Akan conceptual scheme what Westerners call supernatural belongs in the same space as what Africans call natural. Arguing that the nature/supernature distinction as traditionally understood in Western circles was a false distinction, Abraham writes, "To state the metaphysical view in terms of a spiritualizing of nature is to falsify the view altogether. It is to try to state it in terms of a position with which it is in radical conflict, for, in the Akan view, nature was, if you like, supernature antecedently spiritual."[4] And the much maligned Placide Tempels notes in his book *Bantu Philosophy* that Bantu metaphysics should be regarded as an extension of Bantu natural science. He writes, "among the Bantu it seems that their philosophy, like ours, makes no claim to be more than the natural intellectual knowledge of beings. The general principles of the knowledge of forces and of influences also belongs [*sic*] to the realm of natural empirical knowledge of the Bantu."[5]

I am interested in the principle of continuity within the order of understanding to which these two writers seem to be pointing in their attempts to bring alive traditional knowing to their respective readers. Insofar as both of their statements issue from an honest grappling with the indigenous material and maintain some fidelity to that which they describe, it behooves us to include them in the set of belief articulations whose ramifications I am trying to explore in this essay. These beliefs, whatever else one might think of them, point to an attitude of mind, an approach to human knowledge that is best described as grounded in the material circumstances of life. They have an empirical warrant and contain a tough-minded refusal to abandon the anchor that holds them to the original sense of things. Hence, emotions are often found having body parts.[6] Hence, there is an absence of a substantive attribution of mind, as opposed to the adverbial, within the structure of the indigenous languages, a fact that has been nicely described by Kwasi Wiredu.[7] Hence, also speaking of language, there is often no distinction made within the tribal languages between the "he" and the "she" in the matter of pronouns—as if the village, having a profound understanding of persons, and refusing therefore to be sidetracked by issues of gross anatomy, and the multiple surface of disturbances in the distribution of temporal power that often attend the gross anatomical differences—refuses also to play the male vs. female game where such a fundamental instrument as language is concerned because the playing of such a game would tend to reify *person-irrelevant* distinctions where the speech is about persons, not about male or female function.[8]

Since objections usually arise regarding the adequacy of proceeding in village fashion on the question of knowledge of the world, let me add, forthright, some remarks on the issue in the hope of clarifying where I stand. First, we cannot ignore the inbuilt rationality manifested in the structure of the ordinary languages of the human village. We cannot deny that there are unappropriated cognitive powers inherent in the 'tribal' tongues of the world whether they be English, French, Ibo, Akan, or Yoruba. The reason-bound individual philosopher, rationally proceeding, would still have to proceed by making use of the tribal tongue of the respective culture to which he belongs, or the tribal tongue of some other culture that he has adopted. And it is the rational structures of these tongues, these ordinary languages, that sustain his individual rational performances. Quite often, it is not an easy job separating the anterior rationality of the village from the posterior one of the individual.

Second, and on a more specific level, many of the particular notions that philosophers struggle with, notions such as identity and difference, cause and effect, part or whole, appearance or reality, time and eternity, self and others, motion to or from—all of these already have a place on the ground floor, the foundation of the epistemic household; they occupy a corner of the knowledge of things, which is village-accessible. To forget this beginning level without which argumentative philosophy is not possible is very much like an ostrich raising its neck to the clouds oblivious of the fact that that neck is fully attached to a body that is grounded on the earth.

I believe that the philosopher's skepticism regarding the village and its ways is a corollary of the philosopher's own fascination with three things the validity of which, in all circumstances, may be open to question. First, there is the fascination with inference, a fascination so strong that within the discipline inference has become almost like an end in itself. The result is that very often we try to force into an inference mold things that by the nature of the situation are at odds with inference. As is evident, certain particular situations are immediately apprehensible and their logic is such that to talk of inference and conclusion, in the way that philosophers are wont to do, often succeeds in straining usage and casting into question the philosopher's inferential activity. If a soldier marching through a jungle path were to see the left index finger of an enemy soldier sticking out of the greenery, in a well-camouflaged position, he can infer that the finger is a sign of an enemy soldier. But if he sees the enemy soldier dash for cover, he does not see the dashing as a sign of an enemy soldier; he simply sees an enemy soldier dashing—no inference; no conclusion. And here, the point is not the advisability of inference as a way of proceeding towards knowledge, but the inadvisability of playing the inference game in certain particular situations.

Second, there is, joined to the fascination with inference another fascination, this one with rule-guided knowing or rules as such, with articulated governing principles—again another area in which the village is said to be deficient. Most often the complaint is that not only does it, the village, lack argumentative rigor; it also lacks a clear statement of what its formal rules, its principles of procedure, are. Instead, it proceeds in an ad hoc unregimented manner, the result being that unless and until an authoritative body emerges, either of philosophers or law makers, to state formally what is or is not the case, clarity eludes one and all. But, here again, rules have their validation, their very existence, within their situations of use in an untidy world. I am reminded here of H. L. A. Hart's remark regarding the issue of rule-skepticism in the law—how the rule-skeptic is often a disappointed purist who, having failed to see realized on earth the jurist's heaven of concepts, decides that there are no rules at all.[9] But the fact remains that apart from the failed dreams of the system builder, there are rules in the world, and most of them, including informal village rules, do succeed in providing their users adequate guidance. That the rules cannot do all we push them to do, in the way and manner we push them to be done, is very much a part of the human situation, and that is all right as such. Its being so does not have to provoke an epistemological crisis.

Again, just as we must learn when to play and when not to play the inference game, so likewise, we must learn when the rules have functioned sufficient unto their use, and when they have not. By doing this we will be able to establish for the rules in question a parallel existence with somewhat recalcitrant data until one or the other gets modified in a process of mutual accommodation. The principle, if you like, is one of cognitive tolerance and the temper of the village matches very well such an approach to cognition.

And yet a third preoccupation has to do with the problem presented by skepticism itself. Although it is said that the beginnings of modern philosophy can be traced to Descartes's radical doubt, doubt itself carried to a certain extent may become an indication of pathology, not of enlightenment. For the brain that pulls the trigger when things are said to be finally known, thus closing off the doubting channels, this brain is not able to support any affective order if it finds itself perpetually exposed, on a nonstop basis, to the debilitating clutches of unresolved doubt regarding the ordinary things that are in the world. And when affect goes, cognition is bound to follow, depending of course on the severity of the affective loss. It is standard practice in philosophy to talk of cognition, then of affect, but the casual direction of things may well be the other way—sometimes, at any rate. The point here is that there is doubt, and then there is doubt—the doubt of healthy inquiry and the doubt that soon caves in on itself.

This matter of exaggerated solutions to simple problems is one of a kind with the issue of exaggerated diagnosis of simple problems. In the one case we confront the mistake before the fact, and, in the other, the mistake after the fact. Simplicity in the formation of theory, in the presentation of problems and the offering of solutions to problems presented is a goal strongly to be pursued in light of these observations. And this cry for simplicity in the area of theory formation, I would dare suggest, is a cry for a village orientation in the naming and management of things. The demand for simplicity keeps everyone focused and clear as to the tasks at hand; it forces specialists to become more cognizant of when their complex manufacturing has become a hindrance rather than a help, given the tasks to be solved.

In a recent biography of Richard Feynman titled *Richard Feynman: A Life in Science*, John Gribbin and Mary Gribbin write:

> By the time most people learn about Feynman's approach (if they ever do), their brains have been battered by so much mechanics of one kind or another that it is hard to appreciate its simplicity and galling to realize that they could have saved time and effort by learning quantum theory (and classical theory) Feynman's way in the first place. Feynman's approach is not the standard way to teach physics for the same reason that the Betamax system is not the standard format for home videos and the Apple MacIntosh is not the standard for personal computers because an inferior system got established in the market place first and continues to dominate as much through inertia and resistance to change as anything else.[10]

It was Feynman, of course, who brought a simplified integral approach to the conflicting visions of the world projected by classical mechanics, on the one hand, and quantum mechanics, on the other; who helped resolve the conflict between Schrödinger's wave approach to the description of the quantum world and Heisenberg's particle approach to the same. In his own book *The Character of Physical Law*, Feynman stated as his motto that no matter how elegant, how brilliant our guess is, "if it disagrees with experiment, it is wrong." We can fully substitute 'experience' for experiment in the previous passage. For although the two terms are not the same, it is clear that experiment holds the power that it does because it makes things come within the grasp of experiential reality. It is experience that gives experiment its weight in scientific gold.

I have been talking now about such scientific notions as experiment, measurement, and so on. How, the critic might ask, does one reconcile such concerns with the generally unregimented attitude of the village? Isn't the village the very example of a nonscientific cast of mind with its belief in spirits and immaterial agency? Isn't the village's notion of causation a rather strange one when it embraces such things as belief in witchcraft, hexing, psychokinesis, telepathy, action from a distance, dead ancestors who still act in a living world? All of these, so the contention goes, fly in the face of physicalistic explanations of the universe.

In order to explore these objections adequately, it is important to keep the issues that they raise as separate as possible from the cross-cultural contentions, which, charging Eurocentrism and cognitive imperialism, sees all talk of scientific empiricism and rationality as tainted at the source, given Europe's less than worthy intentions toward the rest of the world. As I see it, the issues raised by the objections remain alive whether directed at a traditional African or directed at a Londoner planting onions during the full moon, convinced that they would come out of the ground full of magical powers, so that he or any other Englishman who eats them would be three times as strong as a Frenchman and ten times as strong as an African. And were such a Londoner (after his moon-based onion experience) to write a book titled *Cattle Raiding and Bride Stealing among the English, 1900–1950* convinced that these were indeed the social practices of England in the period described, it would not be up to him to have the last word on the matter. Even the son of a traditional African could join other Englishmen in defending old England from the hallucinations of the Londoner. There is such a thing as evidence, such a thing as a fact, or facts, of the situation.

This brings me to an observation made by Kwasi Wiredu in his book *Philosophy and an African Culture*. The observation is to the effect that charges of superstition, authoritarianism, and anachronism are only possible from a vantage point that is removed in time or space from the target situation being criticized.[11] Otherwise, it is only possible against a background of some other specified assumptions. It is hard, for example, to conceive of a traditional African society thinking of itself as engaged in superstitions or anachronistic practices. That charge would have to be made by others, appropriately distant from the situation, that define the traditional African society. In so far as the latter is concerned, its belief system is in order and needs no correction. The Londoner's example is different and warrants a different sort of consideration. His belief is judged aberrant because not too many other Londoners share it. Were these others to declare that belief a piece of New Age nonsense, then they do so because the belief measured against the background of other beliefs held by contemporary Englishmen is a noncompliant item. Being noncompliant, it has no way of establishing its credentials either by appeal to what is generally believed or by appeal to what is scientifically known to be the case.

And so it is with many of the other situations involving belief in supernatural powers, in the efficacious agency of such things as witches, seers, sorcerers, and diviners, whether or not it includes clairvoyance, precognition, telepathy, or some other kind of abnormal potency. Sometimes a popular belief takes hold, such as not crossing the path of a black cat on Friday, especially if that Friday falls on the 13th of the month. Even nonbelievers in the mysterious powers of black cats or the number 13 often find themselves acquiescing in the tradition of avoidance, as a matter perhaps of rational prudence, with each saying: I don't really believe in this stuff, but I feel uncomfortable challenging it just in case there is something to the belief. Or the hotel manager might say, perhaps, on a more practical note: Why risk losing business by numbering the floor 13 and spooking some of our customers? Why not use the number 12A, instead, and keep all of our clients satisfied?

Because of the pull of causation in the normal activities of our daily life, it is easy to understand the readiness displayed by folks around the world in extending causation to what appears to be unrelated events or naturally disjunct occurrences. As Donald Davidson has put it, "Cause is the cement of the universe; the concept of cause is what holds together our picture of the universe, a picture that would otherwise disintegrate into a diptych of the mental and the physical."[12]

To talk of causation is of course to turn attention to physicalism— physicalism defined as a claim that for each fact in the world there is ultimately a dependence of one sort or another on a prior physical fact, and for each causal explanation a dependence on a prior physical explanation. Philosophers make many controversial claims in the course of their writings, but physicalism, understood at a bottom level, it seems to me, is not one such controversial claim. It cannot be seriously questioned. In any case, as Hartry Field has pointed out, the belief in it as a methodological assumption in the sciences has led to many important discoveries, and as such it stands instrumentally validated. Writes Field, "the implicit acceptance of the doctrine of physicalism on the part of most scientists has led to a successful search for the molecular foundations of genetics and the quantum mechanical foundations of chemical bonding."[13] Furthermore, notes Field:

> Even if there were positive evidence for telepathy that we did not know how to refute, most of us would tend to disbelieve the telepathic claims (and presumably suspect the evidence) simply because it seems so difficult to conceive how such claims could fit with a physicalistic worldview. Of course, given *sufficient* evidence for telepathy, we would look harder for its physical foundations; or we would contemplate giving up the doctrine of physicalism and replacing it by a broader 'unity of science' type doctrine (much as we gave up the doctrine of

mechanism late in the nineteenth century). But this last move is not one
we take at all lightly, and that is what gives the doctrine of physicalism
its methodological bite.[14]

In marshaling these considerations regarding the inescapability of a
physicalistic understanding of the world over and against those claims
that avow the truth of such things as telepathy, Field calls attention to
an issue that lies at the heart of this essay, namely: how does one
reconcile belief in material agency with the belief in nonmaterial
agency? My answer to this question is that in the case of traditional
African society what we have is a belief system that is fully committed
to material agency but that trades on an extended notion of what is
embraced by the material universe. This being so, what we would
have to say in regard to Field's passage quoted earlier is that for traditional society, a material or a quasi-material accounting would have
to be given for the telepathic claims in question. The option of discounting a physicalistic or quasi-physicalistic accounting of the phenomenon in question is simply not there.

Suppose, one reads an account of a young boy, 3 years old, who
digs up a piece of rock and insists that what he has dug up is a dinosaur
egg. He will not let his father have peace until the weary father agrees
to take the rock to be tested at the local Museum of Natural History.
When scientists at the Museum conduct the test they establish conclusively that the piece of rock is indeed a fossilized remains of an egg
laid by a meat-eating egg-laying dinosaur, that it is a fragment dating
back 150 million years to the time when the theropods held sway
during the upper Jurassic Period. Now suppose that this boy does this
sort of thing time and time again, that it happens not once but several
times in an unfailing succession. One imagines that a response would
be that it was chance and chance alone. But truly, the scientific rea-
soned response should be, not that it was chance, but rather that we
simply do not know; that the boy may have powers whose sources we
cannot comprehend but had better not dismiss, especially if he keeps
accurately predicting these things, time and time again. The choice, in
other words, need not be between magic and chance but between
understood physical things and physical things not yet understood.

We can also cite another type of example, this one involving
nonhuman agency. It is known that certain sea-going turtles after
spending their life elsewhere, when it comes time to lay their eggs
somehow manage to navigate a thousand miles or more of uncharted
waters to within a five-mile radius of where they themselves were

hatched, there to lay their own eggs. How do they do it, we ask? The scientist says 'imprinting.' The theologian says it is the hand of God. The villager amazed at the powers of the natural world and the natural creatures that come to action in such a world—actions that project specific efficacies—this villager stays away from grand theory, convinced that the order of causation is unbroken and if powers are assigned, then they remain assigned to palpable physical agents, whether human, animal, botanical, or mineral.

Or, again, take the current electronic revolution and the microchips that power the computers, which make possible things like the Internet, the World Wide Web, and so on. People who build these machines, whether hardware or software, count on the natural powers of silica to complete the circuitry. They believe they know the principles, the way and manner in which the wired devices have been put together, and ordinary folks also believe the principles have all been understood by the experts and there is no mystery remaining. What many cannot answer, of course, is *why* silica, of all the other array of natural substances, has those powers. Having figured out *how* it all works, the villager in all of us is still nonetheless amazed, amazed at the distribution of natural powers and at the fact that it is silica that has those powers, not, for example, compacted okra.

I presume that elevating our discussion so as to take up physics at another level will not change the situation. Thus, in the case of atomic clocks whether we continue to talk of silicon or talk instead of rubidium, hydrogen, or cesium 133, and all of their natural resonances measured in megahertz, the issue still remains one of properties endowing certain powers in certain things. If the physicist tells us that for him cesium is the most electropositive element to be found and that, in defying temperature and atmospheric fluctuations, it is most useful in the construction of atomic clocks whose accuracy can be measured to a deviation of one second every six million years, the villager in each of us still responds: Why cesium, why not vegetable matter?

In addition to this sort of consideration regarding the specifications of material agency, there is also the issue of a type of causation, which though traced on a physical plane, still appears to make little sense as, for example, when cosmologists tell us that the universe, this universe of several billion celestial bodies was brought about from a point of physical matter no larger than a pumpkin seed. Faced with this sort of explanation, the ordinary mind feels acutely disoriented. Better, it says, to seek shelter in a life of faith, to believe in a divine immaterial origin of the universe, than believe in this single-point big bang theory of its origin. One wonders if it is not because of these sorts of strange occurrences within the physical universe that the idea of immaterial causation had come to gain some saliency in the first place. For seen in light of the magnitude of the physical production called the universe, a pinpoint of origin might as well be thought of as spatially nonexistent; as immaterial, in other words.

These remarks gather some interest especially in regard to various types of mind-to-body causal attributions. Consider one example. A morgue attendant has just brought out a body from cold storage to begin preparing it for burial. Soon after, the dead body stirs and begins moving. The morgue attendant immediately collapses out of sheer fright and dies. Now the dead person rejoins the ranks of the living and the alive person joins the ranks of the dead, there to stay for good. While the village explains this situation by reference to ancestral intervention or violations of taboo, the scientifically minded, perhaps Oxford educated, son of the village elder declares it a matter of simple fright. In either explanation, immaterial factors are seen to lie behind the material occurrence in question. (I am assuming here of course that the educated son of the village has already offered a satisfactory explanation as to the dead man's revival along lines of such things as the icy temperature kept him in suspended animation and the thawing jump-started him into life again.)

In any case, apart from this sort of dramatic example, we all do know about psychosomatic causal linkages and how a depressed person, or a person filled with anxiety, very soon begins to manifest physical loss of weight; how stress, overall, leads to various forms of immune deficiency, which leads to growth of illness, which leads to death; hence the scientific field of psychoneuro-immunology and its emphasis on the avoidance of stress, the development of healthy mind habits, and the cultivation of friends, who provide us with strong social support systems.

The details of the immunologist's explanations might lie in the claim that stress unleashes certain hormones and that this in turn lowers one's resistance to disease. But here again, even with this sort of explanation, we are still talking, ultimately, of assumed immaterial factors issuing in material end-products. Unless, of course, psychological factors like stress and anxiety be declared outright to be nothing but a body state. But that is a whole other disputation, one already reflected in the current debate between psychotherapists and psychopharmacologists regarding the best way to classify and treat emotional disorders— whether it is talk that will do the healing, or drugs, or perhaps both in combination. If talking alone does the healing, and it is further assumed that after the patient is healed his brain shows a difference in physical structure, what then do we do with the causal story?

One assumes here that even if brain structure is claimed to be eventually altered by talk therapy and by the pull and push of the interaction between patient and psychotherapist, so that always a new recognizable neuronal pattern can be found on a patient's brain soon after psychotherapy is initiated, talk is still talk, still to be classified in the domain of meaning endowed social relations, not in the domain of measurable psychotropic substances. Thus, if a patient is angry because his wife has just run off with a taxi driver and as a consequence the neurotransmitters in his brain keep firing the more he talks things over with the therapist, and, in firing, keep leaving recognizable neuronal patterns, it would still be best to regard his anger, *qua anger*, as belonging in the domain of matter-silent social relations. That the neurobiologist shows us the mechanisms of affective rage does not render the anger borne of betrayal into a simple matter of neurons laid out in a certain way.

What the physical sciences do, especially the successful special sciences like chemistry, genetics, and so on, is give us useful details about the world—details that are often revealing regarding the *how* of things, the way and manner in which they function. However, when it comes to issues of basic orientation to cognitive questions, such issues as the fundamental patterns of apprehension inherited from the human village, it is doubtful that the received details issuing from the various scientific discoveries will ever succeed in forcing us to abandon them. Give up the belief in physical bodies and it becomes a weird world whose contours defy articulation. Give up the belief that persons have consciousness and think thoughts, that they are something beyond the sum total of the chemical events in their bodies and it becomes, also, a world equally weird. In terms of what it proposes to deny either option fails miserably.

What this suggests is that our efforts at reductionist explanations, if they are to be put to good use, will have to be contained within a range intermediate to the investigation in question. They do not have to be seen as always propelling themselves, with inevitable momentum, to a final resting point that occurs only after all recalcitrant obstacles have been obliterated. Thus, trying to procure the physical basis of mental functioning does not have to lead, inevitably, to a claim regarding the ultimate reducibility of mind to body with no remainder whatsoever. Nor does trying to defend the nonmaterial nature of mental functioning have to lead to a final claim that mind, being mind, is totally independent of the body, that in defying physical location it has to be considered an otherworldly affair.

Again, in this matter, the epistemic temper of the village suggests a way out. It is a temper which, as the saying goes, steadfastly refuses to open a can of worms where nothing can be gained by doing so — where, in actual fact, instead of attaining clarity the original thing we sought to explain finds itself somehow transformed into something else, obscured and unrecognizable. The problem with reductionism is that although it appears to be propelled by the principle of the continuity of inquiry (a principle to which we subscribe and which has guided much in this essay, its methodology and stubborn insistence on going all the way to a pure resting point (once a trajectory has been chosen) exposes it to very serious charges of *exclusion* of unpleasant data found along the way. In an essay titled "Constructivism, Realism, and Philosophical Method," Richard Boyd makes the following sensible observation:

> Insofar as the various areas of human inquiry are interconnected, epistemological theories must satisfy a requirement of integration with the best substantiated results of all the various areas of inquiry. Similarly, once the possibility of experimental metaphysics is acknowledged, any sort of human inquiry must be seen as partially relevant to metaphysics and thus metaphysical theories, too, must face the requirement of integration with the rest of our knowledge.[15]

Thus, in addition to continuity as a principle of inquiry, there is also the principle of the *unity* of inquiry. Whereas continuity might be achieved by forcing everything to remain on the chosen grid that the reductionist presents to us, the concern of unification of all the substantiated data issuing from the various fields of inquiry still has to be attended to, as Boyd so importantly reminds us. Here, again, because the village tends to be inclusive and accommodating, not exclusive, in its approach to matters of moral and physical knowledge, it is well positioned to respect the principle of the unity of inquiry. Its emphasis is placed on what works and on observing what there is in the world. It does this by staying away from high theory and avoiding stipulative definitions with all of the aforementioned difficulties regarding the arbitrary rejection of unpleasant data.

Because the village knows how to keep its silence on certain matters, i.e. how to hold back speech where it is necessary that speech be held back, it is able to avoid many of the problems mentioned earlier. Think now of the notion of an *abiku* among the Yoruba or *ogbanje* among the Ibo. These are children who elect to go through repeated cycles of birth and death. First, they bring joy to their families and the community in the fact of their being born; and then they play mischief with their families' emotion by going right back to the spirit world, just when everyone believes they have come to stay for good. They are children who are caught in between worlds—neither staying put in this world nor staying put in the other one. That these children repeat the cycle of birth and death, that they come and go as they please until the right confining ritual is deployed to stop their mischief, was accepted as part of the metaphysical story of persons. And yet that acceptance did not force the Ibo nor force the Yoruba worldview to postulate an elaborate final-entry sort of theory regarding reincarnation. The ambiguity involved in belief in some children repeating, and others not, is tolerated because the world is an ambiguous place. If some children, because of their physical and mannerism resemblance to a dead ancestor, or to a child recently dead, are seen as repeating, that is all well and good. But it provides no ground for claiming that repetition awaits every child born to the world. Or ground for claiming that there is really no repetition going on, since it would be inconsistent to assign it to some children but not to others.

Is this then one of those signs of the pre-logical mentality of the native? Let those who claim such pre-logicality answer. Whether yes or no, their answer is not a concern of the village. The village's concern, rather, is an explanation, in the immediate, of things observed in the physical world and in the social world of living persons, including the village child whose physical and mannerism characteristics indicate, or appear to indicate, existence split between a here and a there. If village society ignored the need to explain what is clearly perceived to be there, namely the observed characteristics of the born child, that, truly, would be grounds for charging it with illogicality. By its positing a category of beings defined as *abiku* or *ogbanje*, the village rises squarely to the epistemic task before it which, in this case, is the task of explaining what it feels is unusual, and doing so according to the metaphysical resources available to it.

And what we also notice on this issue of the *ogbanje* is that belief in it is a matter of a public philosophy accessible to everyone, a philosophy whose base of understanding is anchored in the doings of the one known physical world, with all of the variegated causal potencies seen as thereto attaching—attaching not simply to the individual things, but to the category of things to which the individual things belong. Thus, the individual *ogbanje* does what he or she does because he or she belongs to a category of beings conceived as *ogbanje*, a category seen as retaining certain special causal powers. The child's *ogbanje* powers, though exercised by it, are not seen as simply residual in him or her but in the defining category. This point could perhaps be made in another way. For example, the reason it sounds odd to call a vegetarian an herbivore is that doing this appears to vest a residual characteristic where it does not belong. For 'herbivore' like 'carnivore' and 'omnivore' belongs to a class of terms whose function is to categorize species, families of things, not primarily individual members of those species, or families of things. Because these terms are not only species-categorizing but species-categorized, their use, outright, to describe individual organisms is bound to be descriptively ambiguous at best; at worst, just plain odd—as in the case just discussed.

These observations obviously leave unanswered some other kinds of questions which might be of concern to a philosopher used to asking those kinds of questions. For example, was the notion of an *ogbanje* already there before individual *ogbanjes* could be so designated, and, if so, then where did the notion come from? And if not, then how could individual *ogbanjes* be seen as instantiations of something not already there? I do not think we have to answer this sort of question, just as we do not have to answer the question of whether there had to be a concept of motorability before there were motor cars, or if motor cars first had to occupy the physical universe before motorability could occupy the conceptual one.

Much of what I have said here in the matter of *ogbanjes/abikus* can also be applied to the consideration of twins (*ibeji* in Yoruba, *ejima* in Ibo). Traditional society no doubt assumed that twins are possessed of certain powers (or are connected to certain powers) because of the universal fact that, whether situated in the village or situated in the metropolis, the experience of encountering twins, especially identical ones, is like an experience of seeing double, an experience not generated in the case of encounters with singly birthed other individuals. But, here again, the powers that are assigned, for good or ill, to this or that specifiable twin, are assigned primarily to the category of beings to which twins belong. These powers speak to a class of embodied persons in a natural universe with other persons. This being so, the agency of twins (or the agencies associated with them) cannot on pain of error be regarded as an altogether spooky otherworldly affair. If twins as a class are said to know what others do not know, or do as others are not able to do, then the belief about *that* arises because of the *observed* physical facts about them, situated as they are in the one common world occupied by them and other non-twin persons. In the end, the metaphysical understanding regarding twins and what they are, or are capable of doing, finds empirical warrant in the observed physical facts, which at the outset provided the grounds for the differential claims regarding them.

It has now become customary to speak of 'the event and its theory.' But what can also be argued is that, strictly speaking, most event descriptions are already burdened with theory. What this means is that should an individual philosopher be so inclined, he or she could go ahead and claim outright that all we have is theory, though, admittedly there is a more or less to the matter. For such a philosopher, since there is a more or less to the matter one can simply conclude that the best way to approach the event/theory distinction is to think (and talk) in terms of a continuum of theories of different levels of sophistication, some on the low, some on the high, end of the classification.

Now, concerning village society, it needs to be pointed out that the construal of all that is encountered, then spoken of, to be a matter of degrees of theory would not necessarily sit very well with the society. This is so because village society is of a down-to-earth empirical persuasion. It would be inclined to maintain a distinction between what is seen to be there and what is believed about, or theorized about, what is seen to be there, since it is the former that provides the observational grounds on the basis of which the village is able to settle any disagreement between the different proclamations of the latter. We could say, in the language of the streets, that whereas theories are a dime a dozen, the thing that is publicly perceived to be there stands in durable fashion, defying the discommonality of reference that theory is heir to. This may be the reason why the *onisegun* or *dibia* (Yoruba and Ibo, respectively)[16] put white chalk around their eyes, or the eyes of initiates, as if to indicate the primacy of sight, the primacy of what sight first encounters. The initiate can believe later, think, interpret, or theorize later. It is understood that for the class of seers, if what they reveal is to be kept separable from the erroneous declamations of others (not excluding lunatic others), then ultimately those revelations have to be defended by appeal to items discovered at ground zero. There is no better way to do this than to appeal to sight and what sight first encounters in this multi-bodied public world. This I take to be the burden of the white chalk around the eyes, for the *dibia*, for the *onisegun*.

My discussion thus far has been aimed to secure certain claims regarding the embodied grounds of knowledge in so far as village society is concerned. It has also been aimed to secure claims regarding the physicality of causal attributions within village society. Now, it will be recalled that Robin Horton in his famous essay "African Traditional Thought and Western Science" takes a dim view of what he considers to be a lack of needed separation between the material and immaterial within traditional modes of thought. He calls attention to the continuity, the undividedness, involved in the village way of handling the body–spirit divide. He writes:

> Both in traditional African cosmologies and in European cosmologies before Descartes, the modern distinction between "mind" and "matter" does not appear. Although everything in the universe is underpinned by spiritual forces, what moderns would call "mental activities" and "material things" are both part of a single reality, neither material nor immaterial. Thinking, conceiving, saying, etc. are described in terms of organs like heart and brain, and actions like the uttering of words.[17]

Now, I suppose that this attribution to African traditional thought of a belief in "a single reality, neither material nor immaterial" is one way of describing what I have been at pains to articulate in this essay. But I find myself hesitant to subscribe to the view that, in the same African schema, everything in the universe could also be understood as "underpinned by spiritual forces." That may be a legitimate description of the pre-Cartesian European village, but its adequacy to describe the African situation is open to question for the simple reason that the spirit–body divide has always been suspect in African usages, whether one considers the metaphysics, simpliciter, or comes at it through crucial expressions in the languages. And that is why, even today, as we look at the so-called tribal tongues, we can without much hesitation agree with Horton that "thinking, conceiving, saying, etc., are described in terms of organs like heart and brain, and actions like the uttering of words." Consider, here, the Igbo expression for "to love" which is "*ifu na anya*," which literally translates as "to see in the eye."[18] Or consider, also in Igbo, the term for depraved wickedness, which is put in terms of "*afo ita mmili*," literally a reference to a stomach deprived of water, dried out, hardened, with no residue whatever of the usual digestive juices.

I bring up these examples by way of showing that in so far as the village was concerned, when it comes to body–mind distinctions, the looseness or ambiguity regarding what constitutes the domain of the physical, and what the domain of the mental, does not necessarily stem from a kind of an ingrown limitation of the village mind, a crudeness or ignorance, unschooled, regarding the necessity of properly differentiating things, one from the other, but is rather an attitude that is well considered given the ambiguous nature of the physical universe, especially that part of it which is the domain of sentient biological organisms, within which include persons described as constituted by their bodies, their minds, and whatever else the post-Cartesian elucidators believe persons are made of or can ultimately be reduced to. My view on the matter is that the looseness or ambiguity in question is not necessarily a sign of indifference to applicable distinctions demanded by an epistemology, but is itself an epistemic stance, namely: do not make distinctions when the situation does not call for the distinctions that you make. In this there is a certain wisdom to the African, as well as the European, village whatever their other differences happen to be.

In the way I have conceived it, when it comes to basic cognitive orientation, the traditional village retains pride of place, and its standards, properly understood, reach beyond assignable localities. For example, it reaches beyond Africa to even the don at Oxford, not to mention the butcher in London, or the farmer out there in the Caucasus. The reason for this is very simple. The sense we had in our villages before we dwelt in the city, that sense refuses to yield its seniority; so that whatever, subsequently, the Oxford don absorbs by way of knowledge in this or that specific academic pursuit, either this retains a junior position measured against the village's seniority in areas where the specific pursuit involves matters of basic cognition, or else it retains first ranking but only in the partial circumstances of the specific pursuit in question. The don cannot have his cake and eat it too. Either he stands in ancestral relations and gives up claims to seniority of speech in these cognitive matters, or else he moves to secondary locations on the epistemic/cognitive grid if he wishes to retain some semblance of speech seniority.

I suppose that there are some who might find themselves resistant to such expressions as 'village orientation toward matters of basic cognition' and who will retort that orientations toward knowledge are attributes of individuals, not of villages. They will say that since the village has no texts on these matters and only individuals do, especially those individuals trained in philosophy, we cannot speak of village orientations in knowledge. But I hope I have made my meaning clear. As I indicated earlier, I do not wish to be drawn into the fruitless debate on the presence or absence of canonical texts. Suffice it to say that the village stands for an original point of departure in epistemic matters, and that, in it, we find the anchor for the settled belief in the obduracy of bodies; the unavoidable fact of a physical universe that is confronted day in and day out by one and all, including the very same individual makers of those prized canonical texts.

Second, in talking about the physical universe, a demand presses itself upon knowers and speakers alike for a unified idiom in reference to referring to the world, and since bodies are primary, it stands to reason that a residual physicalism will attend our referrings, including even the referring to mental sorts of activities, since they are mental activities of embodied individuals. Thus, a physicalistic sort of idiom, even where emotions are involved, or thought or memory involved, will have to be explained, at least partly, by reference to ancestry. Once speech has been ordered by an antecedent primordial belief in a world of material bodies, it is haunted by its ancestry and cannot, without distortion, escape its lineage. While some may think of this in terms of something bad or inelegant, a vestigial contamination bedeviling language use, I tend to think of it as something good, in so far as it keeps us anchored to the original heft of things, and away from the sort of temptation that leads individuals to engage in dreamy talk, in the course of which they postulate chimerical entities without a base of support in the physical world.

Before leaving aside these observations on Horton and the issue of the absence of a mind–matter distinction in traditional thought, let me also make a pertinent additional observation regarding some remarks make by Kwame Anthony Appiah in his essay, "Old Gods, New Worlds," which appears as chapter 6 of his widely discussed book *In My Father's House: Africa in the Philosophy of Culture*. Appiah writes:

> There is a story—probably apocryphal—of some missionaries in Northern Nigeria who were worried about the level of infant mortality due to stomach infections transmitted in drinking water. They explained to "converts" at the mission that the deaths were due to tiny animals in the water, and that these animals would be killed if they only boiled the water before giving it to the children. Talk of invisible animals produced only a tolerant skepticism: the babies went on dying. Finally, a visiting anthropologist suggested a remedy. There were, he said, evil spirits in the water; boil the water and you could see them going away, bubbling out to escape the heat. This time the message worked. These people were "converts;" for the missionaries' appeal to spirits was appeal to demons, to what the New Testament calls "principalities and powers."[19]

Now it seems to me that given what I have said in the preceding pages, the villagers in the story just mentioned were being perfectly rational, steadfastly empirical, in resisting the attempt to impose on them the microbial theory of disease causation. For when they look in the water, they do not see any little animals there; all they see is plain water, maybe dirty water, but still plain water. In effect what the missionaries were asking them to do is to reject the evidence before their eyes, the evidence of their senses. As for the second explanation along lines of invisible spirits being made uncomfortable by the heat of the boiling water and now escaping through the plainly visible steam, again the point needs to be made that since the villagers have had encounters with the steam of boiling water before, and never before saw this as evidence of irate spirits made uncomfortable to the point of wanting to escape, then what is it that is so special about this particular boiling water that its steam ought now to be seen as evidence of resident malevolent spirits jostling to escape? To pose the question this way is to begin to understand the force of special circumstances in the attribution of causal powers within the frame of traditional thought. For invisible spirits to be part of the causal story, at the point of encounter with the missionaries, they must also have been part of the causal story in past situations involving the drinking of water and the getting sick of children.

It will be recalled that Evans-Pritchard had put forward an explanation of casual relations within the frame of traditional thought in which belief in magical powers and invisible agency coexists, and indeed supplements, belief in natural causation. Whether one calls his account a dual causation view of the matter here under discussion, or calls it some other name deemed more appropriate, I think his general meaning is clear. He writes:

> Levy-Bruhl is also wrong in supposing that there is necessarily a contradiction between an objective causal explanation and a mystical one. It is not so. The two kinds of explanation can be, as indeed they are, held together, the one supplementing the other; and they are not therefore exclusive. For example the dogma that death is due to witchcraft does not exclude the observation that the man was killed by a buffalo. For Levy-Bruhl there is here a contradiction, to which natives are indifferent. But no contradiction is involved. On the contrary, the natives are making a very acute analysis of the situation. They are perfectly well aware that a buffalo killed the man, but they hold that he would not have been killed by it if he had not been bewitched.[20]

Now since sameness in event designation may still lend itself to separable but connected causal stories, Evan-Pritchard's move to reject the displacement or exclusion model implied by Levy-Bruhl's approach is perfectly understandable and appears quite justified regarding the African situation. And yet what he proposes regarding the so-called magical accounts ought to be such that the accounts should not be seen as a mere add on, but really as a natural extension dovetailing with the primary causal grid of the material accounts. A view attributed to the British cartographer Timothy Robinson notes of miracles that miracles are explainable, but that it is the explanations that are miraculous. I believe that in our African situation neither what is explained nor the explanation that is offered to explain it can in principle answer to the description "miraculous." This is so, not just because explanations by their nature are supposed to throw light on what is mysterious, not add another layer of mystery to an already mysterious situation, but also because material causation within the African world has such an expansive range that that sort of labeling would not be necessary. Thus, so long as we keep our explanations anchored to primary village understandings, understandings whose singular physicality I have been at pains to elaborate in this essay, there is neither mystery in the event nor in the explanation that is advanced to explain the event.

Now regarding the idea of an expanded notion of material causation within the frame of traditional thought, it will be recalled that earlier on, in the middle sections of this essay, I did try to provide a sort of grounding for it. In particular, I tried to place it within the context of the complex interactions known to obtain in the physical universe—interactions which, though they are not simple, still manage to tell a simple story, namely, that the world is a thoroughly physical place and persons who inhabit the world, being themselves physical entities can have causal powers attributed to them on one and the same undivided plane of material causation shared by other entities and objects also having action in the world. If errors occur in this attribution, they are errors of detail, not of basic orientation. Whether the aforementioned powers are exercised by the mind part of these individuals or by their body part, the attitude of the village is that this is a matter of little relevance. The actors that it, the village, has come to know—whether wizard, witch, ancestor, or just plain *dibia*—since they are physical or quasi-physical agents, these actors possess their powers in a publicly recognized manner and exercise them in an action field that is understood to be a durable part of the material world. Moreover, though they may share an acknowledged power to act from a distance, almost as if in defiance of regular physical laws, the witch's power is not to be confused with the ancestor's, nor the ancestor's with the witch's and neither power is to be confused with the *diabia's*. The agency involved in their respective doings find definition within the cluster of other powers seen as defining each agent's sort of being.

There is often an unspoken assumption, regarding African thought, that any beliefs put forward, or claims made, in the domain of metaphysical attribution remain suspect because its earlier understanding of causal relations in the domain of material attribution is not to be taken seriously, given what is perceived to be an ineradicable imprint of spirit agency. But, as I believe I have shown, that earlier understanding, once it is properly articulated, can be seen not only to be in order but actually to go several steps further in terms of providing a hook for a usable type of metaphysics to latch onto. Thus, the human person while being understood naturally as an embodied specimen also has a range of other actions assigned to it that is not assignable to other material bodies. It alone is capable of becoming an ancestor after the occurrence of physical death, a capability not open to cats, dogs, elephants, or fish of the sea. And ancestorhood, as we know, is part of the continuing process of elderhood, with those who have achieved its status still tied to the living, still invoked as members of an ongoing moral community. This community, which embraces both the living and the dead, not surprisingly, is bound by considerations of mutual concern—paternal care on the part of the ancestors and filial piety on the part of the living.

But what is also interesting, and I believe significant, in the African case, is the way that ancestorhood is not stretched into being a *permanent* feature of any one person's ontological journey. The ancestral stage also finds its relative termination after an adequate passage of time. The ancestor eventually becomes a member of the nameless dead, one fragment among others that constitute an undifferentiated mass of clan or tribal spirits, each, in its final destination, without moral individuation and without a name. At this stage, the human person that came into the world an 'it,' without moral individuation and without a name, goes out of the world an 'it,' also without moral individuation and without a name; the symmetry complete, the destination now final.[21] And that is why in the matter of religion there is not a belief in heaven or hell. Simply put, the metaphysical basis is not there for constituting an otherworldly world appropriate for life for angelic hosts or for hosts who have been damned.

John Mbiti has argued that it is because of the traditional concept of time that the belief in future redemption is lacking. This may be so, but only partly so. The reason for the absence of a salvific future, I argue, is much more radical than the issue of the movement of time from present to past, as opposed to its movement from present to future.[22] I suspect that in addition to the indications already given regarding what is at stake in the general area of African metaphysics, a more fundamental reason for the absence of a belief in a redemptive future has to do with this future's radical departure from known things. It violates the idea of stage linkage, of an incremental approach to the positioning of things and to knowledge, so that what is first in place is allowed to modulate what comes after.

Additional support can be found for this sort of conclusion from considerations relating to the domains of moral and political duty. Generally, morality is seen in light of what 'fits,' what leads to societal harmonization and village flourishing. It is not based on supernatural factors or on the will of God as such. Although the moral domain admittedly contains a ubiquitous reference to ancestors, the ancestors, we recall, are not to be considered supernatural agents but rather as extended natural agents.[23] If we looked carefully into this area, we will again find a familiar pattern; the approach being to stay with what is known and what is accessible, and, later, where metaphysical extensions are called for, then always to be restrained by the anchor of the hardscrabble ordinary world. In this understanding, if something is moral, it is deemed so not because God approves of it; rather, God approves of it because it is moral.[24]

Finally, in the area of political governance, the State's foundation is not sought in some such thing as the divine right of kings, with earthly power seen as a manifestation of divine power, the king on earth a booted messenger of the one above, and delegated with fiduciary authorization to break the bone of the recalcitrant citizen should the need arise. On the contrary, both the king and the king's power come from ancestral arrangements, from an established order secured by the lived history of the group. And should the elders, or kingmakers, find a serious violation on the part of the king of the sort that they consider an unacceptable threat to the community, they are not likely to be restrained by otherworldly considerations in regard to an effort to remove the king.

Again, one secures things from below by reference to known or accessible understandings and if metaphysical extensions are deemed in order, one keeps those extensions usefully joined to the under-standings already in place in such a way as to avoid the sort of epistemic disruption bound to emerge when a discontinuity is allowed in the sequence of accepted beliefs, beliefs that have been grounded from the bottom up.

One question that still remains to be answered though not in any detailed way is the question of the difference, if any, between things as they are in the world and our claimed knowledge regarding those things that are in the world—the difference, that is, between the sense in the original disposition of things and the sense that we make of that sense. For example, a claim that the universe does not make sense can be argued to be quite different from a claim that we cannot make sense of the universe. For although it is the case that *if* the universe does not make sense, we will never be able to make sense of it, yet, on its own, our not being able to make sense of the universe is no guarantee that the universe does not make sense. Since, therefore, the order of things out there and the order of our knowledge of those things can be argued to be separable, I would like to propose that the problem of invisible agency that is said to bedevil the village is not all that different from the problem that we see bedeviling those who consider themselves modern, including *scientifically* modern. For if the villager is thought to be thinking causation along invisible tracks, the modern-day scientist thinking of his quantum world and of the strange particle that he calls the neutrino is not necessarily in any better position regarding the casual story. To claim that neutrinos exist and that they can pass through several trillion miles of lead without leaving a trace is a claim not made less puzzling because it comes from a theoretical physicist in academic garb as opposed to a villager in a tribal one. And yet, despite our puzzlement, we do not proceed to argue that there are ghosts in the physicist's lab and that what he is advancing is a claim regarding ghostly causation, not a material one.

The conclusion we should draw from all of this is that, in the matter of "non-regular" causation in the universe, it is not necessary to conceive of things in magical terms. Rather, what we could, and should, conclude is that the universe is possessed of complex but natural powers and therefore beliefs found among individual persons, or population groups, ought to be judged in light of that natural complexity, in so far as casual attributions are concerned.

And, when we do this, we will find that there are degrees of reasonableness in the matter of our acceptance of these beliefs. Some of the beliefs will be found more reasonable than others and a crucial factor in our assessment would be the strength of the believer or believer's earlier commitment to an underlying materiality regarding the things that are in the world.

Often we hear talk of the marketplace of ideas and of the need to break the collective monopoly of the village regarding what is believed or what is ventured out. But, here, what are we to make of it, this recommended flight from commonly understood things, a flight justified by reference to the marketplace of ideas, or more simply, by noting the breakdown of the common cognitive ground on which individuals formerly stood, so that Mr. Smith is now entitled to strike out on his own and so also Mr. Jenkinjones? Despite the good of freedom projected by the recommendation in question, the worry here is that this freedom to pursue whatever belief one dares, if not properly channeled, could create the possibility of a radical collapse of agreement on basic philosophical issues so that ideological dissension then takes over, with one camp now winning temporary ascendancy and then, later, another camp. One presumes that this is not the best philosophy could offer.

And so we must continue to be concerned with the question of the criteria on the basis of which metaphysical positions are to be judged, especially as these criteria relate to the requirements of common, or village, sense. This sense is something which it is critical that we keep in mind because if we are to complete the task that the historic human village began, it will have to be completed using the deliverances made available by the epistemic village, not necessarily those made available by the attainments of the so-called free marketplace of ideas in which it is assumed that individuals having fiercely battled it out, each to each, we therefore, collectively, have a belief structure much more credible than that yielded by the village world.

Notes

1. This claim that ordinary language carries its share of philosophical freight is evidenced by the ample contributions made to the field of philosophy by the so-called ordinary language philosophers such as J. L. Austin in *How to Do Things with Words* (New York: Oxford University Press, 1962) and Gilbert Ryle in *The Concept of Mind* (London: Hutchinson & Company, 1949).

2. Okot p'Bitek, *African Religions in Western Scholarship* (Kampala: East African Literature Bureau, 1970), 80.

3. Ibid. 85.

4. William Abraham, *The Mind of Africa* (Chicago: University of Chicago Press, 1962), 50.

5. Placide Tempels, *Bantu Philosophy* (Paris: Presence Africaine, 1959), 85.

6. I come back to this issue later towards the middle sections of my chapter.

7. Kwasi Wiredu, *Cultural Universals and Particulars: An African Perspective* (Bloomington: Indiana University Press, 1996), 98–99.

8. It might be argued that linguistic practices separating persons on the pronomial level based on facts of raw gender alone do not have to be seen as carrying meaningful ontological or social implications but are rather matters of linguistic style. That may be so, but the fact of the existence of these separations is still striking enough to merit attention. In any case, as Robin Lakoff has pointed out, "If it is indeed true that our feelings about the world color our expression of our thoughts, then we can use our linguistic behavior as a diagnostic of our hidden feelings about things." See Robin Lakoff, *Language and Woman's Place* (New York: Harper & Row, 1975), 3–4.

9. H. L. A. Hart, "Formalism and Rule-Scepticism," in *The Concept of Law* (New York: Oxford University Press, 1994), 138–40.

10. John and Mary Gribbin and Richard Feynman, *A Life in Science* (New York: Dutton, 1997), 89.

11. Kwasi Wiredu, *Philosophy and an African Culture* (London: Cambridge University Press, 1980), 4–5.

12. Donald Davidson, *Essays on Actions and Events* (New York: Oxford University Press, 1980), 7.

13. Hartry Field, "Physicalism," in *Inference, Explanation and Other Frustrations: Essays in the Philosophy of Science*, ed. John Earman (Berkeley: University of California Press, 1992), 271.

14. Ibid. 272.

15. Richard Boyd, "Constructivism, Realism, and Philosophical Method," in *Inference, Explanation and Other Frustrations: Essays in the Philosophy of Science*, ed. John Earman (Berkeley: University of California Press, 1992), 194.

16. I suppose that "medicine men" or "seers" would be acceptable translations in English of what these African terms represent, though caution is called for, as always.

17. Robin Horton, "African Traditional Thought and Western Science," *Africa* 37.1–2 (1967): 160.

18. One might be tempted to compare or contrast this with that other expression from the English village "apple of my eye," used also to indicate a certain kind of love or tenderness.

19. Kwame Anthony Appiah, *In My Father's House: Africa in the Philosophy of Culture* (New York: Oxford University Press, 1992), 134–35.

20. E. E. Evans-Pritchard, *Theories of Primitive Religion* (Oxford: Clarendon Press, 1980), 89–90.

21. I have, in an earlier essay, discussed this issue of a symmetrical alignment of beginning and final end in the matter of African ontology of the person, showing how the acquisition of norms, within the milieu of communal life, forms the basis of personhood; and how, additionally, at the point of physical death, this personhood does not cease immediately, but instead gradually evaporates over time; see I. A. Menkiti, "Person and Community in African Traditional Thought," in *African Philosophy*, ed. Richard Wright (Washington, D.C.: University Press of America, 1979).

22. John Mbiti, *African Religions and Philosophy* (London: Heinemann, 1969; 2nd ed., 1989); see chap. 3 "The Concept of Time," pp. 15–28 of the 2nd ed.; see also pp. 157–61.

23. Kwasi Wiredu, "African Religions from a Philosophical Point of View," in *A Companion to the Philosophy of Religion*, ed. P. L. Quinn and C. Taliaferro (Oxford: Basil Blackwell, 1997), 39–40.

24. Ibid. 35–36.

EIGHT

WITCHCRAFT, SCIENCE, AND THE PARANORMAL IN CONTEMPORARY AFRICAN PHILOSOPHY

ALBERT MOSLEY

Belief in some form of magic and witchcraft is a common feature of most traditional cultures and continues to manifest itself in many contemporary African societies. The function of such beliefs and their associated practices is to explain and influence the occurrence of events by reference to the causal agency of spiritual entities and psychic forces. Magic and witchcraft are often conflated because of their mutual suppression by Christianity in the evolution of European culture. However, the distinction between them made by E. E. Evans-Pritchard in his study of the Azande of the Sudan remains standard in the anthropological literature. Healers and sorcerers obtain their magical powers through training and operationalize them through techniques, rites, and potions. But a witch "injures by virtue of an inherent quality. A witch performs no rite, utters no spell, and possesses no medicine. An act of witchcraft is a psychic act."[1] Belief in the role of witchcraft assumes that a particular misfortune derives from the intent of someone known to the sufferer to cause that misfortune and that the intent alone is sufficient for causal efficacy. Thus conceived, a witch is a person who causes the harm of someone he or she is in a position to benefit. "The witch is the hidden enemy within the gate."[2] It is in this sense that episodes such as the Stalinist purges and McCarthyism have been characterized as 'witch-hunts.' Conviction, in such cases, is sought on the basis of alleged intent more so than on the basis of overt action. Because of their susceptibility to misuse for social and political ends, accusations of witchcraft are often used by contemporary social scientists as a measure of social tensions and power struggles. While not discounting this function of witchcraft accusations, I believe it is important not to totally dismiss the possibility of the operation of the kind of psychic forces assumed in traditional accounts of witchcraft.

In an essay published in *Second Order* in 1977, I suggested that many of the traditional claims regarding magic and witchcraft could be explained as the effect of the kinds of psychic powers described in parapsychological research.[3] In this essay, I will review a number of issues raised with respect to this claim by the late Prof. Peter Bodunrin.

Parapsychology is typically presented as providing evidence for the existence of the following abilities or powers:

telepathy: the ability to be affected by the current contents of another mind, without sensory intermediaries;
clairvoyance: the ability to be affected by current information about a physical system that is otherwise not available to any mind, without sensory intermediaries;
psychokinesis: the ability to influence physical states, without sensory intermediaries; and
precognition: the ability to obtain information about events that have not yet occurred.

Though stated categorically, these definitions are necessarily tentative because the very nature of such phenomena is a matter of continuing discussion and clarification. The way such powers are to be understood has not been definitively determined. To illustrate, consider the notion of precognition. Is precognition to be conceived of as a future event causing a present experience? Or, should precognition be conceived of as a form of psychokinesis, where a present thought causes a future occurrence? Or should we conceive of precognition as a form of ordinary inference enhanced by information gained by telepathy or clairvoyance in the present?

Suppose at time t1 A dreams that B drowns at a particular spot in river R, and a week later (time t2) B drowns at that location. Is this merely coincidental? Or did (a) B's drowning in R at t2 cause A to dream it at t1? Or did (b) A's dreaming at time t1 that B would drown in R causally influence B to drown in R at t2? Or did A's clairvoyant knowledge of a strong down current at that spot in river R, plus A's telepathic knowledge that B intended to swim there, lead A to infer that B would (be likely to) drown at that location in the river.

Is it possible for a person to cause, by thinking of a particular event in the present, that event to occur in the future? Is it possible for a future occurrence to cause a present perception? Is it possible that inferences are made based on current information acquired telepathically or clairvoyantly? While many African philosophers openly countenanced the possibility of paranormal interactions, few have explored the controversial nature of parapsychological research.

As was his nature not to evade difficult questions, the late Prof. Peter Bodunrin of Nigeria gave voice to many of the questions that others often ignored. Instead, Prof. Bodunrin insisted that we critically examine the evidence for telepathy, clairvoyance, precognition, and psychokinesis and the suggestion that they might serve as sources of knowledge. Applying the yardstick of modern philosophy to the claims made for paranormal powers, Prof. Bodunrin considered such claims wanting.[4]

To illustrate, Prof. Kwame Gyekye has claimed that in Africa "paranormal cognition is recognized, by and large, as a mode of knowing."[5] However, Prof. Bodunrin objected to the claim that an individual might be said to gain knowledge by paranormal means: "let us assume that parapsychological powers do exist. Does para-cognition justify the diviner's prognostication? Suppose I say that tomorrow something very valuable will be delivered to you. Am I justified in saying that? Do I know that?"[6] Here Prof. Bodunrin answers in the negative. In contrast to Gyekye, Mbiti, and many other African philosophers, he suggests that a person who makes a claim based on information gained by paranormal means is not knowledgeable. A psychic may be able to say what will happen in the future, but unless the diviner is able to give reasons for what is said, the psychic does not 'know' that what was said is true. If the psychic's claim is the result of information gained through paranormal channels not available to normal people, then the psychic would be unable to cite evidence that would justify the claim to the non-psychic. Even if what the psychic says is true, the psychic might not be able to justify that assertion to a non-psychic audience. And if non-psychics believed the psychic's predictions, their beliefs would not be justified true beliefs.

It is my contention that here Bodunrin has smuggled in some assumptions about the nature of knowledge that are unwarranted. One way in which paranormal cognition can be understood as a mode of knowing can be illustrated in the distinction between knowing how and knowing that. Just as I may know how to ride a bike without being able to describe and justify how I ride a bike, so certain persons may know how to precognize future events or engage in telepathic encounters without being able to explain how they do this. Clearly, not being able to explain and justify how one does x is no bar to being able to do x. Indeed, being able to explain and justify how one does x is often a poor guide as to how well that person can actually do x. A's knowing how to reproduce x is no guarantee that A will be able to explain how x is reproduced.

Other contemporary philosophers have offered alternatives that challenge Bodunrin's tacit construal of knowledge as justified true belief. Thus, Peter Unger characterizes factual knowledge in such a way that x knows P if and only if it is not accidental that x is right about its being the case that P. So long as a psychic is able to produce responses that are correct more than would be expected purely by chance, the psychic knows what he or she is doing. The psychic has factual knowledge because "it is not at all accidental that he is right about the relevant matters."[7] On this analysis, non-psychics would also be able to know things they were unable to 'adequately' justify, so long as they depended on a reliable source.[8]

For reliabilists, the epistemic justification for a belief derives from its having a reliable relationship with properties of the world that make it true. But the person holding this belief need not know what this relationship is. In response, Laurence Bonjour offers an intriguing set of counterexamples to the reliabilist position. Bonjour uses clairvoyance in order to produce examples where a person may have no way of accounting for a belief, P, they hold except one which may make them appear, even to themselves, as irrational. Nonetheless, from a reliabilist point of view, they are epistemically justified in holding P. Bonjour's examples are as follows:

Case 1: Samantha believes herself to have the power of clairvoyance, though she has no reasons for or against this belief. One day she comes to believe, for no apparent reason, that the President is in New York City. She maintains this belief, appealing to her alleged clairvoyant power, even though she is at the same time aware of a massive amount of apparently cogent evidence . . . indicating the President is at that time in Washington, D.C. Now the President is in fact in New York City, the evidence to the contrary being part of a massive official hoax mounted in the face of an assassination threat. Moreover, Samantha does in fact have completely reliable clairvoyant power under the conditions which were then satisfied, and her belief about the President did result from the operation of that power.[8]

Case 2: Casper believes himself to have the power of clairvoyance, though he has no reasons for this belief. He maintains his belief despite the fact that on the numerous occasions when he has attempted to confirm one of his allegedly clairvoyant beliefs, it has always turned out apparently to be false. One day Casper comes to believe, for no apparent reason, that the President is in New York City, and he maintains this belief, appealing to his alleged clairvoyant power. Now in fact the President is in New York City; and Casper, does, under the conditions which were satisfied, have completely reliable clairvoyant power, from which this belief in fact resulted. The apparent falsity of his other clairvoyant beliefs was due in some cases to his being in the wrong conditions for the operation of his power and in other cases to deception or misinformation.[9]

Case 3: Maud believes herself to have the power of clairvoyance though she has no reasons for this belief. She maintains her belief despite being inundated by her embarrassed friends and relatives with massive quantities of apparently cogent scientific evidence that no such power is possible. One day Maud comes to believe, for no apparent reason, that the President is in New York City, and she maintains this belief despite the lack of any independent evidence, appealing to her alleged clairvoyant power. Now in fact the President is in New York City, and Maud does, under the conditions then satisfied, have completely reliable clairvoyant power. Moreover, her belief about the President did result from the operation of that power.[10]

Case 4: Norman, under certain conditions which usually obtain, is a completely reliable clairvoyant with respect to certain kinds of subject matter. He possesses no evidence or reasons of any kind for or against the general possibility of such a cognitive power or for or against the thesis that he possesses it. One day Norman comes to believe that the President is in New York City, though he has no evidence either for or against this belief. In fact the belief is true and results from his clairvoyant power under circumstances in which it is completely reliable.[11]

Bonjour denies that Samantha is epistemically justified because she ignores evidence for thinking that her belief is false, evidence that indeed may often be more reliable than that provided by her clairvoyant powers. In the second case, Bonjour denies that Casper is epistemically justified in his belief because, though Casper has no evidence against his belief, he does have evidence that his clairvoyant powers are unreliable and should not be trusted. In the third case, Bonjour denies that Maud is epistemically justified in her belief about the President, and he considers her to be irrational because she ignores the massive scientific and social evidence that clairvoyant powers do not exist, despite his acknowledgment that clairvoyant powers are in fact operative in producing Maud's true belief.

Bonjour constructed these three cases in such a way that the believer intentionally ignores either good reasons for the falsity of the belief that the president is in New York or the unreliability of the process by which the belief is acquired, and so can be considered irrational even if the belief is true. In the fourth case, Bonjour concludes that "Norman's acceptance of the belief about the President's whereabouts is epistemically irrational and irresponsible" because, even if there are reliable connections between his powers and the ability to ascertain true beliefs about the world, Norman is not a position to know this.[12] Norman will not go wrong in accepting beliefs generated by the operation of his clairvoyant powers, but from his own subjective perspective, argues Bonjour, it is an accident that his beliefs are true: "the rationality or justifiability of Norman's belief should be judged from Norman's own perspective rather than from one that is unavailable to him [though perhaps available to someone else]."[13]

Thus, Bodunrin's claim that the psychic does not have knowledge appears to gain strong support from Bonjour's arguments. However, it is important to note an important feature of each of Bonjour's examples: none is assumed to possess good reasons for believing in the existence of clairvoyant powers. Rather, we are asked to assume merely that they do in fact have such powers and that they believe they have such powers. Bonjour's strategy is to challenge the reliabilist position "on an intuitive level."[14] And intuitively, in modern Western culture, most people are highly skeptical of clairvoyant powers and are inclined to view anyone claiming such powers to be irrational. But what about cultures in which such powers are not considered exotic and self-refuting?

In his essay "Epistemic Folkways and Scientific Epistemology," Alvin Goldman defends reliabilism against Bonjour's attacks by identifying reasonable beliefs as those obtained by means of psychological processes that have been predetermined to be epistemically virtuous, while unreasonable beliefs are those obtained by processes identified as epistemic vices. Thus, in modern Western culture, processes based on perceptual evidence and 'valid' reasoning are virtuous, but those based on mere guessing or wistful thinking are epistemic vices.[15]

Goldman points out that processes based on telepathy, clairvoyance, psychokinesis, and precognition are also considered vices in modern Western cultures, and any belief acquired using such processes would typically be considered unjustified. Nonetheless, Goldman considers Bonjour's fourth case to be one in which Norman's belief is, not unjustified, but non-justified. For in this case, the clairvoyant power is neither virtue nor vice because Norman has no reasons for or against the existence of clairvoyant powers.[16] However, it is easy to see that if clairvoyant powers were recognized as virtues, as processes that produced true beliefs more often than would be expected by chance, then Norman's beliefs would be considered justified.

Despite Unger's defending a reliabilist orientation, his claim that "a man may know something without his being in any way justified in believing that it is so"[17] appears to invert the relative importance of knowledge and justification. X getting P right more often than expected by chance when P is suggested by process Q may be all that is needed in order for X to be justified in believing that P. It may be that X is sometimes wrong, and P is not the case. But P is still justified when based on Q, even if we are unwilling to say that X knows that P. Thus, a meteorologist may believe that it will rain tomorrow, and be justified in that belief, even though he and we would decline to say that he knows that it will rain tomorrow. Indeed, since no process of producing belief statements is infallible, except perhaps deductive reasoning from premises known to be true, insistence that our true beliefs be known rather than merely justified may be too strong, even in cases not involving paranormal processes.

In any case, reliabilists do provide an alternative to internalists who insist on reasons and theories as necessary for justifications. I am primarily concerned to show that there are many competing conceptions of epistemic justification for knowledge in contemporary analytic philosophy, and Bodunrin cannot assume that being unable to cite good reasons or an adequate theory precludes paranormal cognition, even if it is operative, from producing justified true beliefs.[18]

Prof. Bodunrin also raises questions about the nature of the evidence so often cited in favor of the existence of paranormal phenomena. He considers oral and anecdotal reports suspect because they are resistant to critical examination, often cannot be tested, and involve claims that tend to change their meaning given different interpretations. Moreover, anecdotal evidence of the existence of psychic powers is questionable because so many cases have been shown to involve fraud, where one or more of the participants (intentionally or unintentionally) produced an effect by one means but persuaded others to believe the effect was produced by a different means.[19]

Despite such problems with anecdotal evidence, Bodunrin does acknowledge the existing experimental evidence for the existence of paranormal phenomena, and in this, is much more sympathetic than many contemporary philosophers and psychologists. For most are likely to reflect the views of Ian Hacking who claims that "If ever there was anything refuted by statistics, it is the claims of parapsychology. It follows then that if there are psychic phenomena, they are not of a type systematically reproduced in the laboratory." In Hacking's opinion "every claim to persistent subtle but statistically detectable psychic phenomena has been refuted."[20]

It is surprising that, despite making such bold claims, Hacking sees no need to provide evidence to support them. He makes no reference to the work of J. B. Rhine at Duke University, which introduced the use of the 25-card deck of Zener-cards (five sets of cards, where each card is embossed with either a circle, cross, star, square, and wavy lines). One run consisted of twenty-five attempts to guess the card extracted from the deck (with replacement and shuffling after each draw), and by chance alone should have resulted, on the average, in five correct 'hits' per run. One subject, Hubert Pearce, averaged 7.1 hits per session, a feat that itself would likely occur by chance only once in every twenty-two billion sessions.[21]

Nor does Hacking cite the Ganzfield experiments of Charles Honorton at Princeton University. Ganzfield experiments involve immersing the subject in a homogenous sensory field, typically by placing halved ping pong balls over the subject's eyes, playing white noise through headphones, and inducing relaxation. From thirty-six possible pictures, a computer randomly picks four, and from this four, one is chosen and concentrated on by a sender. The Ganzfield subject is then asked to describe his or her impressions and subsequently is asked to pick out the target from among the four chosen by the computer. For every 100 such sessions, one would expect the subject to pick out twenty-five by chance alone. Instead, the percentage of direct hits was 34%, a rate the odds against which were over a billion to one.[22]

In contrast to Hacking, others capable of evaluating the data statistically believe the evidence is unequivocally positive. Thus, Prof. Jessica Utts of the Division of Statistics of the University of California, Davis, considers the accumulated database of over a century of parapsychological research impressive, especially considering that, since 1882, parapsychology has received fewer resources than conventional psychology currently receives in two or three months. Unlike the phenomena demonstrated in simple experiments in physics and chemistry, the phenomena of parapsychology are statistical in nature. And just as every person who smokes cannot be expected to get lung cancer, so every person involved in Zener card or Ganzfield experiments cannot be expected to exhibit telepathic or clairvoyant effects.[23] Professor Utts concludes:

> In any area involving the natural variability inherent in humans, science progresses by first observing a statistical difference and then attempting to explain it. At this stage, I believe parapsychology has convincingly demonstrated that an effect is present, and future research attempts should be directed at finding an explanation.[24]

Bodunrin considers it to be an essential feature of scientific evidence that similar results must be obtained under similar circumstances. However, he claims, parapsychology has been unable to replicate its most persuasive experimental results. Even in carefully designed demonstrations where the data is recorded automatically and fraud is least plausible, he argues, the experiments have typically not been replicable.[25] But considering the dogmatic rejection of claims for the existence of such phenomena by most philosophers and psychologists, and the meager resources available to those who are willing to grant the existence of such phenomena, it should be understandable why replication has not been easy. Despite the persuasiveness of his studies, Honorton was unable to replicate his findings because his lab at Princeton was denied funds and closed.

As Prof. Sophie Oluwole of the University of Lagos has pointed out, witchcraft could be proven to exist if it could be shown that certain individuals were able to 'practically manipulate' psychic powers.[26] But this need not imply that such 'practical mastery' was demonstrable and repeatable under laboratory conditions. More often than not, knowing how to do something is contingent on tacit factors that both witness and doer are unable to specify.

Replications often fail, not because the effects are illusory, but because the attempts to replicate are not competently executed. This occurs even in physics, where habits of quantization and precision are optimized. As one experimenter commented:

> It's very difficult to make a carbon copy [of an experimental demonstration]. You can make a near one, but if it turns out that what's critical is the way he glued his transducer, and he forgets to tell you that the technician always puts a copy of Physical Review on top of them for weight, well, it could make all the difference.[27]

We can expect this to be even more common with phenomena that are not well understood and that are produced by techniques not based on detailed descriptions of quantifiable properties. Thus, while

Bodunrin may insist on more and better experimental evidence, the failure to experimentally replicate a particular effect is not in itself sufficient evidence that the phenomenon in question does not exist.

Prof. Bodunrin tacitly assumes that experimental evidence provides sufficient justification for scientific theories and that the kind of evidence provided by experiments in the 'hard sciences' is exemplary of the kind of evidence required for all justified beliefs. But even in physics, when certain experimental effects have allegedly been produced by one group (A) but cannot be replicated by another (B), members of the profession can either deny the existence of the alleged phenomena or maintain the existence of the phenomena but deny that the conditions necessary for their production have been properly assembled. The dependence of experimental results on ill-defined tacit factors and the technical skills of the experimenter means that B's failure to replicate A's results need not immediately be taken as proof that A's claims have no merit. "The problem is that, since experimentation is a matter of skillful practice, it can never be clear whether a second experiment has been done sufficiently well to count as a check on the results of the first. Some further test is needed to test the quality of the experiment—and so forth."[28]

H. M. Collins has dubbed this dilemma the "experimenters' regress": B's failure to replicate A's results must itself be replicated by C. But then, C's success or failure in replicating B's results must be replicated by D. And so on. "The experimenters' regress has been shown to lie at the heart of the problem of using experimental replication as a test of replicability; the regress prevents us using experiments alone to establish changes in conceptual order."[29]

Our lack of knowledge about the social and psychological factors involved should caution us against making replications of laboratory evidence a necessary condition for recognizing the existence of psychic abilities and paranormal phenomena. Whether the sender, receiver, or experimenter believes in the efficacy of paranormal communication may itself be an important factor in the experimental protocol.

In situations where experiment cannot provide a conclusive answer regarding the existence of phenomena alleged to occur in other settings, it makes sense to try to ascertain how the phenomena in question might be manifest in practice. Otherwise, misguided laboratory investigations might stifle the display of paranormal interactions, and even successful displays of psi manifested under laboratory conditions might not be the best representations of real life psi.[30] Because lab situations do not involve real needs and interests they may fail to involve the kinds of situations that are typical of the traditional manifestation of psi phenomena.

Bodunrin suggests that what is needed to resolve the issue of the existence of paranormal phenomena is better experimental evidence, but this misleadingly oversimplifies the problem. Even granting that we may need more evidence, that evidence need not be of the variety produced by experimental demonstrations. Indeed, the psi phenomena produced in experimental situations may be no more than a small variety of the kinds produced under various social conditions.

I believe insistence on replicable experimental evidence to establish the existence of paranormal phenomena indicates a commitment to a model of the nature of science that initially may be counterproductive and misleading. What we need, I suggest, may not be more replications of current experiments but an alternative conception of the scientific enterprise that shifts attention from the creation of replicable effects under controlled laboratory conditions to the observation of phenomena in natural settings. This requires that we resist prioritizing experimental over ethnological investigations, and re-acknowledge the importance of the scientific naturalist.[31]

This recommendation challenges the view of science as ideally a form of theoretical inquiry complimented by laboratory experiment. Commenting on the split in biology between experimentalists and naturalists, Ernst Mayr argues that they differ in their methods, they tend to ask different kinds of questions, and their work amounts to alternative research programs. He writes:

> Observation led to the discovery of foreign faunas and floras and became the basis of biogeography; observation revealed the diversity of organic nature and led to the establishment of the Linnaean hierarchy and to the [Darwinian] theory of common descent; observation led to the foundations of ethnology and ecology. Observation in biology has probably produced more insights than all experiments combined.[32]

Darwin was not an experimental biologist, but a naturalist. His methods were those of comparative analysis, not the controlled manipulation of conditions. Hopefully such examples will fortify us against too excessive a reliance on theoretical explanations and experimental evidence as we explore how other contemporary African philosophers have treated these issues.[33]

Bodunrin's perspective is reflected in the views of Chiekh Anta Diop, who argued that quantum theory and the experiments motivated by Bell's Theorem provide a plausible framework for the existence of paranormal phenomena involving action and perception at a distance. Though such interactions appear anomalous relative to the basic assumptions of classical physics, Diop argued that they fit easily within the theoretical and experimental framework of recent developments in quantum physics.[34] Like Bodunrin, Diop believed that if evidence for psychic interactions was to be accepted, that evidence would have to meet the scientific standards set by physics. I, on the contrary, have argued that this strategy might be, if not mistaken, then at best premature.

For the present, let me explore some remarks by Diop that I believe offer fruitful leads for development. Summarizing his view on the difference between traditional African and modern Europeans modes of interaction, Diop writes that if the neuroses currently strangling Europe derive from its individualistic tendencies, then "those of Africa could be linked to the excess of communal life, which erases even the boundary of private life."[35] Here, Diop identifies degenerate individualism as the bane of European culture and degenerate communalism as the bane of traditional cultures. I believe these remarks take on added relevance when combined with the insights of Robin Horton, another important African philosopher.

Robin Horton has argued that gods, ancestors, and other spiritual beings composing the traditional ontology are the theoretical equivalents of electrons, protons, and neutrons of the modern scientific worldview. For Horton, the traditional African healer and the modern physicist "are making the same use of theory to transcend their limited vision of natural causes provided by common sense."[36] Each posits theoretical entities to resolve otherwise anomalous events.

References to gods, ancestors, and spirits typically occur in traditional responses to disease and other afflictions. Throughout traditional Africa, Horton argues, those who survived childhood illnesses did so because they acquired a robust immune system. And in the absence of pharmaceutically active agents, what happened to a person who became ill depended very much on factors that added to or subtracted from the operation of the person's own immune system. "The conjunction of no germ theory, no potent antibiotics, no immunization techniques, with conditions favoring the build up of considerable natural resistance to killer infections, served to [stimulate certain] causal connections in the mind of the traditional healer."[37] The solution was the cultivation and development of ways of enhancing immune system reactions by means that were not purely mechanistic.

Diop's and Horton's remarks lead me to suggest that the social conditions of traditional cultures may have facilitated, while the social conditions of modern cultures may inhibit the display of certain kinds of interactions. In particular, where social organization requires prolonged personal interactions, psychic interactions might (for better and for worse) be enhanced, while social situations in which personal interactions are minimized might inhibit psychic interactions.

Where one's own immune system is one's best defense against illness, any kind of interaction (psychic or symbolic) that increased the effectiveness of the immune system would be beneficial and any kind that decreased its effectiveness would be detrimental. The image of the witch is of one who used symbolic and psychic means to harm, just as the healer was one who used such means to benefit. Though these suggestions may be dismissed as mere speculation, they may also be construed as hypotheses motivated by the field observations of eminent contemporary African philosophers.

Professors Barry Hallen and John Sodipo conducted extensive field interviews with traditional healers and found that both healers and witches were viewed as sharing a common ability to interact using paranormal means. Moreover, those with this ability were as likely to be men as women.[38] The essential difference between healers and witches was in moral rather than in gender terms: the former used their paranormal abilities to help, the latter used similar abilities to harm.

Hallen and Sodipo consider the common assumption that utilization of psychic powers is inherently harmful to be a byproduct of the evolution of Christianity, where traditional European religions were considered to be devil worship by the Catholic Church. However, this was not a feature of traditional African beliefs. Among the Yoruba, there are good effects made possible by paranormal means, and there are bad ones. But this implies no greater condemnation of paranormal interactions than of physical interactions: each can be used to either help or harm.

Hallen and Sodipo's sources, the Babalowo, also distinguished different degrees of paranormal ability, as in the distinction drawn between *alujanun* and *aje*. *Aje* is the power usually attributed to witches, but a power they share with healers, and which allows them to influence distant events. *Alujanun* is an even stronger power that allows a person not only to influence distant events by psychic means, but also to perceive distant events. Those with this power are considered among the most powerful in Yoruba traditional culture.[39] Considering such, Hallen and Sodipo write:

Paranormal perception—telepathy, clairvoyance, and mind reading are all rather typical English language terms in the field sometimes referred to as parapsychology. On a more prosaic level that will allow us to avoid becoming entangled in various theories underlying this controversial field of interest, what the above quotation seems to indicate is that the *alujanun* can both send and receive, the *aje* can only send. This would mean that the power of the *aje* is primarily in the ability to use the second *emi/inu* to do something for it, even if it is distant from the body with which it is associated. The *alujanun* however in some manner for future researchers to look into, is able to know about . . . events that are going on distant from him, as well as to do something about them if he so chooses.⁴⁰

Hallen and Sodipo conclude by encouraging Western-trained intellectuals to collaborate with traditional sages in integrating traditional and modern forms of knowledge, without assuming that the modern form should receive metaphysical priority. Implicit here is the need to go to the settings in which traditional sages operate, instead of insisting that those practitioners be subjected to testing in laboratory settings.⁴¹

The Ghanaian philosopher Kwame Gyekye argues that mediumship, divination, and witchcraft involve modes of cognition that clearly distinguish African from European epistemology. He considers it a nearly universal belief in African cultures, as noted earlier, that "paranormal cognition is recognized, by and large, as a mode of knowing" and that certain individuals are born with special psychic abilities. Telepathy, clairvoyance, psychokinesis, and precognition are "in the African context aspects of divination and spirit mediumship." He writes, "In Africa, these kinds of activities are thought to be the result of the activities of discarnate minds, that is, spirits. Divination thus links the spiritual and physical worlds, and in Africa there are numerous stories of individuals communicating with the dead which, if true, would attest to survival after death."⁴²

Gyekye's conditional acknowledgment of this metaphysic is mirrored in the work of his countryman, the philosopher Kwasi Wiredu. Although Wiredu is best known for his critical stance toward traditional African beliefs, he is also one of the most persistent explorers of traditional African belief systems.⁴³ His work on Akan concepts of mind, religion, morality, custom, logical operations, etc. is unique in terms of its scope and quantity. Wiredu explains that the Akan distinguish the human being into a unity of different aspects: *nipadua* (the body), *amene* (the brain), *adwene* (the mind), *okra* (the life force), and *susuma* (the personality). The *okra* is considered to be a person's double or companion, but of a quasi-physical nature capable of existing independently of the physical body. Medicine men and witches are assumed to be able to communicate with the *okra* of both the living and the dead.[44]

For Wiredu, traditional Akan beliefs held that objects and entities in the land of the ancestors are composed of a 'quasi-material' substance and are analogues of objects in this world. There, the ancestors are believed to continue their activities and require that the living provide them sacrifices and physical offerings. On the other hand, the living depend on the ancestors to provide them with direction, fortitude, strength, and protection from malevolent influences. Because those who have died continue to have a 'quasi-physical' existence, it is possible for certain living members of the community to see and converse with the ancestors.[45] The *okra* of such individuals is assumed to be able to travel between the world of the living and the dead, bringing information that spans both space and time.[46]

It was the intent of parapsychology to provide the naturalistic categories of telepathy, clairvoyance, precognition, and psychokinesis to account for the effects traditionally explained by appeal to spiritualistic agents such as the soul, astral body, or '*susuma*'. Accordingly, possession, a phenomenon that is fairly common in traditional African ceremonies, is typically described in terms of a discarnate spirit taking over the body and personality of a living person. But the possession of a person, Z, by the spirit of a deceased person, Y, can also be accounted for as the telepathic influence of X's memory of Y on Z, inducing Z to manifest mental, physical, and emotional traits characteristic of Y. Such an account does not require the continued existence of Y after Y's physical death, but only that there be some X who remembers Y. However, once the memory of Y is no longer held by a living person, Y could no longer become manifest. This way of viewing possession phenomena fits well with Mbiti's view that ancestors continue to exist in the present (the *Sasa*) as long as someone among the living personally remembers the deceased individual. Once the memory of a person is lost, however, their quasi-material existence ceases, and the deceased is merged into a collective spiritual identity that Mbiti calls 'the *Zamani*.'[47]

But it is not obvious that the naturalistic explanations provided by parapsychology will, in their present form, be sufficient to explain all the phenomena traditionally explained by reference to spiritualistic entities. A strong case can be made that the evidence for reincarnation cannot be adequately accounted for using the categories of telepathy and clairvoyance. For instance, an individual, X, who claims to be the reincarnation of some individual, Y, who lived in the past and is now deceased may, in support of that claim, offer information about that person's life that they could not possibly have been privy to. But for that information to be verified, either some other individual, Z must have been privy to it, or the information must be stored in some form, Z′, which is not available to x. In the first case, however, it could be claimed that X telepathically accesses the information in Z's mind. In the second case, it could be claimed that X clairvoyantly accesses the information stored in source Z′.

However, the experimental models of telepathy and clairvoyance typically only show rates that are better than would be expected by chance, as in the Ganzfield experiments in which subjects would be expected to guess correctly by chance 25 out of 100 tries, but instead scored (on the average) 33 out of 100. The maximum scores in those experiments were achieved by musicians, who scored (on the average) 50 out of 100. A person who was correct 80%, 90%, or even 100% of the time in recounting facts about a life he or she claimed to have lived in another time or place, and who had no access to that information, would exhibit an access to such information that far exceeds the level of access achieved in experimental parapsychology.[48]

Reincarnation, apparitions of the dead, possession, out of the body experiences, and communications with the dead collectively provide evidence that, when critically examined, supports an explanation in terms of the personal survival of individual consciousness after death. But it is a mistake to dismiss such evidence because it is not produced under experimental conditions that can be repeated at will. Experimental evidence that is repeatable is required for knowledge that makes possible causal control, but that need not be a requirement of all knowledge. It is, for example, certainly possible to know what Jones said immediately before he died, without it being necessary to provide experimental evidence to ground that knowledge.[49]

It is not my purpose to resolve the dispute as to whether modern/ naturalistic or traditional/spiritualist categories best account for the kinds of phenomena covered in healing, witchcraft, and reincarnation. While some African philosophers, like Mbiti, show a preference for spiritualistic notions, others, like Sodipo, tend to favor the naturalistic variety. Wiredu is ambivalent in this regard: on the one hand, he recommends that contemporary African philosophers "cast their philosophical nets in their own indigenous conceptual waters"; on the other hand, he wonders whether belief in the ancestors will survive the onslaught of scientific investigation and modern Western assumptions about reality.[50]

At this stage, I believe it is most important to remember that discarnate minds and paranormal abilities are both theoretical explanations for certain phenomena that otherwise are difficult to account for. Discarnate minds are used to explain effects that others propose to explain equally well using the categories of ESP. But the crucial point is not to dismiss such phenomena simply because it is unclear exactly how to account for them.

Conclusion

There is a long history in philosophy and the sciences of belittling traditional, religious, and anecdotal accounts of 'miraculous' events. This remains true of the kinds of phenomena investigated by parapsychology. As Collins puts it: "Parapsychology threatens too much to too many to be easily acceptable. That is why its more uncompromising proponents are forced to live in a world of their own. . . . Their web of concepts, *and the coextensive social network*, has fewer connections with the main network of science than do most scientific fields."[51] Such comments remind us that the choice of a research program has practical as well as epistemological implications. For the investigator interested in these matters, serious entertainment of the existence of spiritual or psychic influences is likely to increase his or her risk of professional marginalization. But appealing for more experimental evidence cannot shield philosophers from having to make uncertain choices. As recent work in the philosophy of science emphasizes, our theories and beliefs are typically underdetermined by the facts. We cannot escape the fate that philosophy, like science, is an inherently shaky game.[52] Let us hope that those interested in African philosophy are more willing to take risks than the majority of their philosophical peers.

I have advanced the possibility of accounting for the belief in magic and witchcraft by reference to the existence of psychic powers of the sort studied in parapsychology as well as by reference to the existence of discarnate minds. However, I do not wish to suggest that perspectives that make neither assumption are not equally (and often perhaps more) important. Accounts abound of individuals being ostracized and even killed, on the pretext that they are witches, so that others may reap political or personal gain. There is a valuable body of literature on this aspect of witchcraft and healing.[53] But I do wish to caution against the categorical denial of the existence of paranormal interactions of the kind attributed to spirits, telepathy, and so on.

I believe an adequate resolution of the question of the existence of paranormal phenomena will require a more explicit concern with the social processes inherent in the generation of evidence. A research program oriented toward studying paranormal phenomena in traditional settings may well appear suspect to those who wish to emulate modernity's status quo. Nonetheless, we must resist the tendency to suppress such research. William James, who was not afraid to pursue the unorthodox, puts the matter thus: "Why do so few 'scientists' even look at the evidence for telepathy, so called? Because they think, as a leading biologist, now dead, once said to me, that even if such a thing were true, scientists ought to band together to keep it suppressed and concealed."[54]

This bias against acknowledging the existence of the paranormal is as much a problem as the nature of the evidence and explanations. Confronting it may help us appreciate that we must be as skeptical of our conceptions of science as we are of our conceptions of witchcraft and the paranormal.

Notes

Parts of this chapter appear as "Witchcraft, Science and the Skeptical Inquirer: Conversations with the Late Prof. Peter Bodunrin," in *Philosophical Papers* 30.3 (Nov. 2001). I thank the editors of that journal for permission to use these materials.

1. E. E. Evans-Pritchard, *Witchcraft, Oracles, and Magic among the Azande* (London: Clarendon Press, 1937), 21.

2. Phillip Mayer, "Witches," in *Witchcraft and Sorcery: Selected Readings*, ed. Max Marwick (Baltimore: Penguin Books, 1970), 45–64.

3. Albert G. Mosley, "The Metaphysics of Magic," *Second Order* 7 (1978): 3–19.

4. "Witchcraft, Magic, and ESP: A Defense of Scientific and Philosophical Skepticism," *Second Order* 7 (1978): 36–50; reprinted in *African Philosophy: Selected Readings*, ed. Albert Mosley (Englewood Cliffs, N.J.: Prentice-Hall, 1995), 371–85.

5. Kwame Gyekye, *Toward an African Philosophy* (New York: Cambridge University Press, 1987), 201.

6. Imagine that a person constantly repeats the statement "This is Thursday." On certain days that statement is true, but this does not mean that the producer of the statement *knows* that the statement is true.

7. Peter Unger, "An Analysis of Factual Knowledge," *Journal of Philosophy* 65.6 (March 1968): 157–70; reprinted in *Philosophers in Wonderland*, ed. Peter French (St. Paul: Llewellyn Publishers, 1975), 281.

8. Laurence Bonjour, *The Structure of Empirical Knowledge* (Cambridge, Mass.: Harvard University Press, 1985), 38.

9. Ibid. 39.

10. Ibid. 40.

11. Ibid. 41.

12. Ibid. 42.

13. Ibid. 44.

14. Ibid. 37.

15. Alvin Goldman, "Epistemic Folkways and Scientific Epistemology," in *Human Knowledge: Classical and Contemporary Approaches*, ed. Paul Moser and Arnold VanderNat (New York: Oxford University Press, 1987), 158.

16. Ibid. 159.

17. Unger, "Analysis of Factual Knowledge," in French, ed., *Philosophers in Wonderland*, 278.

18. Thanks to Ward Jones for prodding me to develop this section.

19. See Bodunrin, "Witchcraft, Magic, and ESP," in Mosley, ed., *African Philosophy*, 374.

20. "Some Reasons for Not Taking Parapsychology Very Seriously," *Dialogue* 32 (1993): 591.

21. D. R. Griffin, *Psychology, Philosophy, and Spirituality* (Albany, N.Y.: SUNY Press, 1997), 78ff.

22. Daryl Bem and Charles Honorton, "Does Psi Exist? Replicable Evidence for an Anomalous Process of Information Transfer," *Psychological Bulletin* 115.1 (1994): 4–18. Honorton's Ganzfield experiments utilized 240 receivers, instead of a few exceptional individuals as in the Rhine experiments.

23. Prof. Bodunrin remarks that if the phenomena of ESP can stand the test of repeatability we may one day succeed in "scienticing" witchcraft and ESP (Bodunrin, "Witchcraft, Magic, and ESP," in Mosley, ed., *African Philosophy*, 378). This suggests that being able to experimentally demonstrate parapsychological phenomena in a manner that was replicable would imply the existence of specific conditions within which paranormal effects could be reliably reproduced. Presumably, this would amount to having identified and extracted the 'active ingredients' of traditional magic and witchcraft, and reproduced them in terms of the experimental phenomena of parapsychology. But I would caution us not to ignore the ostensibly statistical nature of psi phenomena: the existence of a causal relationship between smoking and cancer does not mean we can induce or even expect cancer in every individual case in which a person habitually smokes.

24. Jessica Utts, "Response to Ray Hyman's Report: Evaluation of Program on Anomalous Mental Phenomena" (www-stat.ucdavis.edu/~utts/response.html).

25. See Bodunrin, "Witchcraft, Magic, and ESP," in Mosley, ed., *African Philosophy*, 376ff. Also see H. M. Collins and T. J. Pinch, "The Construction of the Paranormal," in *On the Margins of Science: The Social Construction of Rejected Knowledge*, ed. Roy Wallis, Sociological Review Monograph 27 (Keele, U.K.: University of Keele, 1979), 249ff.

26. Sophie Oluwole, "On the Existence of Witches," *Second Order* 7 (1978): 20–35, reprinted in *African Philosophy: Selected Readings*, ed. Albert Mosley (Englewood Cliffs, N.J.: Prentice-Hall, 1995), 357–70.

27. H. M. Collins, "The Replication of Experiments in Physics," in *Science in Context*, ed. Barry Barnes and David Edge (Cambridge, Mass.: MIT Press, 1982), 103.

28. H. M. Collins, *Changing Order: Replication and Induction in Scientific Practice* (London: Sage Publications, 1985), 2.

29. Ibid. 129.

30. Much like the canned laughter on TV sitcoms compared to humor in real life. See Stephen Braude, *The Limits of Influence: Psychokinesis and the Philosophy of Science* (New York: Routledge and Kegan Paul, 1991), chap. 1, esp. pp. 9–11.

31. The initial founders of the study of paranormal phenomena differed as to whether that study should take an experimental or a naturalistic mode. The experimentalists have, to a great extent, prevailed. See Paul Allison, "Experimental Parapsychology as a Rejected Science," in Wallis, ed., *On the Margins of Science*, 271–92. See also Braude, *The Limits of Influence*, chap. 1.

32. Ernst Mayr, *The Growth of Biological Thought* (Cambridge, Mass.: Harvard University Press, 1982), 32. Mayr explains that the two traditions developed fairly independently of one another until first synthesized in 1937. Also see ibid. 568–70.

33. It may be, as some commentators have suggested, that certain paranormal phenomena are intentional processes that are outside the domain of physics. To illustrate, the existence of jokes is not established by precisely described, replicable experiments. Indeed, jokes are not the kinds of things that are defined by sets of necessary and sufficient conditions. Rather, jokes are a broad set of social phenomena, connected by family resemblances rather than by essential qualities. Traditional forms of healing and injury may in many instances be more like jokes and insults than like sugar and strychnine. The existence of psychic phenomena may be subject to similar considerations. See Braude, *The Limits of Influence*, 56–58.

34. Chiekh Anta Diop, "Does an African Philosophy Exist?" in *Civilization and Barbarism* (Brooklyn, N.Y.: Lawrence Hill Publishers, 1991), 370ff. For a review of the EPR paradox, Bell's Theorem, and the experiments of Clauser and Aspect, see Nick Herbert, *Quantum Reality* (New York: Anchor, 1985), chap. 12, esp. pp. 224–27.

35. Diop, "Does an African Philosophy Exist?" in *Civilization and Barbarism*, 362.

36. See "African Traditional Thought and Western Science," *Africa* 37 (January 1967): 50–71 and (April 1967): 155–87; edited version reprinted in Mosley, ed., *African Philosophy*, 307.

37. See ibid. 309.

38. Barry Hallen and John Sodipo, *Knowledge, Belief, and Witchcraft* (London: Ethnographica Press, 1986).

39. Ibid. 107.

40. Ibid. 110–11. It is important to remember that it could be a "she" that is exhibiting *aje* or *alajuan*, as Hallen and Sodipo point out earlier in their work (p.103).

41. One of the *onisegun* interviewed by Hallen and Sodipo remarked: "There are some people, called *aje*, who are supernatural. But whenever they do any supernatural thing, if you ask them how it is possible for them to do such a thing, they attribute it to the power of *Olorun* [the supreme deity]. *Olorun* is just like something under which persons hide to apply their powers." See ibid. 105.

42. Kwame Gyekye, *An Essay on African Philosophical Thought: The Akan Conceptual Scheme* (New York: Cambridge University Press, 1987), 203.

43. Kwasi Wiredu, "How Not to Compare African Philosophy with Western Philosophy" and "Custom and Morality: A Comparative Analysis of African and Western Concepts of Morals," in *African Philosophy: Selected Readings*, ed. Albert Mosley (Englewood Cliffs, N.J.: Prentice-Hall, 1995).

44. Kwasi Wiredu, "The Akan Concept of Mind," in *Contemporary Philosophy*, vol. 5. *African Philosophy*, ed. Guttorm Floistad (Dordrecht, Netherlands: Nijhoff, 1987), 160–61.

45. "Death and the After-life in African Culture," in *Person and Community*, ed. Kwasi Wiredu and Kwame Gyekye (Washington, D.C.: UNESCO Council for Research in Values and Philosophy, 1992), 137–52.

46. For a more recent treatment of these themes, see Martin Odei Adjei, "The Paranormal: An Inquiry into Some Features of Akan Metaphysics and Epistemology" (MA thesis, University of Ghana-Legon, May 2001). Adjei follows Gyekye in holding that it is the 'sunsum' that is able to leave the body and traverse the divide between the living and the dead. For an enlightening account of the *Ga* notions of the *susuma* and the *kla* as those aspects of the person capable of paranormal encounters, see Joyce Engmann, "Immortality and the Nature of Man in *Ga* Thought," in Wiredu and Gyekye, eds., *Person and Community*, 153–92.

47. See John S. Mbiti, *African Religions and Philosophy* (New York: Anchor, 1970), chap. 3. Excerpted in *African Philosophy: Selected Readings*, ed. Albert Mosley (Englewood Cliffs, N.J.: Prentice-Hall, 1995), 87–115.

48. Robert Almeder, *Death and Personal Survival: The Evidence for Life after Death* (Lanham, Md.: Rowman & Littlefield, 1992), 42–57. Innocent Onyewuenyi, "Philosophical Reapprisal of African Belief in Reincarnation," *International Philosophical Quarterly* 22.87 (Sept. 1982): 157–68.

49. Almeder, *Death and Personal Survival*, 263–66.

50. Wiredu, "The Akan Concept of Mind," 175.

51. Collins, *Changing Order*, 139. But we should not infer from this that the experimental evidence produced by parapsychologists lacks scientific rigor. On the contrary, the experimental procedures of parapsychology are generally recognized to be more rigorous than those of most other human sciences. See Ian Hacking, "Telepathy: Origins of Randomization in Experimental Design," *Isis* 79 (1988): 427–51.

52. See Arthur Fine, *The Shaky Game: Einstein Realism and the Quantum Theory* (Chicago: University of Chicago Press, 1986), chap. 1.

53. See Diane Ciekawy, "Witchcraft in Statecraft: Five Technologies of Power in Colonial and Postcolonial Coastal Kenya," *African Studies Review* 4.3 (1998): 119–41.

54. William James, "The Will to Believe," in *Pragmatism and Classical American Philosophy*, ed. John Stuhr (New York: Oxford University Press, 2000), 233.

NINE

UNDERSTANDING AND ONTOLOGY IN TRADITIONAL AFRICAN THOUGHT

LEE M. BROWN

By "traditional African thought," I mean the philosophical perspectives that were indigenous to sub-Saharan cultures prior to the infusion of Islamic, Judaic, and Christian ideologies. Central to traditional African thought is the belief that the intentions of ancestral spirits can be known. Given those perspectives, ancestral spirits are individuals that were once alive, but are nonetheless still capable of agency. Having agency is to be understood as having a capacity to initiate, on one's own accord, actions that have intended consequences for oneself or for others. It is believed that an awareness of the intentions of ancestral spirits provides grounds for understanding physical occurrences.[1] It also is believed that ancestral spirits are recognizable as such and that each can be identified with its once living human counterpart. This is so even though neither may resemble the other in any sense that is wholly or simply obvious. Furthermore, ancestral spirits are purported to be quasi-material, in the sense that they can manifest themselves in physical objects that have no obviously recognizable characteristics belonging to their prior human counterparts. They can reside, for example, in artifacts such as masks or in living creatures such as cattle.

Such beliefs raise profound questions about the ontological commitments within traditional African cultures. In this essay, I will examine some of those commitments and discuss their viability in light of the theoretical posits of modern Western culture. In question is whether the claims about ancestral spirits should be received only as mere superstition or myth and as void of merit. In so doing, I shall address whether there is something of significance that can be learned from such commitments about the nature of human understanding—about an apparent human propensity to posit unobservables to explain the experiential world.

A fundamental tenet of traditional African culture is that there is more to reality and to the realm of experience than that which is readily accessible through empirical inquiry, and that one can acquire an understanding of natural phenomena by appealing to experiences whose characterizations are not empirically confirmable but are nonetheless warrantably assertible. The warrant is rooted in a felt sense that there are spiritual components to nature that influence experiences and perceptions. It is also rooted in the belief that phenomena that are not readily explainable via empirical means can best be explained by appealing to the causal efficacy of the spiritual components of nature.[2] Underlying this perspective is a commitment to the existence of unobservable entities that can act as causal agents. "Unobservable" refers to purported objects, theoretical posits, that cannot be accessed through the senses or through the enhancement of the senses. Sensory enhancers make accessible to the senses phenomena that would be sensed were we able to get close to them with our senses or were they amplified so as to be detected by our senses. Eyeglasses, microscopes, telescopes, and hearing aids are sensory enhancers. Geiger counters are not sensory enhancers. Geiger counters give us phenomena that must be interpreted—phenomena that are different from the phenomena they are designed to detect. A reading on a Geiger counter bears little resemblance to a particle's decay. That said, there are still instances where whether something is observable or unobservable is a matter of perspective. Nonetheless, the cases of concern herein are not of that type. Few would not understand what was being claimed by the statement, "Souls are not the kind of things that can be observed."

A fundamental tenet of modern Western culture is that science is the primary arbiter of what is real and that which cannot be confirmed or otherwise supported by science is metaphysical fantasy or mere superstition. Although not all of Western religion is supported by empirical inquiry, Western religion is nonetheless not viewed as grounded in metaphysical fantasy or mere superstition. It is viewed instead as grounded in the literature, doctrines, dogmas, reports of revelations, and historical traditions that have shaped civil and political policies and norms. It gives meaning and purpose to its faithful and motivates both scientific inquiry and great art. Moreover, it is grounded in a felt sense that the fundamental claims within its grounding literature, doctrines, and dogmas are true. Consequently, Western religion has given Western civilization a purported moral structure upon which to guide and judge all human behaviors and human interactions. It is from such a grounding that Westerners typically view traditional African culture as rooted in mere myth, metaphysical fantasy, or religious superstition. Traditionally, African culture purportedly lacks the grounding that Western culture is claimed to have.

Unless one is intimately familiar with the ontological commitments of a culture, it is often difficult to appreciate or otherwise understand those commitments. Perhaps through comparing salient aspects of Western and traditional African conceptions of personhood, we can realize a more informed perspective on the foundations for the associated ontological commitments within traditional African culture. Perhaps, also, we can realize a more informed perspective on the foundations for the associated ontological commitments within Western culture. Since the focus will be upon personhood with regard to humans, it is important to make clear the senses of "human" and of "person" that will be used herein. Although the two words are often used as if synonymous, the conditions for the proper usage of each are distinct. A human is an animal that has a specific genome. All and only those having an instance of that genome are human. A person is an individual that is capable of self-consciousness and of self-reflection. Most humans are persons.[3]

Something can be a human without being a person, and something can be a person without being a human. Concerning the former, deceased humans are not persons.[4] Also, it is not wholly obvious that embryos of humans are persons, even though their being human is not seriously contested. Concerning the latter, studies suggest that non-humans can be persons.[5] For example, elephants mourn and mourning requires self-consciousness and self-reflection—and a sense of sorrow as well. Most owners of dogs and cats view their pets as persons and see many of their behaviors as indications of consciousness and of self-reflection. Common to all such perspectives is a felt sense that those characterized as persons have the capacity to relate to the attributer or to its own kind in a manner that humans count as meaningful. Clearly, the attributions are judgments and as such are open to challenge. Nonetheless, there is a common component in almost all such judgments: the purported person is seen as someone to be respected and treated morally as like in kind. By like in kind, the purported person is viewed as having emotional and psychological dispositions that are of a type that are very much akin to those of the attributer.[6] Within Western folk culture—and in many others as well— the having of such dispositions is a defining characteristic of being a person and is viewed typically as sufficient for the attribution of personhood. We should keep in mind that consciousness and self-reflection are required for having such dispositions. A person, we want to say, is the kind of thing that can have a personality. It is mere metaphor to say that this unusual chair or this violin or this computer module has a personality all its own.[7]

Personhood in Traditional African Thought

According to traditional Yoruba philosophical thought, for any individual characterized as a person, its history begins with the infusion of a spirit into a fetus and with the emergent composite accepting a destiny for its life. The spirit is called an *emi'* and the *emi'* gives both human life and consciousness to the fetus. In this sense, the *emi'* is much like the anima in Western culture. The composite of fetus and *emi'* becomes an individual and chooses a destiny. At the reception of the destiny, the individual becomes a person. A person, *eniyan*, is a conscious body that lives out its destiny. At death, the body dies, but the individual giving rise to the person may survive as an ancestral spirit. As an ancestral spirit, the individual is capable of agency and its intentions can be made known to those to whom it chooses to reveal itself. It is important to note that "individual" and "person" are not synonymous. A person is an individual that lives out its destiny. Purportedly, an individual may, at times, fail to live out its destiny and during those times, it is not a person, according to traditional Yoruba thought.

Admittedly, this use of "destiny" is problematic. Having a destiny tacitly implies having a fate, and one cannot escape one's fate. But, like fate, destiny does not purport that every action or behavior is strictly determined, that no occurrence in an individual's life could have been otherwise. It implies instead that some action or behavior in an individual's life is inevitable. There is also a sense in which one's destiny refers merely to a way of living one's life. In such a case, it is not the specific details that are important, but the overall manner in which one's life is lived that is destined. How one gets to or through one's destiny seems open and not fashioned by strict causal chains. Otherwise, we would be as robots and that is not the typical perspective of those who view people as having destinies. Typically, the having of free will is attributed to those with destinies. It is just that at some point in time, something will occur, that cannot be avoided, which was destined to occur. The problem for advancing the notion that people can have destinies is reconciling the tenet that a destiny is something that cannot be avoided—something that is inevitable— with the tenet that someone may fail to follow or realize his or her destiny. Perhaps the conflict resides in the use of "destiny" as a deterministic characterization and the use of "destiny" as something else. That something else does not imply fate, but implies instead a path or way that seems best suited for that which is construed as self-actualization.

To make sense of the Yoruba use of "destiny," destiny cannot be a deterministic concept. A destiny in the Yoruba sense is something that a person ought to embrace, but can do otherwise if he or she chooses. The mandate is derived from having freely chosen a destiny as one's own, and having done so implies having an obligation to embrace the choice and all that unravels from having made the choice. Here, one's destiny and one's fate are different concepts. To speak of some-thing destined is to speak of something fated. But to speak of something beings one's destiny is not to imply anything about what is destined or fated. It is instead to speak of what should occur. "Should" in this case is to be understood normatively and not nomically. The mandate is referenced to a purported normative order in the universe, much like but not equivalent to the mandates of an omnipotent deity. An omnipotent deity can insist that actions be performed that are not performed. Its mandates can be ignored. In like manner, having and following a destiny is something that can be ignored. Hence, having a destiny does not imply having a fate, but given the usage where having a destiny does have such implication, there can be no wavering from that destiny—from that which is inevitable. It would be inconsistent to hold that a person's life has a destiny, in the sense that some life experiences are inevitable, and simultaneously hold that one may live otherwise.

It appears the requirements for being a person within traditional African philosophical thought suggest that the Western concept of person has no viable place in African folk thought.[8] Grounding this perspective is the view that the Western concept of person is essentially dualistic, while the traditional African concept of person is not. Within Western thought, persons can be differentiated and subsequently char-acterized as physical or as nonphysical essences. For example, when making reference to his or her person, the referent can be the individual's body, mind, soul, sense of self, or some combination thereof. In contrast, the traditional African concept of person does not permit such characterizations. Efforts to differentiate a person can result only in components that are not themselves persons. In both Akan and Yoruba, a human that is a person is a composite of body and spirit (mind), and without either, there is no corresponding person. Because of this difference, one may be led to believe that Western perspectives on personhood have no explanatory efficacy in traditional African philosophical thought. For similar reasons, one may be led to believe that traditional African philosophical perspectives on personhood have no explanatory efficacy in Western thought. Holding either position can be viewed as shortsighted.

Western Perspectives on African Conceptions of Personhood

In traditional Yoruba and Akan cultures, ancestral spirits are viewed as persons. Within modern Western cultures, only individuals that have the capacity for consciousness and self-reflection are persons. From a Western perspective, two types of fundamental concerns arise when ancestral spirits are claimed to exist as persons. The first is ontological and the second is epistemological. With respect to the ontological concerns, there are two. An ancestral spirit is an incorporeal being that is the same individual as its once living human counterpart, but without its counterpart's body. Of concern is the sense in which an individual can exist without a living body, and the sense in which an ancestral spirit can be the same individual as its once living human counterpart. Secondly, being a person, in the Western sense of "being a person" requires consciousness and self-reflection. As traditionally understood, both are processes and require life energy. Of concern is the sense in which something that is not alive can be self-reflective or conscious.

Concerning the former, there is no obvious evidence within science to support claims for the existence of incorporeal human beings. Were there such support, it would still not be obvious what would constitute criteria for characterizing something incorporeal as the same individual as its once-living counterpart. However, an *emi'*, once embodied, contains the collective memories of the experiences and associated dispositions of the body to which it gave life. The *emi'*, like the soul, remains after the death of the body. At death, the *emi'* emerges as an ancestral spirit with the collective memories and associated dispositions of its once living human counterpart. Its having those memories and associated disposition can be said to make it the same individual as its human counterpart.

However, having said memories and dispositions seem to require a physical presence. In keeping with this speculation, ancestral spirits could be viewed as contained energy clusters, and as energy clusters, they could have memories and dispositions. This is not far-fetched, since all existent phenomena exist as either matter or as energy and according to physical law, neither can be destroyed and either, in principle, can convert to the other. Hence, just as dielectric materials within, for example, transistors and cables have memories (hysteresis) and associated dispositions (dissipation factor), so can energy clusters.[9] In keeping with this line of thought, an ancestral spirit could be the residual energy cluster of the once-living individual from which it emerged. Its ability to sustain itself is beyond my understanding, but there is a precedent within Western culture that permits the acceptance of such a characterization as true. Western theism posits both an afterlife and an eternal life of joy or of suffering for the souls of those once alive. Moreover, in Western theism, personal identity is preserved beyond the death of the body from which the soul survives. The inability of science to subsume or otherwise capture the posits of Western theism does not undermine the significance of such posits in grounding Western culture.

Concerning the latter, ancestral spirits as energy clusters can be conscious and self-reflective. Modern technology has produced artificially intelligent systems that are functionally conscious and self-reflective. A personal computer's operating systems, such as Microsoft's Windows 2000, is aware of the states of the devices it operates and takes corrective actions when deviations are beyond what it sees as a healthy norm. Also, to some extent, the operation system is able to make corrections to itself when its functioning is less than optimal. This requires it to look upon itself and to see that it is not as it should be. Such a process does not deny Wittgenstein's maxim that the eye cannot see itself, since any such viewing by an electronic or bio-chemical system would be one wherein that which would be viewed would be an immediate past. Nothing in nature is instantaneous and any view of one's self would be a view of one's past, and as long as that past is seen as one's self, there is warrant for characterizing the view as one of self-consciousness or self-reflection. Concerning the capabilities of current artificially intelligent systems, their functions are admittedly limited, but those limitations do not admit of an inability to function as if conscious and self-reflective. Moreover, it has been projected that as memory, system speed, and semantic capabilities are enhanced, the complexity of the processing of artificially intelligent systems will approach that of humans.

Still, given current technology, some artificially intelligent systems display a rudimentary functional consciousness, and in some cases, that functional consciousness takes the form of self-consciousness and self-reflection. All such functions can be modeled as manifestations of energy, and that seems sufficient for giving the nod to characterizing ancestral spirits, in principle, as conscious and self-reflective energy fields. Moreover, it gives a physical foundation for claims about the existence of souls within Western culture. It also allows souls to be persons without their being alive, in the traditional sense of being alive. This is not to equate souls and ancestral spirits, since ancestral spirits are purportedly active causal agents, while souls, after the death of the body, are purportedly passive.

The epistemological concerns are far more challenging, and spec-ulation of the previous sort seems unpromising. Even if there were no concerns about the ontological status of ancestral spirits, claims about ancestral spirits cannot be known to be true unless believing them is warranted. Attributing personhood to something requires that it or others of its kind have evoked compelling reasons for viewing it as having a capacity for consciousness and self-reflection. Hence, if ances-tral spirits are to fall within the extension of the Western sense of "person," they must exhibit evidence of consciousness and self-reflection. Satisfying that condition is also necessary for being a person in the traditional African sense of person. However, it is not obvious what would count as an exhibition of consciousness or self-reflection by something incorporeal. It is one thing to see a behavior and attribute that behavior to a mind or a spirit or soul. It is quite another to see a mind or a spirit. Unless an ancestral spirit has taken residence in something that lends itself to observation, there will be little ground for viewing it as exhibiting evidence for anything. Spiritual and mental phenomena are not directly observable. Moreover, were an ancestral spirit to take residence in an object, unless we had evidence that it was an ancestral spirit that gave rise to our observations, we would have little basis for attributing our observations to an ancestral spirit. Of course, if a rock, plant, or snake were to exhibit self-reflection, that would perhaps count as compelling evidence for attributing the resi-dence of something extraordinary within it. Still, without an observable manifestation: without a display of conscious and self-reflective behavior that could be attributed to an ancestral spirit, we would have no clear justification for attributing consciousness or self-reflection to an ancestral spirit.

In keeping with such concerns, it is not wholly obvious that there is an epistemic warrant for making claims about the existence of ancestral spirits. There is less of a warrant for making claims about the behaviors or the intentions of ancestral spirits. Neither having substantial support leaves African culture open to the criticism of being rooted in metaphysical fantasy and mere religious superstition. However, upon close scrutiny, it becomes apparent that such criticisms are not peculiarly applicable to African culture and that such commitments are no more pervasive or perplexing than those found in Western culture. In Western culture, the most advanced and thorough offered explanations of the physical world are rooted in the theoretical posits of a science whose fundamental components are only accessible by the high priests of quantum physics. Like the ancestral spirits of traditional African culture, the subatomic particles of quantum physics are not readily amenable to observation, and even among the experts, there is debate over the physical reality of such posited entities. Moreover, Western culture provides a precedent for allowing the attribution of personhood to incorporeal beings. Within the traditions of Western monotheism, nonphysical phenomena can be persons without being human. Within Judaism and Islam, Yahweh is by nature incorporeal and is not human, yet Yahweh is viewed as a person.[10]

The truth of such claims is not of immediate significance. Of significance is the highly entrenched Western folk tenet that an incorporeal being can exist and that an incorporeal being can be a person. Significant also is that both are held in light of contrary perspectives from a discipline upon which Western civilization is dependent for its material flourishing. According to modern science, there is no evidence to support the claim that incorporeal conscious beings exist.

Moreover, current scientific research suggests that only mammals have the capacity to be conscious and self-reflective. In spite of these differences, Western folk culture and its science make use of theoretical posits to explain the experiential world, and the theoretical posits of each are only observable by those who accept them as real. That said, the ontological commitments that ground traditional African culture are no more obviously metaphysical fantasy or mere religious superstition that those of modern Western culture. This does not let African culture off the hook, so to speak. It merely places it in the same predicament as modern Western culture when it tries to explain or otherwise account for perplexing phenomena by positing the unobservable.

Learning from the Other

According to traditional African thought, persons are individuals that have chosen a specific destiny and are following the destiny they have chosen. This sense of "person" is unlike that of Western culture, since in Western culture having a destiny is not a necessary condition for being a person. Another difference is that a person in traditional African culture cannot be differentiated as a body and as mind or spirit. The idea of a person being distinct from its body is viewed as incoherent. An individual becomes a person only when its body is infused with a spirit, an *emi'*. Neither body nor spirit alone is a person. An individual can be segmented and discussed as if it is a body or a mind or spirit, but a person cannot.[11]

As in Western culture, a person in traditional African culture is a conscious and self-reflective being. However, according to traditional African thought, it is not the case that something's being conscious and self-reflective is sufficient for its being a person. For example, an *emi'*—the spirit that gives consciousness to the fetus—is characterized as conscious and it is arguably self-reflective, but it is not characterized as a person. It is only when the *emi'* becomes infused within a fetus and a destiny is chosen that a person emerges.

Concerning the *emi'*s being self-reflective, choosing a destiny for oneself implies having an awareness of self and having some perspective on how the given options will affect one's well-being. An assumption here is that in choosing a destiny one has some familiarity with what is being chosen and that one is not merely choosing from, say, a selection of colored boxes whose contents are unknown. Were the choice blind, characterizing one's destiny as something chosen becomes suspect. Moreover, one's destiny is something that is both chosen and accepted.[12] It is one thing to accept an offered gift that is presented in a box. It is quite another to accept the content of the box, especially when the content may be unwelcome, such as when it is powdered anthrax or a poisonous snake. Hence, there appear to be grounds within traditional African thought to characterize the *emi'* as something that can engage in self-reflection.

In opposition one could argue that self-reflection requires two distinct phenomena and that an *emi'*, being a spirit and without body, is but one. That objection is unpromising, since being without a body does not mean being void of components. Constituting a magnetic field are eddies and fluctuations, and those components interact and respond to elements within their environment.[13] Such dynamics give rise to the character of each magnetic field. Like magnetic fields, spirits can be energy fields, and as such have components that permit their being differentiated. Hence, being a spirit does not imply being undifferentiated. Since self-reflection is fundamentally nothing more than a viewing of what is recognized as oneself, and that is a having of a perspective on aspects of one's self, self-reflection could be a possible state for spirits.[14] In fairness, since we grant that capacity to humans where there is no obvious explanation for how self-reflection occurs, we must grant its possibility to spirits.

Destiny as a necessary condition for personhood is problematic. First, the concept infuses a normative feature into ontological concerns. Being a person implies being successful at following a specific path or at actualizing a specific way of life. The Western concept of person is not normative in the same way, in the respect that an individual's lifestyle has no material consequences for its being a person.[15] Instead, the manner in which one lives one's life determines whether one can be said to be good or bad, a success or a failure, or a self-actualized or an undeveloped person. Normative ascriptions are made of persons and the satisfaction of a particular normative prescription is not integral to being a person. It is one thing to say that being able to fail or to succeed at satisfying a normative prescription is required for being a person. It is quite another to say that an individual is a person only if he or she satisfies a particular prescription.

Second, because of the normative requirement for being a person, there is no easily discernible way for determining whether an individual is a person. Given that an individual's destiny, if knowable, is immediately knowable only to herself, and given that an individual may be unaware of her destiny, others have no reliable way of knowing her destiny. Since knowing whether someone is a person requires knowing that the individual is pursuing her destiny, and since there is no obvious way of knowing an individual's destiny or whether the destiny is being pursued, there is no obvious way of knowing that an individual is a person.

On the surface, this appears similar to the Western problem of other minds—the problem of knowing whether some other has mental states. However, a close look reveals that the similarities are superficial. Unlike the problem of other minds, there is no discernible standard for determining whether the criteria for personhood have been satisfied. No matter how closely we observe the behavior of an individual, we have no readily available means for knowing whether her behavior is consistent with behavior that would mimic the realization of her destiny. Since her destiny is only available to us via her report, and since she may be mistaken about her destiny, we at most can only justifiably judge her to be a person on the basis of what she claims to be her destiny. We both can be mistaken and there is no obvious way to determine otherwise. There are no obvious dispositions or behavioral correlations that by analogy point to the satisfaction of the normative criteria for something to be a person.

Arguably, there is a sense in which the Western concept of person is less problematic. The Western concept of person connotes an individual with readily identifiable properties. This is not to say that persons are directly observed. We see bodies and attribute personhood to bodies that manifest characteristics that are associated with being a person. Again, on Western criteria, something is a person if it is conscious and self-reflective. Except in unusual but explainable circumstances, both states are readily identifiable. That is, there are applicable criteria for discerning whether an individual is self-conscious and self-reflective. That being the case, there are applicable criteria for the predication of personhood.

On the other hand, in Yoruba, there is no criterion for personhood whose satisfaction is readily observable. As previously stated, we have no way of knowing if the *emi'* has failed to choose a destiny and we have no way of knowing the particular destiny chosen by an *emi'*. Moreover, we do not know whether the particular path an individual takes to realize its destiny is appropriate for realizing its destiny. Again, "destiny" in the sense used does not imply fate. Since being a person is in part normative, and since we have no way of knowing whether the normative criteria have been satisfied, no particular individual can know that it or some other is a person.

Although the Western and the traditional African requirements for being a person are not equivalent, the Western characterization fosters explanatory efficacy for significant aspects of the traditional African conception of personhood.[16] Moreover, aspects of the Western characterization of person seem better able to ground the capturing of personhood and personal identity across time than does traditional African thought. This is most obvious when characterizing ancestral spirits as persons and when attributing personhood to an individual when there are concerns about its following its destiny.[17] I am not suggesting that Western perspectives on personhood are not flawed or that the traditional African conception of person can or should be reduced to Cartesian dualism.[18] Clearly, each tradition has merit and there is something of significance to be gained from viewing persons from each of the two traditions. Nonetheless, in spite of the tenet that the traditional African conception of persons is not dualistic, Western perspectives on personhood can facilitate our understanding of the ontological commitments that are associated with the traditional African conception of persons. Also, our understanding those associated commitments can facilitate our acquiring a better understanding of the grounding of the ontological commitments within Western culture.

Concluding Remarks

Science emerged out of a response to believed inadequacies in the edicts of religion for accounting for perspectives that were in conflict with what was decreed as obvious by Western religious tradition. Some of faith did not perceive the world as it was characterized by religious teachings. Those who saw otherwise were viewed as not of the faith and were subject to severe reprimand for challenging religious decrees. For example, at sunrise, Galileo did not see the sun rising, but instead saw the horizon descending, and that meant that the earth was moving and not the sun.[19] The offered explanations by Western religion to account for its claim that the earth is at the center of the universe and that the sun revolves around the earth were neither confirmable nor compelling for those who saw otherwise. Science emerged in part to validate the claims of those whose perspectives about nature were different from those of religious teachings. Science offered a neutral methodology for testing hypotheses and for providing the public with means for discerning the truth of the claims about matters of empirical import. The discerning of truth fell upon the public and not solely upon those of the cloth. Ironically, from the perspective of observation alone, the characterization of the universe by religious tradition was no less confirmable than that of Galileo. Moreover, from the point of view of experience, one does not sense the horizon descending when viewing the sun near the horizon in the morning. There is no sensation of the earth moving, but there is one of the sun rising. Apparently, something more was going on in early science than the mere reliance of immediate experience to confirm or disconfirm hypotheses. Early science was appealing to underlying unobservables to support its claims.

Common to both Western science and to African and American folk cultures is a disposition to posit unobservables to help account for experiences. Perhaps this is because there is an underlying tenet in each that there are phenomena that escape notice by the senses that give rise to experience. This tenet is evident in traditional African culture, and since all cultures are rooted in early African culture, it should not be surprising to find significant remnants of African culture in Western culture as well.[20] When the first humans migrated from sub-Saharan Africa to populate the earth as it is now, they took with them the ability to fashion inductions and to make causal inferences. Those who fail to make causal and good inductive inferences do not live long enough to reproduce.[21] That disposition, whether innate or learned is crucial for survival, and its use not being nurtured by a culture predisposes the culture to extinction. That said, cultural differences, for the most part, reflect adaptive responses to the new ecosystems that the surviving migrants encountered.

We seem to have a tendency to generalize when doing so is critical to survival or, at the least, when it is felt important to do so. It appears also that our coming to understand some phenomenon rests upon our seeing that phenomenon as an instance of something more generally understood: as an instance of a noticed pattern. Humans are extraordinarily well adept at finding patterns and at fashioning correlations. The correlations can be between the physical, as in the case of the laws of thermodynamics, and between the abstract as in the case of the axioms of Euclidean geometry. And, as is our concern, they can be between the abstract and the physical as in the case of positing unobservables to explain observables: to use the theoretical posits of quantum mechanics and religion to account for the experiential world. We come to an understanding by seeing that which is in question as an instance of a believed order or pattern or as something more fundamental that grounds that which is in question. It is by virtue of our seeing new information as an instance of a believed pattern or of something viewed as more fundamental that we subsequently come to have an understanding of new information.[22] Hence, having an understanding of why p is true is tantamount to having a meaningful perspective on how or on why p is true. This is tantamount to seeing that or how p is related to something previously accepted.[23]

Common to each culture is a belief in the existence of underlying unobservable phenomena that determine or otherwise influence the universe as understood through human experience. Moreover, common to each culture is a belief in forces or in some forms of energy or order that follows its own rules and is not answerable to any life form to which we have access. Traditional African folk culture and Western folk culture focus primarily upon submitting to and embracing that which is believed to determine or fashion the universe, while Western science tries to discover the rules that govern the universe. From the perspectives of folk cultures, efforts by science to discover the essence of what determines and fashions the universe will prove fruitless. It is believed that knowing reality on the level pursued by science can only be achieved by transcending the barriers imposed by the mind and body when trying to see without distortion and delusion. Ironically, such a perspective seems supported by the inability of science to observe its most basic posited particles without introducing changes in what science is attempting to observe.

We perhaps should keep in mind that beliefs in the existence of a spiritual world and that beliefs in things like physical transformations are not unique to traditional African culture. Native American culture embraces the notion that there are nonobservable life forms—spirits and life essences—that can reside in birds, bears, and streams. Also, transubstantiation is an integral part of Roman Catholic dogma. The communion wafer and wine are claimed to be literally transformed into the body and blood of Christ when consumed during communion. The two are claimed to become one—Christ incarnate—even though when examined after consumption, each retains its pre-consumed chemical identity.[24] Of significance here is the highly endorsed Western folk wisdom that in spite of the obviously powerful contributions from science to the acquisition of human understanding, there are spiritual and physical components of nature that escape notice by science and that the characterizations of those components are true nonetheless.[25]

Hopefully, it is now apparent that the unobservables that ground Western religions share the same credibility problems as those of traditional African religions when viewed under the purview of modern science. A plausible position to take is that science, in the long run, provides the most likely method for discovering what is true, and that the grounding posits of both religious traditions are pre-theoretic and should be abandoned when in conflict with science. On the other hand, it is equally plausible that Olodumare fashioned the world unveiled by science, but that many of the purported facts of science are not as science claims.[26] For example, the age of the earth could be as suggested within the Old Testament—no more than 7,000 years.[27] It could also be the case that archeological finds that are dated as pre-historic are otherwise. In other words, dinosaurs never walked the earth, and the unearthed bones and other relics that indicate life and an evolving universe prior to 7,000 years ago are merely either an aberration in our assessment methodology or a reflection of the universe as it was made at the time of creation. To conjecture from Russell's "five minute hypothesis," just as it is logically possible that the world came into existence just as we know it only five minutes ago, it is logically possible that it came into existence 7,000 years ago. This is not to blast science or to support creationism. It is instead to be mindful that we do not know which, if either, cosmology is correct. There are good grounds for accepting either, but both could be false. Both are stories fashioned by the ontological commitments of the cultures from which the stories evolve. Those commitments are a reflection of what the most influential members of a community have accepted as what they see as the most plausible reasons for their experiences being as they are. As a matter of social practice, those perspectives become institutionalized and heralded as true.

The advantage that science has over religion is that science offers theories that explain, while religions do not, except in those cases where the offered explanations are not testable. The scriptures of religions are not really theories. They are instead stories that offer means to finding meaning in life and directions for how best to live one's life. Still, it is obvious that most humans have a feeling of being connected to life in ways that are not readily explicable by science, and that one of the most fundamental and meaningful components of human interactions is a phenomenon that has to date escaped the measure of science. That phenomenon is love.

It could be that the ability to survive is partly a function of our abilities to look for underlying causal correlations. The practice is evident in all cultures and on one reading, the more technologically based cultures have brought forth, so to speak, a more evolved theoretical foundation for accounting for experiences. However, on another reading, science may have lost sight of the spiritual component that sprang from African culture that is still dominant in Western folk culture. Love, loyalty, courage, empathy, and the like are sentiments of significance that set humans apart from most other kinds of organisms. That which we feel in our hearts has as much significance and reality to us as what we experience through our skins, eyes, ears, tongues, or noses. From the perspective of traditional African thought, it is not a big leap to go from a felt presence of something familiar that is unseen or unheard to: "That was my grandfather trying to get my attention. My grandfather's having being dead for twenty years is of no consequence. What is of consequence is that the information he has now given me will save my mother's life. It was something about her that only he knew, and had not I been open to receiving him, she would have died." There are countless credible experiences of fantastic occurrences that escape the notice of science. There are also many ordinary occurrences that escape explanation by science, such as the flying of bumblebees, the audible differences between interconnecting audio cables, and the lifting of an automobile by a mother to free her trapped child. Although each culture has offered explanations for all phenomena, neither culture has provided explanations for all phenomena.

From the perspective of a traditional African medicine man, the Western leap from geocentric astronomy to heliocentric astronomy seems no less great than would be the leap from viewing persons as conscious and self-reflective beings with an embraced destiny to viewing persons as resonate energy packets. The same can be said for the leap from the uttered words of a poet to the magnetic states of a storage disk, or from water to electrically charged particles. Medicine men manipulate energy, and to borrow from the Aristotelian accident/substance distinction, ordinary experiences of the world are of accidents and not of the underlying substance. It could very well be the case that all things are energy fields fashioned by the subatomic particles posited by quantum physicists. It could also be the case that some combinations of those fields form conscious and self-reflective entities that have causal efficacy and that escape notice by those who lack the appropriate sensitivity to them. This is pure speculation, but neither approach to explaining phenomena is complete, and perhaps a fresh synthesis can yield a more fruitful model for understanding the believed foundations of life that apparently have not yet been explained. In keeping with that speculation, just as the small particles of quantum physics are prevented, by the particles we use to observe them, from following what would otherwise be their natural course, the otherwise natural manifestations of the spirit world could be blocked from observation by our perceived presence in their world.

Notes

1. Those having access to ancestral spirits possess knowledge about the world that is not had by those who lack access to ancestral spirits. Those having

access are viewed as important members of their communities and as such have honorific positions within their communities.

2. The spiritual component of nature is an incorporeal component that has consciousness, in the sense that it has an awareness of nature much as do humans, and it has a capacity to initiate responses to its perceptions.

3. There are more humans alive today than have lived in the past, and most all those alive are conscious and capable of self-reflection.

4. Speaking of a body as a deceased person is a figure of speech. It is the body of something that was once a person—a human body once alive with thoughts and feelings and so on.

5. See Marc Bekoff, "Animal Emotions: Exploring Passionate Natures," *Bioscience* 50.10 (2000): 861 for numerous references to discussions on this topic, including Charles Darwin, *The Expression of the Emotions in Man and Animals*, 3rd ed. (1872; rpt. New York: Oxford University Press, 1998); J. Goodall, *Through a Window* (Boston: Houghton-Mifflin, 1990); and J. Poole, "An Exploration of a Commonality between Ourselves and Elephants," *Etica and Animalia* 9 (1998): 85–110.

6. Its converse can be equally compelling: treat the other in a manner opposed to how one would want oneself to be treated so that the other will suffer. Suffering requires a measure of self-reflection that is not required for being in pain. History shows that those not treated as like in kind are either deeply depersonalized or are not viewed as persons. For example, although slave brokers and slave owners in America were typically Christian, they did not view slave trade as morally wrong or sinful. It was believed that Africans lacked characteristics that were essential for having a soul and as such lacked the spiritual, intellectual, and moral base shared by all persons. Africans were viewed as biologically less evolved than Caucasians and were ranked between chimps and humans. Personhood was then viewed as physically derived, in the sense that it was seen as a property that emerged with the biology that made an individual fully human. It was also thought that the soul was given only to animals of a specifically evolved type. Although Africans who were applauded for displaying 'fully human' talents could be treated as persons, that consideration was materially limited and did not imply actual personhood. It meant only that special treatment could be given by those who saw an African as manifesting behaviors that typically were manifested only by persons—that is by Caucasians. Hence, enslavers could see themselves as God-fearing and moral because those enslaved were like cattle or other animals over which Caucasian domination was seen as natural. Social Darwinism reinforced that perspective and nurtured racial oppression. On the other hand, this perspective does not accommodate the justification for the less than legal unions between Caucasian males and African women, since bestiality was considered a sin.

7. I owe this perspective to Dr. David R. Kurtzman.

8. This perspective was gathered from conversations with various scholars of African philosophical thought. It is specifically representative of the perspectives of Kwasi Wiredu, Segun Gbadegesin, and Kwame Gyekye.

9. Hysteresis and dissipation factor are technical terms and are here used to make mention of a characteristic of materials that are affected by an applied voltage. For example, when a voltage is applied to an ideal capacitor and subsequently removed the applied voltage remains in the capacitor. The capacitor can be said to have a memory. When shorted, an ideal capacitor will lose all its applied voltage. To speak of the capacitor as having hysteresis is to speak of its reluctance to dissipate the voltage it has memorized. The rate at which the voltage completely leaves the capacitor is the dissipation factor of the capacitor. Semiconductors, such as transistors, have a capacitance in their junctions, and their capacitance, when shorted, is more reluctant to dissipate an impressed voltage than say a vacuum tube. This disposition affects any new voltage input to the device in an additive fashion. In this sense, we can speak of a transistor as having a greater disposition to distort a signal than a vacuum tube.

10. References to God as a man are references to gender rather than to sex and as such they imply no consequences for biological attributions to God.

11. Analogously, there was a short-lived Christian proposal that was offered to permit early abortions. During medieval times, it was believed that God's spirit was not placed within the developing embryo until it was no longer possible for twins to evolve. The thinking at the time was that if the soul were placed in an embryo that had not completed its development into two or more fetuses, each fetus would have only part of a soul. It was believed that only after the receipt of the soul would an individual become a person.

12. Gbadegesin compares the choosing of a destiny to the choosing of a spouse. See Segun Gbadegesin, *African Philosophy: Traditional Yoruba Philosophy and Contemporary African Realities* (New York: Peter Lang, 1991), 46–53.

13. A magnetic field is a phenomenon induced by currents that produce a force that attracts or repels materials that would be similarly affected when placed near a magnet.

14. From a Zen Buddhist perspective, one can only exist in the present, so when self-reflecting, one is reflecting upon one's views of one's past self. Such actions provide perspectives. When one is one's true self—an undifferentiated self—there is no awareness of past or future or present. There is only awareness. When there is only awareness there is no thought. There is an apperception of time only when there is a recognition of difference, and when one is without thought and only aware, there is no perception of difference and hence no perception of time. It is in this sense that we can be eternal. When in a state of *mushin*, time has no beginning or end.

15. An exception to this can be found in early American culture. The dominant culture showed an inability or unwillingness to view African Americans as persons because of differences in cultural aesthetics and associated behaviors.

16. Reference here is made to the criteria for using "person" within each of the two cultures.

17. The Western perspective better addresses the metaphysical concerns, but does not tell us how to go about recognizing persons. So, the epistemology remains problematic—as it does for Western religion and Western science.

18. *P* being explained by *q* does not imply that *p* can be reduced to *q*.

19. According to religious dogma at the time of Copernicus, the earth was at the center of the universe and the sun and all else moved around the earth. However, it was the earth's rotating on its axis that accounted for the changes from day to night to day, and not either body moving around the other.

20. Current science tells us that all humans emerged from sub-Saharan African between 200,000 and 65,000 years ago and subsequently populated the earth as we now know it.

21. From where this claim originated I do not know. I remember it from a 1973 preliminary examination in epistemology during my graduate study at the University of Michigan.

22. As a point of clarification, having an understanding is not the same as having knowledge. My claim that "I understand that *p* is true" can be false, while still having an understanding that *p* is true. My beliefs about *p* can be misguided or otherwise mistaken, or my beliefs about that which subsumes *p* may be false or inappropriate. Having an understanding is analogous to being certain that some proposition is true. Being certain does not imply that one's belief is true. To have an understanding is to appreciate, assimilate, or integrate information into or by virtue of one's existing beliefs.

23. As in the case of visual perception, seeing something red and seeing that something is red are not equivalent observations. While the second does, the first does not presuppose having a concept of what it is to be red or an understanding of when it is appropriate to use the word "red." Seeing something red and understanding that it is red require something quite different. The first is immediate in the sense that it is a mere experience without cognitive processing. Understanding that something is red requires an appeal to a phenomenon other than our immediate experience. The appeal is to either our understanding of when it is appropriate to use the word "red" to characterize the phenomenon experienced, or the appeal is to our understanding of what it is to be red or to appear red.

24. This reflects the Aristotelian distinction between substance and accident (Aristotle, *Categories*, 5). Namely, that which something is may be quite different from how it appears when observed. All scientific analyses of the wafer and of the wine reveal the essential characteristics of each, both before and after they have been consumed. Neither the body nor the blood of Jesus has been discovered upon analyzing the consumed host during the Eucharist. Nevertheless, according to Catholic dogma, their not being found is to be expected, since in this context, the substance of Jesus is only revealed as the substance of bread and wine.

25. The virgin birth of Jesus, the ascensions of Mary and of Jesus, and the parting of the Red Sea by Moses are examples of physical occurrences for which science has provided no account.

26. Olodumare is the god of the Yoruba religion. Like Yahweh, Olodumare is that which has all perfections. Unlike Yahweh, Olodumare does not get angry or jealous and it does not have favorites (Exodus 34:14 Tanakh). Hence, Olodumare is viewed as the Supreme Being and not as merely god.

27. See Henry Halley, *Halley's Bible Handbook* (Grand Rapids, Mich.: Zondervan, 1965), 32–33.

SELECTED BIBLIOGRAPHY OF EPISTEMOLOGICAL AND METAPHYSICAL PERSPECTIVES IN AFRICAN PHILOSOPHICAL THOUGHT

Abimbola, Wande. "The Yoruba Concept of Human Personality." *La Notion de Personne en Afrique Noire, Centre National de la Recherche Scientifique* 544 (1975): 73–89.

Abraham, W. Emmanuel. "Sources of African Identity." In *Person and Community.* Ed. Kwasi Wiredu and Kwame Gyekye. Washington, D.C.: CRVP, 1992.

Aja, Egbeke. "The Power of the 'Word' in Traditional African (Igbo) Metaphysics: A Pragmatic Perspective." *Cont Philosophy* 14.4 (1992): 1–4.

Alfa, Samuel Audu. "The African Philosophical Concept of Time and its Metaphysical and Epistemological Ramifications." Ph.D. diss., Drew University, 1988.

Anyanwu, Kane Chukwulozie. "The Meaning of Ultimate Reality in Igbo Cultural Experience." *Ultimate Reality and Meaning Journal* 7 (1984): 84–101.

—————. "A Response to A G A Bello's Methodological Preliminaries." *Ultimate Reality and Meaning Journal* 14 (1991): 61–69.

Apostel, Leo. *African Philosophy: Myth or Reality.* Philosophy and Anthropology 2. Atlantic Highlands, N.J.: Humanities Press, 1981.

Appiah, Kwame Anthony. *In My Father's House: Africa in the Philosophy of Culture.* New York: Oxford University Press, 1992.

Beck, Simon. "Counterfactuals and the Law." *South African Journal of Philosophy* 12.3 (Aug. 1993): 62–65.

Bell, Richard H. *Understanding African Philosophy: A Cross-Cultural Approach to Classical and Contemporary Issues.* New York: Routledge, 2002.

Bidney, David. "On the Concept of Culture and Some Cultural Fallacies." In *Ideas of Culture: Sources and Uses.* Ed. F. C. Gamst and E. Norbeck. New York: Holt Rinehart and Winston, 1976.

Blakeley, Thomas J. "The Categories of MTU and the Categories of Aristotle." In *African Philosophy: An Introduction*. Ed. Richard Wright. New York: University Press of America, 1979.

Bodunrin, P. O. "The Question of African Philosophy." *Philosophy* 56 (1981): 61–179.

————. "Witchcraft, Magic, and E. S. P.: A Defense of Scientific and Philosophical Scepticism." *Second Order* 7.1 and 2 (1978): 36–50.

Buckley, A. D. *Yoruba Medicine*. Oxford: Clarendon Press, 1985.

Bwele, Guillaume. "Axes du temps en Afrique et en Occident." *Quest* 5.2 (1991): 48–62.

Carew, G. Munda. "A Critique of John S. Mbiti's Traditional African Ontology." *Quest* 7.1 (1993): 78–91.

Chukwudieze, Emmanuel. *African Philosophy: An Anthology*. Oxford: Blackwell Publishers, 1997.

Coetzee, P. H., and A. P. J. Roux. *The African Philosophy Reader*. New York: Routledge, 1998.

Collingwood, R. J. *An Essay on Metaphysics*. Chicago: Gateway, 1972.

Conradie, Anna-Louize. "Africa." In *Handbook of World Philosophy*. Ed. John R. Burr. Westport, Conn.: Greenwood Press, 1980.

————. "Republic of South Africa." In *Handbook of World Philosophy*. Ed. John R. Burr. Westport, Conn.: Greenwood Press, 1980.

Dalfovo, A. T. *The Foundations of Social Life*. Washington, D.C.: CRVP, 1992.

Dukor, Maduabu. "African Cosmology and Ontology." *Indian Philosophical Quarterly* 16.4 (1989): 367–91.

Dukor, Maduabuchi. "God and Godlings in African Ontology." *Indian Philosophical Quarterly* 17.1 (1990): 75–89.

Dzobo, N. K. "African Symbols and Proverbs as Sources of Knowledge and Truth." In *Person and Community*. Ed. Kwasi Wiredu and Kwame Gyekye. Washington, D.C.: CRVP, 1992.

————. "The Image of Man in Africa." In *Person and Community*. Ed. Kwasi Wiredu and Kwame Gyekye. Washington, D.C.: CRVP, 1992.

————. "Knowledge and Truth: Ewe and Akan Conceptions." In *Person and Community*. Ed. Kwasi Wiredu and Kwame Gyekye. Washington, D.C.: CRVP, 1992.

————. "Values in a Changing Society." In *Person and Community*. Ed. Kwasi Wiredu and Kwame Gyekye. Washington, D.C.: CRVP, 1992.

Emmet, Dorothy. "Haunted Universes." *Second Order* 1 (1972): 34–42.

English, Parker, and Kibujjo Kalumba. *African Philosophy: A Classical Approach*. Englewood Cliffs, N.J.: Prentice-Hall, 1996.

Engmann, Joyce. "Immortality and the Nature of Man in Gara Thought." In *Person and Community*. Ed. Kwasi Wiredu and Kwame Gyekye. Washington, D.C.: CRVP, 1992.

Evans-Pritchard, E. E. *Witchcraft, Oracles and Magic among the Azande*. Oxford: Clarendon Press, 1976.

Eze, Emmanuel C. *African Philosophy: An Anthology.* Oxford: Blackwell, 1998.
————. *Post Colonial African Philosophy: A Critical Reader.* Oxford: Blackwell Publishers, 1997.
————. "Rationality and the Debates about African Philosophy." Ph.D. diss., Fordham University, 1993.
————. "Truth and Ethics in African Thought." *Quest* 7.1 (1993): 4–19.
Fennema, J. G. "The Discussion of Identity among African Philosophers." In *I, We, and Body: First Joint Symposium of Philosophers from African and from the Netherlands.* Ed. Heinz Kimmerle. Amsterdam: Grüner, 1989.
Frye, Charles A. "Einstein and African Religion and Philosophy." In *Einstein and the Humanities.* Ed. Dennis P. Ryan. New York: Greenwood Press, n.d.
Gbadegesin, Segun. "Destiny, Personality and the Ultimate Reality of Human Existence: A Yoruba Perspective." *Ultimate Reality and Meaning* 7.3 (1984): 165–78.
————. "God, Destiny, and Social Injustice: A Critique of a Yoruba Ifa Belief." In *The Search for Faith and Justice in the Twentieth Century.* Ed. Gene James. New York: Paragon Press, 1987.
————. "Kwame Nkrumah and the Search for URAM." *Ultimate Reality and Meaning* 10.1 (1987): 14–28.
Gbadegesin, Segun, and Oladimeji Alo. "The Theme of Causation and Contemporary Work Attitude among Nigerians." *ODU: A Journal of West African Studies* 31 (1987): 15–31.
Gluckmann, Max. "Social Beliefs and Individual Thinking in Tribal Society." In *An Essay on African Philosophical Thought: The Akan Conceptual Scheme.* Ed. Kwame Gyekye. New York: Cambridge University Press, 1987.
Green, Helen Bagenstose. "Temporal Attitudes in Four Negro Subcultures." *Stadium Generale* 23 (1970): 571–86.
Gyekye, Kwame. "The Akan Concept of a Person." *International Philosophical Quarterly* 18 (1978): 277–87.
————. *An Essay on African Philosophical Thought: The Akan Conceptual Scheme.* Cambridge: Cambridge University Press, 1987.
————. "Person and Community in African Thought." In *I, We, and Body: First Joint Symposium of Philosophers from Africa and from the Netherlands.* Ed. Heinz Kimmerle. Amsterdam: Grüner, 1989.
————. "Person and Community in Akan Thought." In *Person and Community.* Ed. Kwasi Wiredu and Kwame Gyekye. Washington, D.C.: CRVP, 1992.
————. "Philosophical Relevance of Akan Proverbs." *Second Order* 4 (1975): 45–53.
————. *Traditions and Modernity: Philosophical Reflections on the African Experience.* New York: Oxford University Press, 1997.
Hallen, Barry. "Indeterminacy, Ethnophilosophy, Linguistic Philosophy, African Philosophy." *Philosophy* 70.273 (1995): 377–93.

Hallen, Barry, and J. O. Sodipo. *Knowledge, Belief, and Witchcraft: Analytical Experiments in African Philosophy*. London: Ethnographica, 1997.

————. "Robin Horton on Critical Philosophy and Traditional Thought." *Second Order* 6.1 (1997): 81–92.

Horton, Robin. "African Traditional Thought and Western Science." *Africa* 37.1 and 2 (1967): 50–71; 155–87.

————. "Destiny and the Unconscious in West Africa." *Africa* 31 (1961): 110–16.

————. "The Kalabari World-View: An Outline and Interpretation." *Africa* 32.3 (1962): 197–220.

————. "Paradox and Explanation." *Philosophy of Social Science* 3 (1973): 231–56.

————. "Paradox and Explanation: A Reply to Mr. Skorupski, Part II." *Philosophy of Social Science* 3 (1973): 289–312.

————. *Patterns of Thought in Africa and the West*. Cambridge: Cambridge University Press, 1994.

Hountondji, Paulin. *African Philosophy: Myth and Reality*. Bloomington: Indiana University Press, 1983.

Idowu, Bolaji. *God in Yoruba Belief*. Lagos: Longmans, 1962.

Imbo, Samuel Oluoch. *An Introduction to African Philosophy*. Lanham, Md.: Rowman & Littlefield, 1998.

Irele, Abiola. "Culture and the National Idea." *African Philosophical Inquiry* 1.2 (1987): 123–39.

Isichel, Elizabeth. *The Ibo People and the Europeans*. London: Faber and Faber, 1973.

Jackson, Michael, and Ivan Karp. *Personhood and Agency: The Experience of Self and Other in African Cultures*. Uppsala Studies in Cultural Anthropology 14. Washington, D.C.: Smithsonian Institution Press, 1991.

James, George G. M. *Stolen Legacy*. New York: Philosophical Lib., 1954.

Keita, Lansana. "African Philosophical Systems: A Rational Reconstruction." *Philosophical Forum* 9 (1997): 169–89.

————. "Jennings and Zande Logic: A Note." *British Journal for the Philosophy of Science* 44.1 (1993): 151–56.

Kessler, Gary E. *Voices of Wisdom: A Multicultural Philosophy Reader*. Belmont, Calif.: Wadsworth, 1992.

Kimmerle, Heinz, ed. *I, We, and Body: First Joint Symposium of Philosophers from Africa and the Netherlands*. Amsterdam: Grüner, 1989.

————. "The Question of Truth in Africa: From a European Perspective." *Philosophy Soc Act* 19.3 (1993): 41–47.

Kudadjie, J. N. "Towards Moral Development in Contemporary Africa." *Person and Community*. Ed. Kwasi Wiredu and Kwame Gyekye. Washington, D.C.: CRVP, 1992.

Kwame, Safro. "Feminism, African Philosophy and the Rejection of Dualism: An Essay in Metaphilosophy." Ph.D. diss., University of Cincinnati, 1989.

————. *Readings in African Philosophy: An Akan Collection*. Lanham, Md.: University Press of America, 1995.

Lawuyi, Olatunde. "The Tortoise and the Snail: Animal Identities and the Ethical Issues Concerning Political Behaviors among the Yoruba of Nigeria." *Second Order* [New Series 1.2] (1988).

Lewy, Guenter. *Religion and Revolution*. New York: Oxford University Press, 1974.

Louw, Tobias J. G. "Gerhard A. Rauche's Philosophy of Actuality: The Work and Thought of an Individualist South African Philosopher." *Man World* 26.2 (1993): 181–97.

Louw, Tobias J. G., and Gerhard A. Rauche, eds. *Selected Philosophical Papers*. Fort Hare, South Africa: University Press, 1992.

Lowie, R. H. *Culture and Ethnology*. New York: Boni and Liveright, 1917.

Makinde, M. A. "An African Concept of Human Personality." *Ultimate Reality and Meaning Journal* 7 (1984): 189–200.

————. *African Philosophy, Culture, and Traditional Medicine*. Athens: Ohio University Press, 1988.

————. "Immortality of the Soul and the Yoruba Theory of Seven Heavens [Orun Meje]." *Journal of Cultures and Ideas* 1 (1983): 31–59.

————. "A Philosophical Analysis of the Yoruba Concepts of Ori and Human Destiny." *International Studies in Philosophy* 17.1 (1985): 53–69.

Masolo, D. A. *African Philosophy in Search of Identity*. Bloomington: Indiana University Press, 1994.

Mbiti, John. *African Religions and Philosophy*. London: Heinemann, 1969.

————. *Concepts of God in Africa*. London: Heinemann, 1970.

Menkiti, Ifeanyi A. "Person and Community in African Traditional Thought." In *African Philosophy: An Introduction*. Ed. Richard Wright. New York: University Press of America, 1979.

Minkus, Helaine K. "Causal Theory in Akwapim Akan Philosophy." In *African Philosophy: An Introduction*. Ed. Richard Wright. New York: University Press of America, 1979.

Morley, Peter. "Culture and the Cognitive World of Traditional Medical Beliefs: Some Preliminary Considerations." In *Culture and Curing: Anthropological Perspectives on Traditional Medical Beliefs and Practices*. Eds. Peter Morley and Roy Wallis. Pittsburgh: University of Pittsburgh Press, 1978.

Mosley, Albert. *African Philosophy: Selected Readings*. Englewood Cliffs, N.J.: Prentice-Hall, 1995.

————. "The Metaphysics of Magic: Practical and Philosophical Implications." *Second Order* 7.1 and 2 (1978): 3–19.

Mudimbe, V. Y. *The Invention of Africa: Gnosis, Philosophy and the Order of Knowledge*. Bloomington: Indiana University Press, 1988.

Murphy, John W., and John T. Pardeck. "Technology and the Manufacture of Madness: A New Dimension." *Philosophy and Social Act* 12 (1986): 59–66.

Murungi, John. "Toward an African Conception of Time." *International Philosophical Quarterly* 20 (1980): 407–16.

Nasseem, Zubairi. "African Heritage and Contemporary Life." In *The Foundations of Social Life*. Ed. A. T. Dalfovo and others. Washington, D.C.: CRVP 1992.

Nebuwa, Imma Emeka. "On the Nature of African Philosophy: An Inquiry on What is Actually African Philosophy and the Process of the Discovery of Its Nature." Ph.D. diss., Pontificia Universitas Gregoriana (Vatican), 1989.

Nnoruka, Sylvanus Ifeanyi. "African Culture and the Quest for Truth." *Philosophy Today* 43.4 (1999): 411.

Northrop, Filmer Stuart Cuckow, and Helen H. Livingston. *Cross-Cultural Understanding: Epistemology in Anthropology*. New York: Harper & Row, 1964.

Nwala, Uzodinma. *Igbo Philosophy*. Lagos: Literamed, 1985.

Nyasani, Joseph M. "The Ontological Status of 'I' and 'We' in African Philosophy." In *I, We and Body: First Joint Symposium of Philosophers from Africa and from the Netherlands*. Ed. Heinz Kimmerle. Amsterdam: Grüner, 1989.

Ocaya, Victor. "Ultimate Reality and Meaning According to the Acholi of Uganda." *Ultimate Reality and Meaning Journal* 11 (1988): 11–22.

Oduyoye, Mercy Amba. *Hearing and Knowing: Theological Reflections on Christianity in Africa*. Maryknoll, N.Y.: Orbis, 1986.

Okafor, F. U. "Legal Positivism and the African Legal Tradition." *International Philosophical Quarterly* 24 (1984): 157–64.

Okolo, Chukwudum Barnabas. "The African Person: A Cultural Definition." *Indian Philosophical Quarterly* 6 (1989): 67–74.

————. "The African Person: A Cultural Definition (An Essay in African Philosophy." *Indian Philosophical Quarterly* 15 (1988): 99–107.

Oladipo, Olusegun. "An African Conception of Reality: A Philosophical Analysis." Ph.D. diss., University of Ibadan, 1988.

————. "Reason, Identity, and the African Quest: The Problems of Self-Definition in African Philosophy." *Africa Today* 42.3 (1995): 26.

Oluwole, S. B. "On the Existence of Witches." *Second Order* 7.1 and 2 (1978): 20–35.

Onwuanibe, Richard C. "The Human Person and Immortality in Ibo (African) Metaphysics." *Philosophy Research Archives* 6.1411 (1980).

Onyewuenyi, Innocent C. "A Philosophical Reappraisal of Africa Belief in Reincarnation." *International Philosophical Quarterly* 22 (n.d.): 157–68.

Oshita, Oshita O. "Some Aspects of Person in an African Tradition." *Journal of Social Philosophy* 24.2 (1993): 235–42.

Owolabi, Kolowole A. "The Quest for Method in African Philosophy: A Defense of the Hermeneutic-Narrative Approach." *Philosophical Forum* 32.2 (2001).

Oyelaran, Olascope, and others. *Obafemi Awolowo: The End of an Era?* Ile-Ife: Obafemi Awolowo University Press, 1988.

P'Bitek, Okot. "On Culture, Man, and Freedom." In *Philosophy and Cultures*. Ed. Odera Oruka and D. A. Masolo. Nairobi: Bookwise Ltd., 1983.

Peachey, Paul, John Kromkowski, and George F. McLean. *The Place of the Person in Social Life*. Washington, D.C.: CRVP, 1991.

Penner, Hans H. "Rationality, Ritual, and Science." In *Religion, Science, and Magic: In Concert and in Conflict*. Ed. Jacob Neusner, Ernst S. Frerichs, and Paul Virgil M. Flesher. New York: Oxford University Press, 1989.

Petitjean, Patrick, Catherine Jami, and Ann Marie Moulin. *Science and Empires: Historical Studies about Scientific Development and European Expansion*. Dordrecht, Netherlands: Kluwer, 1992.

Price-William, D. H. "A Case Study of Ideas Concerning Diseases among the Tiv." *Africa* 23 (1960): 123–31.

Prinsloo, E. D. "Understanding the World: Personal and Impersonal Idioms." *South African Journal of Philosophy* 12.4 (1993): 103–11.

Ross, Stephen D. *The Ring of Representation*. Albany, N.Y.: SUNY Press, 1992.

Rotimi, Ola. *The Gods are Not to Blame*. London: Oxford University Press, 1971.

Ruch, E. A., and K. C. Anyanwu. *An Introduction to the Main Philosophical Trends in Contemporary Africa*. Rome: Catholic Book Agency, 1984.

Serequeberhan, Tsenay. *African Philosophy: The Essential Readings*. New York: Paragon House, 1991.

—————. *The Hermeneutics of African Philosophy: Horizon and Discourse*. New York: Routledge, 1994.

Shutte, Augustine. "Umuntu Ngumuntu Ngabantu: An African Concept of Humanity." *Philosophy of Theology* (1990): 39–54.

Skorupski, John. "Science and Traditional Religious Thought III & IV." *Philosophy of the Social Sciences* (1973): 209–30.

Sodipo, J. O. "Philosophy in Pre-Colonial Africa." In *Teaching and Research in Philosophy*. Paris: UNESCO, 1984.

Sogolo, Godwin. "On the Socio-Cultural Conceptions of Health and Disease in Africa." *Africa: Rivista trimestrale di studi e documentazione dell' Istituto Italo-Africano* 41.3 (1986): 390–404.

Taiwo, Olufemi. "Legal Positivism and the African Legal Tradition." *International Philosophical Quarterly* 25 (1985): 197–200.

Tambiah, Stanley. *Magic, Science, Religion, and the Scope of Rationality*. Cambridge: Cambridge University Press, 1990.

Tempels, Placide. *Bantu Philosophy*. Paris: Presence Africaine, 1969.

Uzukwu, E. Elochukwu. "Igbo World and Ultimate Reality and Meaning." *Ultimate Reality and Meaning Journal* 5 (1982): 188–209.

Wamba-Dia-Wamba, Ernest. "Philosophy of African Intellectuals." *Quest* (1991): 4–17.

Washington, Johnny. "A Commentary on Oshita O. Oshita's Analysis of the Mind–Body Problem in an African World View." *Journal of Social Philosophy* 24.2 (1993): 243–47.

Wiredu, Kwasi. "The African Concept of Personhood." Presented at Conference on African-American Perspectives on Biomedical Ethics at Georgetown University, Washington D.C., December 1990.

————. "The Akan Concept of Mind." *Ibadan Journal of the Humanities* 3 (1983).

————. "Can Philosophy be Intercultural?" *Diogenes* 46.4 (1998): 147.

————. *Cultural Universals and Particulars: An African Perspective.* Bloomington: Indiana University Press, 1996.

————. "Death and the Afterlife in African Culture." In *Person and Community.* Ed. Kwasi Wiredu and Kwame Gyekye. Washington, D.C.: CRVP, 1992.

————. "Moral Foundations of an African Culture." *Person and Community.* Ed. Kwasi Wiredu and Kwame Gyekye. Washington, D.C.: CRVP, 1992.

————. *Philosophy and an African Culture.* Cambridge: Cambridge University Press, 1980.

————. "Universals and Particulars in Religion from an African Perspective." *Journal of Humanism and Ethical Religion* 3.1 (1990).

Wiredu, Kwasi, and Kwame Gyekye. *Person and Community.* Washington, D.C.: CRVP, 1992.

Wright, Richard. *African Philosophy: An Introduction.* New York: University Press of America, 1984.

INDEX OF NAMES

INDEX OF SUBJECTS